Negotiating Thinness Online

The Cultural Politics of Pro-anorexia

Gemma Cobb

 Routledge
Taylor & Francis Group

LONDON AND NEW YORK

First published 2020 by Routledge

2 Park Square, Milton Park, Abingdon, Oxon OX14 4RN

605 Third Avenue, New York, NY 10017

Routledge is an imprint of the Taylor & Francis Group, an informa business

First issued in paperback 2021

British Library Cataloguing-in-Publication Data
A catalogue record for this book is available from the British Library

Library of Congress Cataloging-in-Publication Data
Names: Cobb, Gemma, 1981- author.
Title: Negotiating thinness online : the cultural politics of pro-anorexia
/ Gemma Cobb.
Description: Abingdon, Oxon ; New York, NY : Routledge, 2020. |
Series: Gender, bodies and transformation | Includes bibliographical
references and index.
Identifiers: LCCN 2019046182 (print) | LCCN 2019046183 (ebook) |
ISBN 9781138589223 (hardback) | ISBN 9780429491795 (ebook)
Subjects: LCSH: Body image in women. | Anorexia—Social aspects. |
Online social networks. | Obesity in mass media. | Human body
in mass media.
Classification: LCC HQ1219 .C63 2020 (print) | LCC HQ1219 (ebook)
| DDC 306.4/613082—dc23
LC record available at https://lccn.loc.gov/2019046182
LC ebook record available at https://lccn.loc.gov/2019046183

ISBN: 978-1-138-58922-3 (hbk)
ISBN: 978-1-03-217545-4 (pbk)
DOI: 10.4324/9780429491795

Typeset in Bembo
by Integra Software Services Pvt. Ltd.

MIX
Paper from
responsible sources
FSC
www.fsc.org
FSC™ C013985

Printed in the United Kingdom
by Henry Ling Limited

ss Online

This book interrogates the thin ideal in pro-anorexia online spaces and the way in which it operates on a continuum with everyday discourses around thinness. Since their inception in the late twentieth century, pro-anorexia online spaces have courted controversy: they have been vilified by the media and deleted by Internet moderators. This book explores the phenomenon during its tipping point where it migrated from websites and discussion forums to image-centric social media platforms – all the while seeking to circumvent censorship by, for instance, repudiating 'pro-ana' or adopting hashtags to obfuscate content. The author argues that instead of being driven further underground, 'pro-ana' is blurring the boundaries between normative and deviant conceptions of thinness. Situating the phenomenon in relation to accepted constructions of thinness, promulgated by establishments as far ranging as medicine and women's magazines, this book asks if 'pro-ana' holds the potential to critique that which has long been considered normal: the culture of compulsory thinness. Engaging with debates including the current climate of postfeminism and neoliberalism, digital censorship, the pre-eminence of white, middle-class, heterofemininity, and the articulation of pain in realising the thin ideal, *Negotiating Thinness Online* examines what happens when the margins and the mainstream merge.

Gemma Cobb is a Lecturer in Media at the University of Brighton, UK. Her research interests include gender, the body and digital culture.

Gender, Bodies and Transformation

Series editor: Meredith Jones

Brunel University London, UK

This series explores the intersection of two key themes in relation to scholar-ship on bodies: gender and transformation. Bodies are gendered via biology, culture, medicine and society, such that gender, so deeply and intimately connected to identity, is a crucial part of any thorough analysis of the body. At the same time, bodies are – and have always been – sites of transform-ation, whether through 'natural' processes such as pregnancy, illness and ageing, or the more eye-catching, 'unnatural' transformations of cosmetic sur-gery, violence, extreme bodybuilding or dieting, cross-species transplantation, elective amputation or tattooing.

Interdisciplinary in scope and welcoming work from a range of approaches, including cultural and media studies, sociology, gender studies, feminist theory, phenomenology, queer studies and ethnography, *Gender, Bodies and Transformation* publishes scholarly examinations of contemporary cultural changes that are relevant to both gender and the transformation of bodies, whether in single bodies or between bodies.

Also in the series

Out Online
Trans Self-Representation and Community Building on YouTube
Tobias Raun

The Emergence of Trans
Cultures, Politics and Everyday Lives
Edited by Ruth Pearce, Igi Moon, Kat Gupta and Deborah Lynn Steinberg

Negotiating Thinness Online
The Cultural Politics of Pro-anorexia
Gemma Cobb

For more information about this series, please visit: www.routledge.com/ Gender-Bodies-and-Transformation/book-series/ASHSER1393

This book is dedicated to anyone who has sought thinspiration – pro-ana or otherwise. I hope, in some small way, it contributes towards a better understanding of a much-maligned phenomenon.

Contents

Tables

Acknowledgements

This book began as part of my doctoral degree at the University of Sussex and was completed whilst working at the University of Brighton. It would not have been possible without the support (both practical and emotional) of many people. I only wish I could thank them all by name.

I am indebted to Meredith Jones, whose faith in my work and generous support as I embarked on post-PhD life has been invaluable. I am immensely grateful to my supervisors: Niall Richardson and Sharif Mowlabocus. Sharif's kindness and insight continued long after the PhD and enabled me to complete this book. I must thank the following organisations for supporting my research: the University of Sussex Doctoral School for the AHRC scholarship which funded this project, the School of Media, Film and Music at Sussex for their resources, and the British Library and the National Library of Scotland for the use of their archives. Thank you to Alice Salt at Routledge for her advice and patience during the preparation of the manuscript. I am hugely grateful to the wonderful people in the doctoral community during my time at Sussex, many of whom have become lifelong friends. Special thanks to Lizzie Reed, Tanya Kant and Mid Hayder.

Parts of this book include revised, edited and updated versions of previous publications. An earlier version of my work on the disavowal of pro-ana online spaces, which appears in chapter three and briefly in chapter two, was originally published in *Fat Studies* in the article, '"This is *not* pro-ana": Denial and disguise in pro-anorexia online spaces' (2017). Reproduced with the permission of Taylor and Francis. Revised elements of my work on intersectionality in chapter four previously appeared in *Critical Studies in Fashion & Beauty* in my 2016 article, '"The Jenner genes definitely helped her": Kardashian, Jenners and the intersectional politics of thinness'.

Finally, I am fortunate enough to be surrounded by incredibly supportive – and patient – family and friends. To my parents, Barbara and David, and my sisters, Anna, Laura and Alice, I am eternally grateful – without their love and encouragement I would never have written a word. Last and by no means least, I would like to thank Lefteris Zenerian whose tremendous love and support and brilliant humour have been, and remain, a lifeline – from thesis to book and beyond.

Introduction

'Girls in danger'

In the summer of 2001, *The Observer* published an article on the risks posed by a new online phenomenon: pro-anorexia sites; its central concern was the threat these sites presented to 'vulnerable girls' (Hill 2001, p. 10). It would become but one of many pieces to incite panic around burgeoning pro-anorexia culture, and it typifies the kind of reporting the subject continues to attract. The headline, 'Girls in danger as anorexics give weight-loss tips on web' (ibid.), suggests young women are a threat to other young women: the anorexic is both at risk and the risk itself. Media reporting on the visible anorexic body still follows a similar narrative, and in an article on emaciated YouTube celebrity Eugenia Cooney, *The Express* asks, 'Would you want YOUR daughter idolising this stick-thin YouTube star?' (Delgado 2016). The piece reiterates the risk this young woman presents to other young women and cites a petition calling for Cooney to be banned from YouTube. It is not only articles such as these that demand pro-anorexia online spaces receive sustained critical investigation, but cultural understandings of femininity as alternately dangerous and in need of protection which underpin the phenomenon. This book, then, calls into account such misconceptions by examining pro-anorexia online spaces in relation to everyday understandings of gendered compulsory thinness. To do so, it interrogates a range of sources across pro-anorexia culture, as well as the mainstream construction of the thin ideal. The central claim of this book is that pro-anorexia online spaces expose the blurred boundaries between so-called 'disordered' and 'normal' body practices. At the same time, censorship and media vilification are hastening pro-anorexia culture's absorption into the mainstream and as a result, differentiating between pro-anorexia and health and beauty guidance is increasingly difficult.

Pro-anorexia, or 'pro-ana' – the truncated form of pro-anorexia which has been adopted by users and commentators alike and which I will use hereafter – has no clear-cut definition. Indeed, much of what this book grapples with is how to identify pro-ana when much of it has merged beyond recognition with mainstream thinness culture. Pro-ana online spaces emerged in the form of websites towards the end of the twentieth century (Burke 2012). However, as this book demonstrates, they have altered considerably. In the simplest sense, pro-ana is an online phenomenon that operates across a raft of websites, forums, and social media; and although it has no singular aim, broadly speaking, it operates to provide users with support on living with *anorexia nervosa*. This ranges from recovery advice, through to 'tips and tricks' on how to successfully starve, and 'thinspiration' – a portmanteau of 'thin' and 'inspiration', also contracted to 'thinspo'. Thinspo comprises the posting of images of thin models, celebrities, and users themselves with the intention of inspiring weight loss.

In line with scholars across academic disciplines, I work from the following position: that pro-ana online spaces reject the medical model of passive suffering (Bell 2009; Day and Keys 2008a, 2008b, 2009; Gailey 2009) creating an active phenomenon that continually adapts (Polak 2010, p. 85) and refuses erasure (Ferreday 2003, p. 293, 2009). Pro-ana online has been likened to a 'sanctuary' and safe space for anorectics (Dias 2003), a form of 'social capital' (Tierney 2008) and a 'secret society' where support is given, and friendships are formed (Cantó-Milà and Seebach 2011). Emma Bond (2012) found that although bullying occurred at times, users were generally supportive of one another. Thus, as Sarah R. Brotsky and David Giles conclude,

> it seems that the support on offer on pro-ana websites is – for all the scare stories about "purging tips" and users egging one another on with their latest BMIs – little more than sympathetic companionship in a safe, anonymous and largely sympathetic environment.
>
> (2007, p. 106)

However, because of the constant threat of censorship and deletion, pro-ana users attempt to safeguard their spaces by assuming various methods of disguise: primarily by adopting discourses of health and beauty. These tactics have led to their spaces becoming increasingly normalised. As such, I locate the pro-ana phenomenon within the broader landscape of postfeminist neoliberalism: that is, rather than positioning it as either pathological or to be celebrated, I argue that pro-ana culture is exemplary of the contradictory demands on twenty-first century femininity perpetrated by postfeminism.

Ultimately, this book captures pro-ana culture during its tipping point where it shifted from discussion-based forums and websites to more image-centric social media, all the while being subject to censorship and deletion by Internet moderators. Consequently, most of the data analysed in this book no longer exist; having since been removed, either by Internet moderators or by users themselves. This study then constitutes the preservation of an important cultural artefact: the transient phenomenon of pro-anorexia.

Scholarship

Pro-ana online spaces have received critical consideration across a range of academic disciplines including sociology, feminist media studies, health psychology, and computer science. For the purposes of this study, I understand the scholarship from two main perspectives: health sciences and socio-cultural studies (see Casilli et al. (2012) for a detailed breakdown of the disciplinary fields in which the pro-ana phenomenon has been examined). As I have suggested, pro-ana spaces do not have one overriding aim and scholars agree that they are 'heterogeneous and [...] serving a number of sometimes conflicting purposes' (Day and Keys 2009, p. 88); that 'the voice of pro-ana is not homogeneous and therefore should not be collapsed in to a uniform group' (Strife and Rickard 2011, p. 216; see also Miah and Rich 2008, p. 92; Yom-Tov et al. 2016). Notwithstanding, as the *Observer* and *Express* articles cited above demonstrate, the response to these spaces by the mainstream media has been one of moral panic, treating pro-ana spaces as monolithic and calling for deletion, which is simply not constructive (Ferreday 2003, 2009; Miah and Rich 2008; Polak 2010; Pollack 2003; Yeshua-Katz and Martins 2013). The nervousness around these spaces, however, is not limited to media reporting, and research within the health sciences has tended to take the phenomenon's assumed threat as a starting point.

The health science perspective

A body of research within the health sciences has set out to investigate the *risks* pro-ana online spaces present to non-users (Bardone-Cone and Cass 2006; Custers and Van Den Bulck 2009; Jett et al. 2010; Pan and Peña 2017). Other studies have attempted to quantify the spaces' harm levels (Borzekowski et al. 2010; Lapinski 2006; Lewis and Arbuthnott 2012), even if researchers were ultimately unable 'to confirm or disconfirm the harmful effects of pro-ED websites that have been announced in the popular press' (Rouleau and von Ranson 2011, p. 531). Such research positions pro-ana online spaces as potentially hazardous, thus coinciding with the media panic around the phenomenon. For instance, although Linda C. Andrist does critique wider cultural imperatives to thinness, she nonetheless excludes references to pro-ana sites in her article 'because of the potential danger' they pose, to which she adds: 'unfortunately, readers who want to find these sites can do so easily' (2003, p. 121). Likewise, a report in *The Lancet* notes the importance of raising awareness around eating disorders yet expresses trepidation that drawing attention to pro-ana sites could increase their use (Christodoulou 2012, p. 110). Similar concerns were documented by Carolien Martijn et al. (2009): recognising the unfeasibility of outright censorship, they conclude that placing warning texts before pro-ana sites is an effective strategy for reducing the sites' 'potential harmful effects on naïve viewers' (p. 144), although they do not address the practicalities of identifying pro-ana sites in the first place. Others, such as Megan A. Moreno et al. (2016), have called for social media platforms to improve their Content Advisory warnings so as to protect users from potentially harmful material (see also Chancellor et al. 2016). However, as I argue throughout this book, the lines between pro-ana and the everyday espousal of thinness are increasingly blurred. Invariably, a pro-ana space may disguise itself as a health motivation blog, or a women's magazine may borrow from pro-ana discourse (chapter three attends to this in detail). Thus, accurately classifying spaces as pro-ana or not for the purposes of content moderation is a Herculean task.

Anna M. Bardone-Cone and Kamila M. Cass (2006), who argue that pro-ana sites have a negative impact on users, advocate for censorship on the individual level. They urge parents to 'use the technology available to "block" pro-ana websites from being viewed on home computers, or to place home computers with Internet access in a public part of their home where monitoring could occur' (Bardone-Cone and Cass 2006, p. 261). Such recommendations assume that users of pro-ana sites are exclusively young people who live with their parents and are not technologically savvy enough to find such sites by any means. Interestingly, eight years later the design of this study was replicated by Monique J. Delforterie et al. who conclude that, on the contrary, 'viewing a pro-ana website might *not* have detrimental effects on body satisfaction, positive and negative affect, or appearance self-efficacy in young, *normal* weight women' (2014, p. 334, emphases added). Although the paper concedes that pro-ana sites may not be as dangerous as initially expected, it nonetheless perpetuates the binary of what is a 'normal' weight and what is not. In spite of this, some research has emphasised the agency pro-ana culture affords its users (Crowe and Watts 2014) and its opportunities for identity-building (Fox et al. 2005; Giles and Newbold 2011; Smith et al. 2015). As David C. Giles and Julie Newbold show, in some spaces, new members must go through strict initiation processes to assess the authenticity of their claims to being pro-ana: those found to be, 'a mere "wannabe," or, worse still, a "normal" or a "dieter" ' (2011, p. 420) will be frozen out.

Nonetheless, scholars working from health science perspectives generally agree that healthcare professionals and caregivers must listen to pro-anorectics if they are to better understand both the phenomenon and anorexia itself (Brotsky and Giles 2007; Csipke and Horne 2007; Custers and Van Den Bulck 2009; Gale et al. 2016; Gooldin 2008; Harshbarger et al. 2009; Norris et al. 2006; Oksanen et al. 2015; Tierney 2008; Yeshua-Katz and Martins 2013; Yom-Tov et al. 2012). Antonio Casilli, Fred Pailler, and Paola Tubaro warn that censorship can only lead to pro-ana spaces being driven further underground and becoming entirely inaccessible to healthcare givers and policy makers (2013, p. 95). Although I do not deny the importance of such professionals, and of parents and caregivers, having a better understanding of the pro-ana phenomenon – indeed they must be part of the conversation – my contention is that it cannot be reduced to a clinical issue. If healthcare professionals require an understanding of the phenomenon to inform their work, then equally do those who work in the media and fashion industries. As Susan Bordo rightly points out in her work on eating disorders, 'the prevailing medical wisdom [...] has failed, over and over, to acknowledge, finally and decisively, that we are dealing here with a *cultural* problem' (2009, p. 53, emphasis in original). Pro-ana online spaces and much of the research surrounding them underscores this more than ever.

The socio-cultural perspective

Although existing research on pro-ana within the health sciences has undoubtedly provided important insights into the phenomenon, many of its recommendations situate pro-ana as an isolated problem, rather than part of a culture underpinned by compulsory thinness. However, my primary claim – a claim that provides the motivation for this book – is that pro-anorexia and mainstream culture are irrevocably entwined. This research then, takes a feminist socio-cultural approach to the phenomenon. In their overview of academic writing on the pro-eating disorder phenomenon, Casilli et al. (2012) found a dearth of gender studies research, even though Karen Dias's (2003) feminist approach to pro-ana sites was one of the most cited pieces of work (Casilli et al. 2012, p. 133). What this suggests is the simultaneous need for, and importance of, gender studies research into pro-ana online spaces. The purpose of this book is to begin to address this gap.

During the early days of pro-ana websites, Deborah Pollack published an article asking what the feminist response to the phenomenon should be, suggesting that it 'can be seen as a line of flight', as an affront to oppressive structures (2003, p. 249). At the same time, she urged us to be careful not to 'create new possibilities for the pro-anorexic subject to become a symbolic martyr' (ibid.). Katy Day and Tammy Keys responded directly to Pollack's call, concurring that 'feminist theorists should also be hesitant about romanticizing pro-eating disorder websites as political statements' (2009, p. 94). Day and Keys highlight the contradictory nature of pro-ana sites, arguing that users both comply with and resist feminine beauty ideals (2008a, 2008b, 2009). Thus, feminist scholarship on the pro-ana phenomenon has drawn attention to its capacity to destabilise the status quo. Dias, for instance, reads pro-ana as parodying impossible ideals of thinness (2003, p. 42) and locates it within third-wave feminism. Debra Ferreday suggests the phenomenon is 'challenging what it sees as the hypocrisy of a society that positions anorexics as sick, while continually celebrating and displaying extremely thin bodies' (2003, p. 286). Equally, Natalie Boero and C.J. Pascoe suggest that framing these sites as a problem 'is also a way to deflect attention from larger cultural messages around eating and body size found in mainstream media outlets which are not so different from the ones promulgated on these sites' (2012, p. 36). They argue that the urgency to repudiate and remove pro-ana online spaces means they are not being adequately explored (ibid.; see also Miah and Rich 2008, p. 92).

Other feminist research on pro-ana culture takes a more celebratory approach. For Michele Polak, it is 'more powerful than anything [she has] ever seen before online' and deserves recognition (2010, p. 85) and Jeannine A. Gailey (2009) argues that pro-ana users 'have become active participants in deciding how they will hurt rather than succumbing to passive gender role stereotypes' (p. 106). Debbie Ging and Sarah Garvey (2018) are optimistic about the visibility of pro-ana content on Instagram, conceiving it as a means of awareness-raising and stimulus for debate around eating disorders. Mebbie Bell (2009), however, is more measured, insisting that: 'instead of a polarized reading of pro-anorexia as either "good" or "bad" [...] pro-anorexia must be read as pro-anas often insist: as a struggle, individually contextualized within and against medical discourse' (p. 158). Feminists agree that censorship is futile, with Nicole Danielle Schott and Debra Langan (2015), for instance, suggesting that Tumblr's public service announcements to warn viewers of pro-ana content merely reinforce patriarchal control over women. Whilst some scholars see feminist potential in the phenomenon, Eliza Burke views it 'as *symptomatic* of the same power structures that feminists have argued help to produce anorexia in the first place' (2012, p. 51) and Su Holmes suggests that because of pro-ana users' individualism, they have 'no clear affinity with the feminist approaches which persistently foreground the culture-bound nature of eating disorders' (2015, p. 116). Nonetheless, pro-ana culture is in constant flux and as Burke argues, we must 'continue to ask new questions about the nature of this production as anorexia occupies new fields of representation' (2012, p. 51). This is what this book seeks to do: to develop new understandings of the ever-changing pro-anorexia phenomenon through a feminist framework.

In search of pro-ana: methodological and ethical considerations

The main source of data in this book is drawn from a trawl of the pro-ana online landscape (chapter two is an empirical study of women's magazines to which I attend separately). Finding such content online is a challenge, both methodologically and ethically. A forum full of activity one week may have ground to a halt the next; a hashtag search on Instagram can yield thousands of posts one day and nothing the next. From the outset, I had to modify my intended methodological approach and adapt to the elusive texts I was seeking to analyse. Such modification set the precedent for a project whose methods have constantly needed to evolve in order to respond to the shifting landscape of digital culture.

As a result of censorship by Internet Service Providers, webhosting services, and forum moderators, pro-ana content 'is now more scattered and more secretive' (Ferreday 2009, p. 214) and users are renowned for engaging in 'an elaborate game of cat and mouse to remain one step ahead of the "authorities" ' (Crowe and Watts 2014, p. 3). At times during the research process, it felt that I became (however, unwillingly) another authority from which they sought to hide. Of course, an assumption here is that these groups do not want to be found and that research into them is ethically problematic. This was something I grappled with constantly: as a feminist, my research was motivated by the need to break the silence (see Ryan-Flood and Gill 2010, p. 3) and overturn the misconceptions around pro-ana, yet in so doing, this would inevitably draw attention to these spaces. As Ysabel Gerrard reminds us, 'there should be sound justifications for exposing a marginalized community's secrets' (2018, p. 6). My aim from the outset was to contribute a better understanding of pro-ana texts, and in so doing, provide a critique of thinness culture. It was crucial that my methodological approach was executed in such a way that pro-ana users were protected. I, therefore, sought to be self-reflexive throughout, from data collection to writing up and publication.

Research to date into pro-ana online has adopted various methods, from interviewing pro-ana users face-to-face (Rich 2006), over email, Skype, or telephone (Williams and Reid 2010; Yeshua-Katz and Martins 2013), through e-questionnaires (Rodgers et al. 2012), and surveys of forum users (Ransom et al. 2010). Gavin et al. (2008) adopted a method akin to lurking, whereas other researchers have chosen to become more directly involved by joining publicly available sites and forums under pseudonyms (Gailey 2009), and participating in discussions (Fox et al. 2005). Nic Crowe and Mike Watts (2014) befriended 'gatekeepers', seeking their permission to join forums, as well as conducting interviews with pro-ana users. Similarly, Natàlia Cantó-Milà and Swen Seebach (2011) undertook a combination of discourse analysis of posts and interviews with former pro-ana users. One study in particular stands out where the researcher masqueraded as a pro-ana user and entered private forums in an attempt to better understand the phenomenon (Brotsky and Giles 2007).

The preferred method of enquiry for a number of scholars has been to focus solely on the online content rather than users themselves (see, for example, Burke 2012; Ferreday 2003 2009; Gerrard 2018; Polak 2010; Strife and Rickard 2011; Vellar 2018). This would be my chosen method too, and in line with Ferreday (2009), I approach online spaces as texts. Although I use the term 'space' interchangeably with 'text', I do not regard online spaces as places we visit, as distinct from our everyday lives, but rather, I conceive them as a form of representation. As Elizabeth H. Bassett and Kate O'Riordan have argued, 'the Internet can thus be perceived as a form of cultural production, in a similar framework to that of the print media, broadcast television and radio' (2002, p. 236). Pro-ana online spaces are inherently intertextual and a key facet of pro-ana culture is the selecting, curating, and marking of existing images as pro-anorexic or thinspirational. Although I recognise that human subjects have created these cultural objects (and I have taken in to account ethical considerations accordingly), this project did not seek to directly engage with these people as authors. With online texts, we can never truly know who the author is or how 'real' they are (Ferreday 2009, p. 207; see also Hine 2000, p. 120): these artefacts exist solely online, and 'to demand that ethnographic research always incorporate meeting residents in the actual world for "context" presumes that virtual worlds themselves are not contexts' (Boellstorff 2008, p. 61). This book then places importance not on who created these texts, but how they are used and the meanings they produce. It is also worth noting that although some authors directly referenced having an eating disorder, either at the time of posting or in the past, many did not, and it is possible that such texts were created by individuals who wanted to lose weight and used pro-ana culture as a way of servicing this. Either way, the discourses these spaces construct are the point of interrogation for this book. As a result, I deemed it unnecessary to engage in 'embodied ways of knowing' and instead approached these online spaces as cultural formations (Markham 2005, p. 808).

Despite this, a central concern when carving out my methodological approach was that of privacy. Early on in this study, I made the decision to focus solely on publicly available pro-ana content (see also Boero and Pascoe 2012; Borzekowski et al. 2010; Day and Keys 2008a; Dias 2003; Giles and Newbold 2011; Miah and Rich 2008). Although I expressly did not enter any password-protected spaces or engage with users, there were times when, as Holmes also concedes, I felt guilty being in a ' "private" public space' (2015, p. 103). Indeed, just because there is a wealth of publicly accessible data online, it does not mean that it is there for the taking – whether by researchers, companies, or private individuals (see Zimmer 2010). Hence, Helen Nissenbaum's (2010) concept of 'contextual integrity' is instructive here: 'what people care most about is not simply *restricting* the flow of information but ensuring that it flows *appropriately*' (p. 2, emphases in original). When I began this research, the *inappropriate* flow of pro-ana content was already well under way. Algorithms would generate diet advertising on my personal social media accounts if I was logged in when I searched pro-ana terms (see also Bond 2012) and, as I discuss later, my search engine queries yielded several sites presenting as pro-ana spaces in order to market weight-loss products. The lack of ethical consideration on the part of the advertisers requires more discussion than can be undertaken in this book, but as R. Benjamin Shapiro and Pilar N. Ossorio warn: 'the goals of most academic research surely have as much social value as selling more products to SNS users. Providing marketers greater access than academic researchers to people's online information would be an ethically dubious outcome' (2013, p. 2). In short, I would make certain that my data would *flow* in such a way that new understandings about pro-ana culture's relationship to mainstream thinness culture could be proffered. Consequently, analysis of the boundaries between what constitutes legitimate acts of body disciplining, such as those promoted by the women's magazines explored in chapter two, and the 'marginal' pro-ana spaces that such acts of censorship construct is central to this book.

As a feminist researcher, I consider the privacy and anonymity of the individuals who use pro-ana online spaces paramount. Having received approval from my university's ethical review board, I took steps to ensure that the integrity of users and their spaces would in no way be comprised. I did not set up a user account for any of the forums or social media platforms, nor did I interact with members and password-protected accounts were not accessed. An important consideration when using publicly available data is that it cannot be traced back to its author via search engines. Hence, this book adopts 'fabrication [as] a sensible and ethically grounded solution for protecting privacy in arenas of shifting public/private contexts' (Markham 2012,

p. 341), following Amy Bruckman's (2001) system of 'heavy disguise' to ensure that any sensitive online data are rendered anonymous and untraceable.[1] In line with Bruckman's guidance, I have given pseudonyms to all usernames, websites, and discussion threads, and all quotations have been paraphrased. Links for individual posts have been omitted entirely. Importantly though, I have created pseudonyms and paraphrased quotes in such a way that their provenance is obscured, but the overall sentiment is retained. Finally, the mode of textual analysis I employ has allowed me to build up a set of themes that further conceals the specific provenance of the data. In short, this research did not involve participant-observation, but a text-based study of digital culture.

Mapping the terrain

Pro-ana online is a vast phenomenon that operates across many online platforms and as a result, produces a considerable amount of data. For a researcher, this is both a blessing and a curse, and I had to make several decisions from the outset to render this project manageable. A key decision was around search terms. Pro-ana is often linked to 'pro-mia', the truncated form of pro-bulimia, which is used to indicate that a person is actively engaging in *bulimia nervosa*: binge eating followed by practices to prevent weight gain, such as vomiting (American Psychiatric Association 2013, p. 345). Nonetheless, as Andy Miah and Emma Rich (2008) found, spaces which espouse disordered eating tend to focus more on anorexia than bulimia and use pro-ana as an umbrella term. Consequently, throughout this book, I refer to spaces as pro-ana, rather than pro-mia, or 'pro-ED', for example, the truncated form of 'pro-eating disorders', which arguably may appear more representative but is used much less. The other key term that occurs throughout this book is thinspo. Although thinspo finds its origins in pro-ana culture, it has begun to mean simply that one is inspired by an image of thinness without necessarily having an eating disorder. As a result, pro-ana and thinspo were the key terms that guided this research and enabled me to set the boundaries of this project, albeit with the confidence that I was capturing a broad range of data.

In order to chart the pro-ana landscape, my first task was to undertake two sets of online searches, inputting 'pro-ana' and 'thinspo', respectively, into four search engines – *Google, Bing, Yahoo,* and *Ask* – and recording the respective results from pages 1, 2, 5, and 8. I then selected for further investigation the links that appeared most frequently. By carrying out simple queries, I sought to replicate the kind of search undertaken, for example, by 'young people without requiring technical expertise (rather than by using a more technically complex route)' (Bond 2012, p. 15). However, it has long been established that search engine tools are not neutral (Hine 2000, p. 89) and that ' "raw data" is an oxymoron' (Gitelman and Jackson 2013; see also Gillespie 2014). Given the controversial status of pro-ana online, it is likely that results had previously been removed from searches and that the data examined in this book had already been manipulated by the search engines that ordered them. Whilst this study does not deal with 'pure' data, it nevertheless dovetails with the spaces produced from searches undertaken by the everyday user.

The more commonly listed hyperlinks generated by these searches led to forums and websites, a vast number of which were no longer being updated, or whose content appeared frozen. In other cases, the listed hyperlinks led to notices indicating that the site had been removed. As I continued with my research, it seemed that, increasingly, pro-ana content had migrated and would not be as easy to find as I had initially thought. Nonetheless, I took screenshots of these 11 frozen spaces and included them for analysis (see Appendix, Table 1). The search results that yielded active spaces were primarily those on microblogging platform – Tumblr – and social networking sites – Instagram and Pinterest – as well as bulletin board – Reddit – even if some of the results were simply noting that hosts had banned pro-ana content. This produced 14 active, publicly available spaces from which I took screenshots and made field notes over four months (see Appendix, Table 2), although during the research period, a number of these were frozen or removed.

In addition to these spaces, my searches yielded six pro-ana 'marketing' spaces: blogs and websites that were ostensibly user-led, but closer inspection revealed that they were selling dieting products and using pro-ana lexicon to do so. These spaces were recorded for analysis too (see Appendix, Table 3). As a result of their not being 'genuine' pro-ana sites, I quote from them verbatim and provide links to them in the bibliography (although the majority have since been frozen or deleted). Finally, my searches also produced two spaces that focused exclusively on recovery (see Appendix, Table 4). As I have pointed out, pro-ana spaces are not monolithic: some forums and sites describe themselves as pro-ana but feature recovery content and *vice versa*. These two spaces, however, were dedicated solely to recovery, but because they arose from my searches, I included them for analysis.

Having noted that content was predominantly arising on social media spaces, I then undertook a second round of searches on Tumblr, Pinterest, and Webstagram[2], the searchable web browser for Instagram. What I found here altered the trajectory of my research. These platforms have all taken steps to remove pro-ana content, advising users accordingly in their respective policies (moves that I discuss in detail in chapter three), but this censorship meant that initial searches on these platforms suggested that there was ostensibly very little pro-ana content to be found. Echoing my first round of search engine results, it seemed that pro-ana had once again been and gone. In spite of this, the platforms varied in how strictly they adhered to their content removal policies: Instagram suggested that pro-ana and thinspo simply could not be found, and although Pinterest yielded results for pro-ana and thinspo, content was not updated over time, thereby appearing frozen like many of the older sites and forums. Tumblr was less stringent: 'pro-ana' and 'thinspo' were not blocked, but the terms did generate Content Advisory warnings. Users were tagging posts with 'thin' and 'ana' to identify their content as pro-ana and ensure against censorship and I wanted to see if the same was happening on other platforms too. It was: a search for 'thin' and 'ana' on Webstagram produced posts with numerous other hashtags. I was intrigued by terms such as #thynspiration and #thynspo; it seemed that users were circumventing censorship and deletion with obscure spellings and terms. Clicking the hyperlink for #thynspo generated images with accompanying hashtags such as #thinspoooo, the variations upon which seemed endless. Table 1 below indicates the results generated by #thinspoooo; it appeared that pro-ana users were in a linguistic battle with Instagram; and 111,366 photos tagged with thinspoooo suggested that they were winning.

Each hashtag search produced new spelling variations on thinspo and pro-ana, as well as yielding new terms such as 'bonespo'. During the research period, 'bonespo' appeared to be a relatively new coinage because, across each of the social network sites examined, it generated results without warning statements. It seemed it was yet to arouse the suspicion of platform moderators, although by the end of the four-month period, it was triggering content warnings. I, therefore, moved through various iterations of key terms in order to establish a method for capturing my primary data, all the while modifying my searches as hashtags took me on different routes. For instance, when I discovered a new term, provided it was generating a significant number of results, such as the first variation of thinspoooo in Table 1, I interrogated it further and took screenshots for analysis (see Appendix, Table 5). The evolving linguistic culture of pro-ana

Table 1 Hashtags and images generated by a search for '#thinspoooo'

Hashtag	Number of images
#thinspoooo	111,366
#thinspooooo	5,460
#thinspoooooo	228
#thinspooooooo	119
#thinspooooration	71
#thinspooooooooo	13
#thinspoooooooooo	7
#thinspooooooooooo	6
#thinspooooooration	4
#thinspooooogirl	3
#thinspooooorational	3
#thinspoooooooooooo	3
#thinspooooooooooooo	2
#thinspooooooi	1
#thinspoooooooooooooooo	1

and the 'cat and mouse game' that users appear to be engaged in with key social media platforms ensures that one can never fully map the terrain of pro-ana online. However, using the technique identified here, I was able to secure a sizeable amount of data and towards the end of the fourth month, the results produced by my searches were reaching saturation point.[3]

Scope of the book

This book is about women (broadly defined) and although as I have emphasised, anorexia is by no means exclusive to young girls, the data this study yielded suggest that *pro*-anorexia is. My argument is not that men, non-binary, or transgender people cannot be (pro-)anorexic, but that contemporary Western culture frames anorexia as a specifically female concern because it is on a continuum with the demands of normative femininity (Bordo 1989, [1993] 2003; Malson 1998; Wolf 1991). All too often normative femininity is presented as white, able-bodied middle-class, cisgendered, and heterosexual. Eating disorders may affect people of all ages and genders but, as I suggested above, the media response to pro-ana has focused on the threat it presents to *young women*. Consequently, I argue that both the representation of pro-ana culture by the media and the content within the spaces themselves bring to the fore understandings of women's inferior position in contemporary Western culture – whether cis or trans.

It is worth noting that during the research process, very little content arose which did not assume a cis female subject (whether in forum threads or image boards), but if I searched for 'male pro-ana' and 'male thinspo', for example, the results were plentiful. This gendered separation is reflective of culturally dominant beliefs that men do not suffer from eating disorders and those that do are deemed non-normative (see Herzog et al. 1990). Research into such pro-ana content is much needed but it requires more discussion than can be undertaken in this book. In the spaces examined in this study, a female subject was simply assumed; my aim is to interrogate such assumptions.

Feminism, postfeminism, and neoliberalism

This book situates contemporary femininity within a postfeminist neoliberal framework, and although an in-depth history of feminism is beyond its scope, one cannot understand postfeminism without feminism. Therefore, I would like to briefly address some fundamental points around feminism before moving on to a discussion of the key debates in postfeminism. Defining feminism is a complex task; for the purpose of this book though, it is useful to think of it, as many scholars do, in waves.[4] These waves are by no means exhaustive but can operate as a tool for situating the current tendency towards postfeminism.

The second wave, which emerged in the 1960s and spans the seventies and eighties, is most pertinent to an understanding of postfeminism. It comprises many trajectories, but here I will attend to four: radical feminism, black feminism, liberal feminism, and socialist feminism. Radical feminism was borne out of the Civil Rights Movement and the New Left where women of colour had been side-lined (Bryson 2003). Viewing the patriarchy as the source of women's oppression 'radical feminists articulated the earliest and most provocative critiques of the family, marriage, love, normative heterosexuality, and rape' (Echols 1989, p. 3), but they rendered women of colour invisible (Bryson 2003, p. 183). Subsequently, black feminists, such as bell hooks (2015), highlighted this double oppression in the Civil Rights Movement and in feminism alike. For hooks, works such as Betty Friedan's (1963) *The Feminine Mystique* demonstrated that the writer 'had been socialized to accept and perpetuate racist ideology' (hooks 2015, p. 137). *The Feminine Mystique*, which focused on the plight of white, middle-class women epitomises liberal feminism. Concerned with legislative reform and women's participation in mainstream political and economic life, this form of feminism adumbrates the individualism of neoliberal feminism we see today (Krolokke and Sorensen 2006, p. 11). By contrast, second-wave socialist feminism argued for a politics that also incorporated 'widely differing structures and experience of that oppression in different societies, periods of history and social classes' (Barrett 1980, p. 4). Although socialist feminist Nancy Fraser does not address postfeminism by name, her account of the way second-wave feminism and neoliberalism 'prospered in tandem' (2013, p. 218) helps to explain the current postfeminist climate. She calls for feminism to realign with Left-wing politics, suggesting that whilst as a movement it may have grown enormously, it is now 'susceptible to serving the legitimation needs of a new form of capitalism' (Fraser 2013, p. 223; see also Rottenberg 2014, p. 433).

The third-wave of feminism that emerged during the 1990s sought in some way to remedy this, with proponents such as Rebecca Walker – who coined the term 'third-wave' – advocating for an activist approach to feminism, rather than a theoretical stance (Genz and Brabon 2009). Although the third-wave is radical in its ideas, Tram Nguyen argues that '[it] is troubled by divisions within its still-forming body of activism and theories, as well as by postfeminist seductions' (2013, p. 157). Third-wave feminism, like postfeminism, is characterised by contradictions and individualism. Recently, scholars have explored the possibility of a fourth-wave of feminism, one they suggest is borne out of Internet-based feminist activism and presents a direct affront to postfeminism (Munro 2013; Retallack et al. 2016). Whilst there is undoubtedly important feminist work happening both online and offline, my critical enquiries suggest that postfeminism is far from over. Therefore, in line with Rosalind Gill (2016), I advocate for the 'value and utility of a continued attention to postfeminism' (p. 625).

Angela McRobbie defines postfeminist culture as one which 'positively draws on and invokes feminism as that which can be taken into account, to suggest that equality is achieved' (2004, p. 255). For McRobbie, postfeminism is not simply a backlash against feminism, rather it 'comprises the coexistence of neo-conservative values in relation to gender, sexuality and family life [...] with processes of liberalization in regard to choice and diversity' (2009,

p. 12). It is, therefore, characterised by contradictions (Tasker and Negra 2007, p. 8), where, for instance, 'choice and self-improvement sit side-by-side with surveillance, discipline and the vilification of those who make the "wrong" "choices" ' (Gill 2007, p. 163). The *right* choices are those that have been sanctified by normative femininity, meaning that 'women's relationship to the "choosing subject" is the product of social processes and conditioning which are not of their own choosing' (Budgeon 2015, p. 308). Ironically then, for all its claims to choice, postfeminism imposes restrictions upon which choices can be made and by whom. The ideal postfeminist subject is 'white, straight, able-bodied and middle class' (Winch 2013, p. 3; see also Ringrose and Walkerdine 2008), thus leaving little space for those who do not occupy such intersections of privilege. A disregard for social inequalities means that this new feminist culture lacks 'emancipatory potential' (Scharff 2011, p. 274). Unlike feminism, in which solidarity and collective action are key to social change, for postfeminism, 'the solution to injustice is to work on the self' (Gill 2016, p. 617). It is because of postfeminism's focus on the self, as well as its contradictory and depoliticising qualities, that scholars including Gill (2007) and Christina Scharff (2012) have argued of its striking similarities with neoliberalism (see also Gill and Scharff 2011, p. 7).

Wendy Brown (2005) suggests that neoliberalism, which began as a set of economic policies based on free trade, deregulation, and minimum state intervention, has now become a political project that has permeated the self. She argues that 'it figures individuals as rational, calculating creatures whose moral autonomy is measured by their capacity for "self-care" – the ability to provide for their own needs and service their own ambitions' (Brown 2005, p. 42; see also Ringrose and Walkerdine 2008). For Shelley Budgeon, 'key forces contributing to the functioning of neoliberalism and postfeminism include individualization, feminization, co-optation and depoliticization' (Budgeon 2015, pp. 304–305). Such forces operate insidiously, obscuring the inequalities they perpetuate. This book, in a small way, seeks to unveil their workings through an investigation into pro-anorexia online spaces, which, as I will show, are a product of postfeminist neoliberalism.

Motivations and self-reflection

Although, I believe, it is important to set out my own motivations for writing this book and to state where I am personally located in the phenomenon of pro-ana, I acknowledge that in attempts to be self-reflexive, one risks centring the self and thereby 'eclipsing and de-authorizing the articulations of others' (Skeggs 2004, p. 128). It would, however, be disingenuous not to state why I pursued this research and how I arrived at this point. The impetus to write this book stems from the personal and the political: my experiences as a woman in a culture that demands a slender body, and my position as a feminist that impels me to fight such oppressive structures. My first encounter with pro-ana online spaces was not as a researcher, but as an interested user.

I was in my twenties, entering another phase in my life where I would undergo extreme dieting and, to be blunt, I was intrigued. I pored over images of emaciated models – although, in fairness, I did not need to go to pro-ana sites to find them: I trawled through the 'tips 'n' tricks' on weight loss, noting that many of them I had tried already. From eating only soup, to taking diet pills; from obsessive jogging, to laxatives, and weight-loss tea – it was years of reading women's magazines, of looking at other women, and of lessons learned from growing up with three sisters, that taught me I would never be thin enough. To me, pro-ana online was an inevitable response to the way women are made to feel about their bodies. I was angry, but not in the least bit surprised.

My desire to be perfectly thin did not sit well with my identifying as a feminist, and for a long time, I struggled to reconcile to the two. Feminists have argued that this focus on physical appearance can be 'profoundly disempowering' (Bartky 1990, p. 85; see also Chernin 1981; Wolf 1991); that it 'keeps [women's] energies directed toward personal change rather than political change' (McKinley 1999, p. 108; see also Hartley 2001, p. 64). Certainly, maintaining a diet of under 500 calories a day – as I have intermittently over the years – leaves energy for very little else. Nonetheless, I carried on, ashamed that I was fat and unattractive, and ashamed that, as a feminist, I should have known better. I may have failed at femininity, but I was also failing at feminism.

I have not touched a diet now since 2012 and it is no small coincidence that since this time, I have been engaged in the research that has now become this book. I am not daring to suggest that any person with body issues should undertake academic research to free themselves. That would be absurd and only result in the kind of self-centred research Beverley Skeggs (2004) warns against. However, in the process of working on this project, I have had the privilege of engaging with a range of feminist writers who have helped me understand that the thin ideal operates as a form of social control and that feminism need not be incompatible with femininity. Being able to do this on such an immersive level is an opportunity I have been afforded because of my middle-class position, a privilege denied to many. As such, during the course of this research, I have endeavoured to be self-reflexive; to recognise that not everybody will regard compulsory thinness through the lens of feminism. This is not to say that I am now no longer susceptible to the pervasive thin ideal, that some academic armour now shields me from the desire to lose weight. Absolutely not, and there were certainly times when I looked at the images of flat stomachs and thigh gaps yielded by my research and had a stab of yearning, however perverse that may sound. I know my experience of body hatred and confusion is not unique and my reason for sharing it is because it is indicative of 'the tense relationship that many feminists experience between the ideology of accepting our bodies as they are, the critique of normative body ideals and practices, and the desire for them' (Throsby and Gimlin 2010, p. 114). In a society which values thinness, aligning it with health and self-worth, whilst repudiating fat (Bordo [1993] 2003; Lupton 1996; Sobal and Maurer 1999), resistance can be hard work and the ramifications far-reaching. This occurs to such a degree that in contemporary Western culture, 'the imperfect body has become the sign of an imperfect character' (Gimlin 2002, p. 5). The thin ideal is about much more than body weight, and this book seeks to explicate that.

When I tell people about my research, they tend to respond in one of two ways, either with concern and sadness, or with disbelief: '*pro*-anorexia?' they exclaim, checking they heard correctly. That anyone would actively pursue anorexia sounds preposterous to most people, but for many of the very same individuals, eating 'clean', going to the gym, dieting before a holiday, all seem perfectly reasonable. To be clear, I am not arguing that healthy-eating and keeping fit are the same as self-starvation and obsessive exercising; rather, that the everyday body discipliner and the pro-anorectic operate on a continuum and as I will show, they have increasingly little distance between them.

It is my intention for this book to present analyses of pro-ana texts which engage with the multitude of readings their authors have brought to them, however, I recognise that my interpretation of these texts has produced this research and that they 'present a particular reality of the object of analysis' (Markham 2005, p. 802). Whilst I have made every attempt to approach the pro-ana phenomenon as impartially as possible, as Mary Maynard argues 'no feminist study can be politically neutral, completely inductive or solely based in grounded theory. This is a contradiction in terms' (1994, p. 23; see also Jones 2008, p. 2). That is, I selected posts for analysis that I felt were instructive. Finally, the data I draw on in this book are from a snapshot in time and are an illustrative representation of pro-ana online culture during the shift in its landscape, rather than an exhaustive depiction.

A note on language and referencing

As will become clear as this book progresses, pro-ana online spaces have their own rhetoric: this is partly a result of attempts to circumvent censorship, and partly a means of creating an exclusive group. For instance, I regularly refer to alternative spellings of thinspo, such as 'thynspo' and 'thinspoooo', as well as other terms users have coined. Furthermore, users adopt the terms 'Ana' and 'Mia' as both nouns and adjectives, thereby indicating the extent to which eating disorders have pervaded their identities, stating for instance, 'I am Ana'. Another term that arises regularly is 'EDNOS', the acronym for 'Eating Disorder Not Otherwise Specified' (American Psychiatric Association 2000, p. 594).[5]

As outlined above, I have given pseudonyms to sites, forums, and threads, and paraphrased all direct quotes. As a result, standard referencing was not possible, nor in this instance, was it logical. I, therefore, use the following citation method: all websites, blogs, and forums that can be considered pro-ana are indicated in italics in brackets – for example, (*Guide to Ana*). In the case of social media posts, they are indicated via the hashtag or key word through which I found them – for example, 'an Instagram post generated by #proanna…'. These in-text citations do not refer to a full reference in the bibliography, instead, I direct the reader to the appendix where they will be able to see a list of all hashtag and key word searches in alphabetical order and their respective platforms. Finally, all other online spaces, whether news sources or pro-ana marketing sites, for instance, follow standard Harvard referencing with the author and date in brackets, are not italicised, and therefore appear in the bibliography in the usual way.

Chapters

This book is divided into six central chapters: the first two are contextual and explore the medical and popular culture frameworks respectively from which pro-ana online spaces emerge; the remaining four attend to the spaces them- selves. Chapter one addresses the historical inception of the medical gaze during the European Enlightenment before examining the impact this had on understandings of the female body and subsequently on disordered eating. Since anorexia has been theorised as both protest against and compliance with the constraints of normative femininity, this chapter considers the possibilities for resistance under the medical gaze. The second contextual chapter comprises empirical research into a set of women's magazines. It explores how these mainstream texts police women's bodies through discourses which disguise such calls to discipline – devices which I argue in later chapters are brought to the fore by the pro-ana phenomenon.

Turning to pro-ana online spaces, chapter three interrogates the changes they have undergone since their inception: it first considers the original pro-ana landscape before attending to its current incarnation on social media platforms. Building on the discourses of disguise identified in the pre- vious chapter, I show how pro-ana users adopt such discourses to legitimise their texts – the result of which is contributing towards the normalising of their culture. Chapter four develops these claims to normalisation, arguing that despite research continually refuting common sense understandings of anorexia as a white, middle-class, heterofeminine concern, the depiction of the anorectic in pro-ana online spaces conforms to such an image. In so doing, pro-ana online spaces highlight the extent to which the thin ideal operates around privileged social categories.

In chapter five, I look to the role of pain in pro-ana culture, showing how it is presented either as a beneficial investment or a self-destructive compul- sion. This chapter then, argues that pro-ana online spaces expose the extent to which pain is presented as necessary for realising the thin body required of not only anorexia, but normative femininity. This anticipates the final chapter that asks if this controversial phenomenon has the potential to form a counterpublic capable of redressing current understandings of the gendered culture of compulsory thinness. Following case study analysis of a selection of women-led publics, I argue that pro-ana should be read as a *postfeminist coun-terpublic* in that it contains the potential to disrupt the hegemonic order, but this is being hampered by the political climate in which it is situated.

Notes

1 Bruckman proposes four levels of disguise when using data gathered from the Internet. Depending on the sensitivity of the data, she advises they should be approached thus: 'on a continuum from no disguise, light disguise, moderate disguise, to heavy disguise' (2001, np).
2 During the research period, Webstagram was the optimum way to view Instagram posts in a web browser.
3 In some cases, – Pinterest for example – censorship meant the same posts were continually generated by a search term, in other cases, posts conforming to a type began to recur. At this point I ceased data collection. I then selected the central two months of data for analysis as these were the most complete: the first month having been very much trial and error, and the fourth and final month being highly repetitive. I selected days at random across the two month period, omitting recurring posts, which resulted in approximately 260 pages of text from forums, blogs, and websites (including screenshots from the frozen sites) and 1,459 unique posts resulting from hashtag and keyword searches (of which there were 567 Instagram posts; 432 Tumblr posts; 360 Pinterest posts; 100 Reddit posts). I then coded the data for dominant themes in both text and image; themes which would formulate the subject of each of the analysis chapters in this book.
4 See Charlotte Krolokke and Anne Scott Sorensen (2006) for detailed analysis on the three waves of feminism.
5 The fourth edition, text revision of the *Diagnostic and Statistical Manual of Mental Disorders* describes EDNOS as follows: 'for disorders of eating that do not meet the criteria for any specific Eating Disorder' (American Psychiatric Association 2000, p. 594). However, in the most recent publication of the *DSM*, EDNOS has been renamed 'Other Specified Feeding or Eating Disorder' (American Psychiatric Association 2013, p. 353). EDNOS is still popularly used in pro-ana online spaces.

References

American Psychiatric Association. (2000) *Diagnostic and Statistical Manual of Mental Disorders*, 4th edn, text revision (DSM-IV-TR). Arlington, VA: APA.
———. (2013) *Diagnostic and Statistical Manual of Mental Disorders*, 5th edn, (DSM – 5). Washington, DC: APA.
Andrist, L.C. (2003) 'Media images, body dissatisfaction, and disordered eating in adolescent women', *Adolescent Health*, 28(2), pp. 119–123.
Bardone-Cone, A.M. and Cass, K.M. (2006) 'Investigating the impact of pro-anorexia websites: A pilot study', *European Eating Disorders Review*, 14, pp. 256–262.
Barrett, M. (1980) *Women's Oppression Today: Problems in Marxist Feminist Analysis*. London: Verso.
Bartky, S.L. (1990) *Femininity and Domination: Studies in the Phenomenology of Oppression*. New York: Routledge.
Bassett, E.H. and O' Riordan, K. (2002) 'Ethics of Internet research: Contesting the human subjects research model', *Ethics and Information Technology*, 4(3), pp. 233–247.

Bell, M. (2009) '"@ the Doctor's Office": Pro-anorexia and the medical gaze', *Surveillance & Society*, 6(2), pp. 151–162.

Boellstorff, T. (2008) *Coming of Age in Second Life: An Anthropologist Explores the Virtually Human*. Princeton, NJ: Princeton University Press.

Boero, N. and Pascoe, C.J. (2012) 'Pro-anorexia communities and online interaction: Bringing the pro-ana body online', *Body & Society*, 18, pp. 27–57.

Bond, E. (2012) 'Virtually anorexic – Where's the harm? A research study on the risks of pro-anorexia websites'. Available at: www.ucs.ac.uk/SchoolsAndNetwork/Faculty-of-Arts,-Business-and-Applied-Social-Science/Department-of-Children,-Young-People-and-Education/Virtually%20Anorexic.pdf (Accessed February 2014).

Bordo, S. (1989) 'The body and the reproduction of femininity: A feminist appropriation of Foucault', in Jaggar, A.M. and Bordo, S. (eds.) *Gender/Body/Knowledge: Feminist Reconstructions of Being and Knowing*. New Brunswick, NJ: Rutgers University Press, pp. 13–33.

———. ([1993] 2003) *Unbearable Weight: Feminism, Western Culture and the Body*, 10th anniversary edition. Berkeley: University of California Press.

———. (2009) 'Not just "a white girl's thing": The changing face of food and body image problems', in Malson, H. and Burns, M. (eds.) *Critical Feminist Approaches to Eating Dis/orders*. London: Routledge, pp. 46–59.

Borzekowski, D.L.G., Schenk, S., Wilson, J.L., and Peebles, R. (2010) 'e-Ana and e-Mia: A content analysis of pro–eating disorder web sites', *American Journal of Public Health*, 100(8), pp. 1526–1534.

Brotsky, S.R. and Giles, D. (2007) 'Inside the "pro-ana" community: A covert online participant observation', *Eating Disorders: The Journal of Treatment & Prevention*, 15(2), pp. 93–109.

Brown, W. (2005) *Edgework: Critical Essays on Knowledge and Politics*. Princeton, NJ: Princeton University Press.

Bruckman, A. (2001) *Studying the Amateur Artist: A Perspective on Disguising Data Collected in Human Subjects Research on the Internet*. Available at: www.nyu.edu/projects/nissenbaum/ethics_bru_full.html (Accessed February 2014).

Bryson, V. (2003) *Feminist Political Theory: An Introduction*, 2nd edn. Basingstoke, Hampshire: Palgrave Macmillan.

Budgeon, S. (2015) 'Individualized femininity and feminist politics of choice', *European Journal of Women's Studies*, 22(3), pp. 303–318.

Burke, E. (2012) 'Reflections on the waif: Images of slenderness and distress in pro-anorexia websites', *Australian Feminist Studies*, 27(71), pp. 37–54.

Cantó-Milà, N. and Seebach, S. (2011) 'Ana's friends. Friendship in online pro-ana communities', *Sociological Research Online*, 16(1), unpaginated.

Casilli, A., Pailler, F., and Tubaro, P. (2013) 'Online networks of eating-disorder websites: Why censoring pro-ana might be a bad idea', *Perspectives in Public Health*, 133(2), pp. 94–95.

Casilli, A.A., Tubaro, P., and Araya, P. (2012) 'Ten years of ana: Lessons from a transdisciplinary body of literature on online pro-eating disorder websites', *Social Science Information*, 51, pp. 120–139.

Chancellor, S., Pater, J., Clear, T., Gilbert, E., and Choudhury, M.D. (2016) '#thyghgapp: Instagram content moderation and lexical variation in pro-eating disorder communities', *CSCW*, Proceedings of the 19th ACM Conference on Computer-Supported Cooperative Work & Social Computing, pp. 1201–1213.

Chernin, K. (1981) *The Obsession: Reflections on the Tyranny of Slenderness*. New York: Harper Perennial.

Christodoulou, M. (2012) 'Pro-anorexia websites pose public health challenge', *The Lancet*, 379, 14 January, p. 110.

Crowe, N. and Watts, M. (2014) '"We're just like Gok, but in reverse": Ana girls – Empowerment and resistance in digital communities', *International Journal of Adolescence and Youth*, 21(3), pp. 1–14.

Csipke, E. and Horne, O. (2007) 'Pro-eating disorder websites: Users' opinions', *European Eating Disorders Review*, 15, pp. 196–206.

Custers, K. and Van Den Bulck, J. (2009) 'Viewership of pro-anorexia websites in seventh, ninth and eleventh graders', *European Eating Disorders Review*, 17, pp. 214–219.

Day, K. and Keys, T. (2008a) 'Starving in cyberspace: A discourse analysis of pro-eating-disorder websites', *Journal of Gender Studies*, 17(1), pp. 1–15.

———. (2008b) 'Starving in cyberspace: The construction of identity on "pro-eating -disorder" websites', in Riley, S., Burns, M., Frith, H., Wiggins, S., and Markula, P. (eds.) *Critical Bodies: Representations, Identities and Practices of Weight and Body Management*. Basingstoke, Hampshire: Palgrave Macmillan, pp. 81–100.

———. (2009) 'Anorexia/bulimia as resistance and conformity in pro-Ana and pro-Mia virtual conversations', in Malson, H. and Burns, M. (eds.) *Critical Feminist Approaches to Eating Dis/orders*. London: Routledge, pp. 87–96.

Delforterie, M.J., Larsen, J.K., Bardone-Cone, A.M., and Scholte, R.H.J. (2014) 'Effects of viewing a pro-ana website: An experimental study on body satisfaction, affect, and appearance self-efficacy', *Eating Disorders*, 22(4), pp. 321–336.

Delgado, S. (2016) 'Eugenia Cooney: Would you want YOUR daughter idolising this stick-thin YouTube star?', *Express*, 29 October. Available at: www.express.co.uk/news/world/726539/Youtube-video-anorexia-Eugenia-Cooney-petition-ban-Euge nia-Cooney (Accessed January 2017).

Dias, K. (2003) 'The ana sanctuary: Women's pro-anorexia narratives in cyberspace', *Journal of International Women's Studies*, 4(2), pp. 31–45.

Echols, A. (1989) *Daring to Be Bad: Radical Feminism in America 1967–1975*. Minneapolis: University of Minnesota Press.

Ferreday, D. (2003) 'Unspeakable bodies: Erasure, embodiment and the pro-ana community', *International Journal of Cultural Studies*, 6(3), pp. 277–295.

———. (2009) *Online Belongings: Fantasy, Affect and Web Communities*. Oxford: Peter Lang.

Fox, N., Ward, K., and O'Rourke, A. (2005) 'Pro-anorexia, weight-loss drugs and the Internet: An "anti-recovery" explanatory model of anorexia', *Sociology of Health & Illness*, 27(7), pp. 944–971.

Fraser, N. (2013) *Fortunes of Feminism: From State-Managed Capitalism to Neoliberal Crisis*. London: Verso.

Friedan, B. (1963) *The Feminine Mystique*. New York: W.W. Norton & Company Inc.

Gailey, J.A. (2009) '"Starving is the most fun a girl can have": The pro-ana subculture as edgework', *Critical Criminology*, 17, pp. 93–108.

Gale, L., Channon, S., Larner, M., and James, D. (2016) 'Experiences of using pro-eating disorder websites: A qualitative study with service users in NHS eating disorder services', *Eating and Weight Disorder*, 21, pp. 427–434.

Gavin, J., Rodham, K., and Poyer, H. (2008) 'The presentation of "pro-anorexia" in online group interactions', *Qualitative Health Research*, 18(3), pp. 325–333.

Genz, S. and Brabon, B.A. (2009) *Postfeminism: Cultural Texts and Theories*. Edinburgh: Edinburgh University Press.

Gerrard, Y. (2018) 'Beyond the hashtag: Circumventing content moderation on social media', *New Media & Society*, 20(12), pp. 4492–4511.

Giles, D.C. and Newbold, J. (2011) 'Self- and other-diagnosis in user-led mental health online communities', *Qualitative Health Research*, 21(3), pp. 419–428.

Gill, R. (2007) 'Postfeminist media culture: Elements of a sensibility', *European Journal of Cultural Studies*, 10(2), pp. 147–166.

————. (2016) 'Post-postfeminism?: New feminist visibilities in postfeminist times', *Feminist Media Studies*, 16(4), pp. 610–630.

Gill, R. and Scharff, C. (2011) 'Introduction', in Gill, R. and Scharff, C. (eds.) *New Femininities: Postfeminism, Neoliberalism and Subjectivity*. London: Palgrave Macmillan, pp. 1–15.

Gillespie, T. (2014) 'The relevance of algorithms', in Gillespie, T., Boczkowski, P., and Foot, K. (eds.) *Media Technologies: Essays on Communication, Materiality, and Society*. MA: MIT, pp. 167–193.

Gimlin, D.L. (2002) *Body Work: Beauty and Self-Image in American Culture*. Berkeley: University of California Press.

Ging, D. and Garvey, S. (2018) '"Written in these scars are the stories I can't explain": A content analysis of pro-ana and thinspiration image sharing on Instagram', *New Media & Society*, 20(3), pp. 1181–1200.

Gitelman, L. and Jackson, V. (2013) 'Introduction', in Gitelman, L. (ed.) *"Raw Data" Is an Oxymoron*. Cambridge, MA: MIT Press, pp. 1–14.

Gooldin, S. (2008) 'Being anorexic hunger, subjectivity, and embodied morality', *Medical Anthropology Quarterly*, 22(3), pp. 274–296.

Harshbarger, J.L., Ahlers-Schmidt, C.R., Mayans, L., Mayans, D., and Hawkins, J.H. (2009) 'Pro-anorexia websites: What a clinician should know', *International Journal of Eating Disorders*, 42, pp. 367–370.

Hartley, C. (2001) 'Letting ourselves go: Making room for the fat body in feminist scholarship', in Braziel, J.E. and LeBesco, K. (eds.) *Bodies Out of Bounds: Fatness and Transgression*. Berkeley: University of California Press, pp. 60–73.

Herzog, D.B., Bradburn, I.S., and Newman, K. (1990) 'Sexuality in males with eating disorders', in Andersen, A.E. (ed.) *Males with Eating Disorders*. New York: Brunner/Mazel, Inc., pp. 40–53.

Hill, A. (2001) 'Girls in danger as anorexics give weight-loss tips on web', *The Observer*, 12 August, p. 10.

Hine, C. (2000) *Virtual Ethnography*. London: Sage.

Holmes, S. (2015) '"That perfect girl is gone": Pro-ana, Anorexia and *Frozen* (2013) as an "eating disorder" film', *Participations: Journal of Audience and Reception Studies*, 12(2), pp. 98–120.

hooks, b. (2015) *Ain't I a Woman: Black Women and Feminism*, 2nd edn. New York: Routledge.

Jett, S., LaPorte, D.J., and Wanchisn, J. (2010) 'Impact of exposure to pro-eating disorder websites on eating behaviour in college women', *European Eating Disorders Review*, 18, pp. 410–416.

Jones, M. (2008) *Skintight: An Anatomy of Cosmetic Surgery*. Oxford: Berg.

Krolokke, C. and Sorensen, A.S. (2006) *Gender Communication Theories and Analyses: From Silence to Performance*. Thousand Oaks, CA: Sage.

Lapinski, M.L. (2006) 'StarvingforPerfect.com: A theoretically based content analysis of pro-eating disorder web sites', *Health Communication*, 20(3), pp. 243–253.

Lewis, S.P. and Arbuthnott, A.E. (2012) 'Searching for thinspiration: The nature of Internet searches for pro-eating disorder websites', *Cyberpsychology, Behavior, and Social Networking*, 15(4), pp. 200–204.

Lupton, D. (1996) *Food, the Body and the Self*. London: Sage.

Malson, H. (1998) *The Thin Woman: Feminism, Post-structuralism, and the Social Psychology of Anorexia Nervosa*. New York: Routledge.

Markham, A.N. (2005) 'The methods, politics, and ethics of representation in online ethnography', in Denzin, N. and Lincoln, Y. (eds.) *Handbook of Qualitative Research*, 3rd edn. Thousand Oaks, CA: Sage, pp. 793–820.

———. (2012) 'Fabrication as ethical practice', *Information, Communication & Society*, 15(3), pp. 334–353.

Martijn, C., Smeets, E., Jansen, A., Hoeymans, N., and Schoemaker, C. (2009) 'Don't get the message: The effect of a warning text before visiting a proanorexia website', *International Journal of Eating Disorders*, 42, pp. 139–145.

Maynard, M. (1994) 'Methods, practice and epistemology: The debate about feminism and research', in Maynard, M. and Purvis, J. (eds.) *Researching Women's Lives from a Feminist Perspective*. London: Taylor & Francis, pp. 10–26.

McKinley, N.M. (1999) 'Ideal weight/ideal women: Society constructs the female', in Sobal, J. and Maurer, D. (eds.) *Weighty Issues: Fatness and Thinness as Social Problems*. New York: Aldine de Gruyter, pp. 97–115.

McRobbie, A. (2004) 'Post-feminism and popular culture', *Feminist Media Studies*, 4(3), pp. 255–264.

———. (2009) *The Aftermath of Feminism: Gender, Culture and Social Change*. London: Sage Publications Ltd.

Miah, A. and Rich, E. (2008) *The Medicalization of Cyberspace*. Abingdon, OX: Routledge.

Moreno, M.A., Ton, A., Selkie, E., and Evans, Y. (2016) 'Secret society 123: Understanding the language of self-harm on Instagram', *Journal of Adolescent Health*, 58, pp. 78–84.

Munro, E. (2013) 'Feminism: A fourth wave?', *Political Insight*, 4(2), pp. 22–25.

Nguyen, T. (2013) 'From SlutWalks to SuicideGirls: Feminist resistance in the third wave and postfeminist era', *Women's Studies Quarterly*, 41(3 & 4), pp. 157–172.

Nissenbaum, H. (2010) *Privacy in Context: Technology, Policy, and the Integrity of Social Life*. Stanford, CA: Stanford University Press.

Norris, M.L., Boydell, K.M., Pinhas, L., and Katzman, D.K. (2006) 'Ana and the Internet: A review of pro-anorexia websites', *International Journal of Eating Disorders*, 39, pp. 443–447.

Oksanen, A., Garcia, D., Sirola, A., Näsi, M., Kaakinen, M., Keipi, T., and Räsänen, P. (2015) 'Pro-anorexia and anti-pro-anorexia videos on YouTube: Sentiment analysis of user responses', *Journal of Medical Internet Research*, 17(11), unpaginated.

Pan, W. and Peña, J. (2017) 'The exposure effects of online model pictures and weight-related persuasive messages on women's weight-loss planned behaviors', *Journal of Health Communication*, 22(10), pp. 858–865.

Pinterest. (2014) Available at: www.pinterest.com (Accessed July 2014).

Polak, M. (2010) '"I think we must be normal … there are too many of us for this to be abnormal!!!": Girls creating identity and forming community in pro-ana/mia websites', in Weber, S. and Dixon, S. (eds.) *Growing Up Online: Young People and Digital Technologies*, 2nd edn. New York: Palgrave Macmillan, pp. 83–96.

Pollack, D. (2003) 'III. Pro-eating disorder websites: What should be the feminist response?', *Feminism & Psychology*, 13(2), pp. 246–251.

Ransom, D.C., La Guardia, J.G., Woody, E.Z., and Boyd, J.L. (2010) 'Interpersonal interactions on online forums addressing eating concerns', *International Journal of Eating Disorders*, 43, pp. 161–170.

Reddit (2014) Available at: www.reddit.com/ (Accessed July 2014).

Retallack, H., Ringrose, J., and Lawrence, E. (2016) '"Fuck your body image": Teen girls' Twitter and Instagram feminism in and around school', in Coffey, J., Budgeon, S., and Cahill, H. (eds.) *Learning Bodies: The Bodies in Youth and Childhood Studies*. New York: Springer, pp. 85–103.

Rich, E. (2006) 'Anorexic dis(connection): Managing anorexia as an illness and an identity', *Sociology of Health & Illness*, 28(3), pp. 284–305.

Ringrose, J. and Walkerdine, V. (2008) 'Regulating the abject: The TV make-over as site of neo-liberal reinvention toward bourgeois femininity', *Feminist Media Studies*, 8(3), pp. 227–246.

Rodgers, R.F., Skowron, S., and Chabrol, H. (2012) 'Disordered eating and group membership among members of a pro-anorexic online community', *European Eating Disorders Review*, 20, pp. 9–12.

Rottenberg, C. (2014) 'The rise of neoliberal feminism', *Cultural Studies*, 28(3), pp. 418–437.

Rouleau, C.R. and von Ranson, K.M. (2011) 'Potential risks of pro-eating disorder websites', *Clinical Psychology Review*, 31, pp. 525–531.

Ryan-Flood, R. and Gill, R. (2010) 'Introduction', in Gill, R. and Ryan-Flood, R. (eds.) *Secrecy and Silence in the Research Process: Feminist Reflections*. Abingdon, OX: Routledge, pp. 1–11.

Scharff, C. (2011) 'The new German feminisms: Of wetlands and alpha-girls', in Gill, R. and Scharff, C. (eds.) *New Femininities: Postfeminism, Neoliberalism and Subjectivity*. London: Palgrave Macmillan, pp. 265–278.

———. (2012) *Repudiating Feminism: Young Women in a Neoliberal World*. Farnham, Surrey and Burlington, VT: Ashgate Publishing Company.

Schott, N.D. and Langan, D. (2015) 'Pro-anorexia/bulimia censorship and public service announcements: The price of controlling women', *Media, Culture & Society*, 37(8), pp. 1158–1175.

Shapiro, R.B. and Ossorio, P.N. (2013) 'Regulation of online social network studies', *Science*, 339, pp. 1–2.

Skeggs, B. (2004) *Class, Self, Culture*. London: Routledge.

Smith, N., Wickes, R., and Underwood, M. (2015) 'Managing a marginalised identity in pro-anorexia and fat acceptance cyber communities', *Journal of Sociology*, 51(4), pp. 950–967.

Sobal, J. and Maurer, D. (1999) 'The social management of fatness and thinness', in Sobal, J. and Maurer, D. (eds.) *Interpreting Weight: The Social Management of Fatness and Thinness*. New York: Aldine de Gruyter, pp. 3–8.

Strife, S.R. and Rickard, K. (2011) 'The conceptualization of anorexia: The pro-ana perspective', *Affilia*, 26(2), pp. 213–217.

Tasker, Y. and Negra, D. (2007) 'Introduction: Feminist politics and postfeminist culture', in Tasker, Y. and Negra, D. (eds.) *Interrogating Postfeminism: Gender and the Politics of Popular Culture*. Durham: Duke University Press, pp. 1–25.

Throsby, K. and Gimlin, D. (2010) 'Critiquing thinness and wanting to be thin', in Gill, R. and Ryan-Flood, R. (eds.) *Secrecy and Silence in the Research Process: Feminist Reflections*. Abingdon, OX: Routledge, pp. 105–116.

Tierney, S. (2008) 'Creating communities in cyberspace: Pro-anorexia web sites and social capital', *Journal of Psychiatric and Mental Health Nursing*, 15, pp. 340–343.

Tumblr (2014) Available at: www.tumblr.com/(Accessed July 2014).

Vellar, A. (2018) '#anawarrior identities and the stigmatization process: An ethnography in Italian networked publics', *First Monday*, 23, p. 6.

Webstagram (2014) Available at: www.web.stagram.com (Accessed July 2014).

Williams, S. and Reid, M. (2010) 'Understanding the experience of ambivalence in anorexia nervosa: The maintainer's perspective', *Psychology & Health*, 25(5), pp. 551–567.

Winch, A. (2013) *Girlfriends and Postfeminist Sisterhood*. Basingstoke, Hampshire: Palgrave Macmillan.

Wolf, N. (1991) *The Beauty Myth: How Images of Beauty Are Used against Women*. New York: Harper Perennial.

Yeshua-Katz, D. and Martins, N. (2013) 'Communicating stigma: The pro-ana paradox', *Health Communication*, 2(5), pp. 499–508.

Yom-Tov, E., Brunstein-Klomek, A., Hadas, A., Tamir, O., and Fennig, S. (2016) 'Differences in physical status, mental state and online behavior of people in pro-anorexia web communities', *Eating Behaviors*, 22, pp. 109–112.

Yom-Tov, E., Fernandez-Luque, L., Weber, I., and Crain, S.P. (2012) 'Pro-anorexia and pro-recovery photo sharing: A tale of two warring tribes', *Journal of Medical Internet Research*, 14(6), unpaginated.

Zimmer, M. (2010) '"But the data is already public": On the ethics of research in Facebook', *Ethics and Information Technology*, 12(4), pp. 313–325.

1 Medicine, maladies and *anorexia nervosa*

I take the psychopathologies that develop within a culture, far from being anomalies or aberrations, to be characteristic expressions of that culture; to be, indeed, the crystallization of much that is wrong with it.
(Bordo [1993] 2003, p. 141)

The folding into each other of pathologised, therapeutically intended and normative constructions and practices suggests instead the need to disrupt the normative rather than scapegoat the therapeutically intended.
(Malson 2008, p. 39)

For Susan Bordo, we might better understand a culture through interrogation of its designated ills; for Helen Malson, it is a culture's norms that must be probed. The pro-anorexia phenomenon offers an opportunity to critique *both* factions: it has been pathologised in the press and in scholarship, yet all too often its texts are indistinguishable from normative constructions of the female body. In order to appreciate how pro-ana online spaces came to be, first we must attend to the cultural landscape from which they emerged. As such, the first two chapters of this book are contextual, interrogating the disciplining of the female body within medicine and popular culture, respectively. In this first chapter, I explore the history of the medical gaze, tracing the way the female body has been discursively produced by medicine. As I highlighted in the introduction to this book, the pro-ana phenomenon has been examined at length in the health sciences and has, therefore, been framed as a medical issue. However, pro-ana's relationship with medicine is more complex than this and feminist and socio-cultural scholars of the phenomenon read it as an affront to medical authority (Bell 2009; Day and Keys 2008a, 2008b, 2009; Gailey 2009). Mebbie Bell, for instance, argues that pro-ana spaces '"teach" individuals how to perform a "normal" body in order to evade the regulatory authority invested in the medical gaze' (2009, p. 152). Thus, whilst there is important work on pro-ana in the health sciences, to read it as solely medical disregards the extent to which it is constituted by mainstream thinness culture. To be clear, my argument is not that anorexia is borne out of young women's uncritical consumption of media images of thin bodies (cf. Malson 2009, p. 143), nor do I suggest that *pro*-anorexia is. Rather I propose that pro-ana culture utilises media images of thin bodies *as well as* the language of health and medicine in order to service its aims. In so doing, it disrupts the constructed boundaries between acceptable and pathological renderings of thinness.

This chapter, then, outlines how the medical gaze became an almighty force in Western culture, specifically attending to the impact this has had on women. It is divided into four sections. The first explores the development of the medical gaze during the European Enlightenment; the second interrogates how the medical gaze played a part in the subordination of women: their removal from the medical profession and subsequent objectification – here I attend to the medicalisation of the female body and the construction of norms of femininity. This leads to the third section where I explore the cultural construction of *anorexia nervosa*. I suggest the way anorexia has been utilised as a form of social control is symptomatic of the treatment of women's bodies in Western culture, as well as the ubiquity of disordered eating. In the final section, I interrogate opportunities for resistance under the medical gaze.

The development of the medical gaze

Any discussion of the Western medical gaze must begin by looking to the Enlightenment period. It is well documented that during this time Western culture witnessed a significant shift in medical knowledge and practice: it was a process whereby doctors were conceptualised, through a discourse of scientific objectivity and authority, as the arbiters of bodily meaning. As societal faith in an all-powerful God was waning, belief in the abilities of the medical practitioner was growing, and medicine came to replace religion (Ehrenreich and English 1979; Hepworth 1999; Turner 1996). As Foucault argues, 'In the patient's eyes, the doctor becomes a thaumaturge' (1967, p. 275), and as the doctor's power grew, the patient ceased to be actively involved in their own medicalisation: 'only an external fact; the medical reading must take [the patient] into account only to place him [sic] in parentheses' (1973, p. 7). This dehumanising process rendered all individuals subservient to the medical gaze, regardless of gender. The gaze sought to penetrate all aspects of society, 'growing in a complex, ever-proliferating way until it finally achiev[ed] the dimensions of a history, a geography, a state' (Foucault 1973, p. 29). Foucault calls this manifestation of control on the micro and macro levels, 'bio-power', suggesting that it 'was without question an indispensable element in the development of capitalism' (1976, pp. 140–141). Illness and morbidity had to be prevented in order to maintain a productive workforce and 'this preventive focus later became instrumental in structuring a national health care system in England' (Hepworth 1999, p. 21). Thus, as Martin Hewitt reminds us, 'the entrance of the human sciences into administration was not guided by humanitarianism but by the advent of disciplinary technologies' (1983, p. 243).

Control over the population then, was enacted through technologies of normalisation where bodies came to be differentiated and managed by their proximity to or aberrance from the norm (Foucault 1973, 1976). As such, what was considered healthy and what was considered normal became interchangeable – a legacy that persists. For instance, in the present day, the healthy citizen is encouraged to use the Body Mass Index (BMI) calculator to determine whether they are of a healthy weight, through measurement against a regulatory norm (Czerniawski 2007). Technologies of normalisation are by no means limited to the regulation of body weight though: Miah and Rich (2008, p. 53) note that public health websites such as the NHS and BBC not only provide advice on disease prevention, but they also feature lifestyle advice more broadly. Deborah Lupton views such guidance as 'a form of pedagogy, which like other forms, serves to legitimize ideologies and social practices by making statements about how individuals should conduct their bodies' (1994, p. 31). Consequently, *health* is deployed as a means of obscuring *unhealthy* practices, a device which, as I show in later chapters, pro-ana users adopt in order to safeguard their spaces. Used in this way, health is reduced to discourse because, as Foucault argues, 'power is tolerable only on condition that it mask a substantial part of itself. Its success is proportional to its ability to hide its own mechanisms' (1976, p. 86). If the disciplinary practices in which we engage are recast as necessary for our own good, we are much more likely to enact them. Simon J. Williams therefore suggests that health is 'a contested notion and an *elusive* phenomenon' (2003, p. 42; emphasis added). What it means to be healthy is increasingly ambiguous which, in turn, renders it susceptible to appropriation, whether by public health services, the diet industry or – as I will argue – creators of pro-ana online spaces.

Above all, contemporary culture elides good health and weight loss: 'Reformulated as health maximising, weight-loss practices, particularly dieting, have now been made to appear necessary, beneficial and hence seemingly above reproach' (Malson 2008, p. 29). The impact that this has had on understandings of 'obesity'[1] is therefore extensive: it is widely seen as dangerous; as a health threat in need of prevention (Cogan 1999, p. 231). Compulsory thinness and the avoidance of 'obesity' are often framed as moral obligations and scholars of Fat Studies have argued that if one is 'obese', one is understood to be a moral failure (Hartley 2001; Haworth-Hoeppner 1999; LeBesco 2004). This has led to a repudiation of the fat body in Western culture, which is both justified and encouraged. As Cecilia Hartley (2001, p. 65) points out, 'fat-phobia is one of the few acceptable forms of prejudice left in a society that at times goes to extremes to prove itself politically correct'. If 'obesity' and fatness are conflated with illness (LeBesco 2004, p. 30) then thinness has, albeit fallaciously, come to be read as a marker of good health and good morals (Bordo [1993] 2003). In this current (Western) climate of plenty, only the most disciplined individuals are able to achieve thinness. This, in turn, makes the quest ever more elusive.

Dieting as a moral obligation, however, is not new and Bryan S. Turner locates it within nineteenth century control of disease, whereby cleanliness of both the masses and the individual corresponded with one another:

The diseases of civilization were to be countered by personal salvation and clean water. The dietary management of the body was thus parallel to the management of water and sanitation in the environment, since both were aimed at moral control of impurity.

(1982, p. 165)

Cleanliness and dietary management are both concerned with 'policing the boundaries of the body, by maintaining strict control over what enters and what leaves the body's orifices' (Lupton 1994, p. 32). As I discuss in chapter four, thinness and cleanliness continue to be elided and this discourse manifests in pro-ana online spaces and mainstream guidance around healthy-eating alike. Although self-regulating the body through diet may sound Foucauldian, Turner (1992) points out that in Foucault's examination of Jeremy Bentham's Panopticon, he overlooks the science of diet and its relationship to capitalism. Turner argues that the provenance of the dietary regime lies in the work of eighteenth-century physicist to the elite, George Cheyne, who advised upper-class individuals on how to control their weight through careful eating and exercise; practices which then permeated all strata of society (1992, p. 192). What began as a specific lifestyle for the elite became an aspiration for all, but this was not a lifestyle for the poor, rather for 'people who could afford to eat, ride horses and enjoy the luxury of a regular vomit' (Turner 1992, p. 190). Thus, possession of a slim body was not simply a means of showing one's distance from the working class, rather, as Bordo points out, 'the gracefully slender body announced aristocratic status; disdainful of the bourgeois need to display wealth and power ostentatiously' ([1993] 2003, p. 191). Thinness, as it is today, was a way of indicating one's refinement, but only the refined had the resources to achieve it. Consequently, the thin *cum* healthy body is not accessible to everyone: it is located at the intersection of a range of privileges, as chapter four's critical enquiries demonstrate.

More widely, the political economy of medicine maintains a number of systemic inequalities. According to Foucault, this stems from what he calls 'the great confinement' in the classical age where those believed to be disruptive to order, 'the unemployed, the idle, and vagabonds', were very literally incarcerated (1967, p. 50). The poor and disenfranchised were alternately confined and deployed to contribute to the economy: 'cheap manpower in the periods of full employment and high salaries; and in periods of unemployment, reabsorption of the idle and social protection against agitation and uprisings' (Foucault 1967, p. 51). This meant that even those who departed from socially acceptable norms were rendered useful during this time. Although confinement does not operate so literally today, there are still many instances in which medicine is deployed to increase an individual's capabilities and thus make them useful under late-capitalism. Using examples such as the prescription of anti-depressants or meditation to divert patients' attention from socio-economic factors which may be impeding them, Lupton argues that 'in their relative dominance over patients, doctors are empowered to make statements that reinforce dominant capitalist ideologies by directing patients' behaviour into non-threatening channels' (1994, p. 108). In this way, medicine colludes with capitalism to shore up the status quo by, at times literally, anaesthetising its subjects. The medical gaze thus operates as a form of social control on both the individual and societal level. Through bio-power, we become self-regulating, self-disciplining citizens. Our quest may be one which aims for good health, but health, as we have seen, is often deployed to obscure practices which uphold the hegemonic order. Nowhere is this more prominent than in the treatment of women by medical authority.

The medical gaze and women

Foucault's account of the birth of modern medicine, whilst important to this study, neglects to address the position of women. In order to make way for medical authority as we now know it, women were effectively ousted from the profession and rendered passive objects of a gaze, which would ensure their subordination for centuries to come (Ehrenreich and English 1979). This crucial moment deserves sustained discussion: consequently, the remainder of this chapter, whilst drawing upon a Foucauldian framework, focuses on the side-lined history of women and medicine. As I have shown, medical discourse has long impelled individuals to engage in regulatory practices which it legitimates under the umbrella of science, a form of 'objective' authoritative knowledge. But the development of this knowledge, together with the process by which it was legitimated, was by no means neutral; rather as I will now explore, it was masculine.

Barbara Ehrenreich and Deidre English's (1979) important work on women's expulsion from the medical profession describes how their mutual support networks were effectively destroyed in the name of medical legitimation. Women were isolated from one other and subsequently made dependent upon those same men who had banished them. The purging of midwives in the early twentieth century was a pinnacle moment in ensuring women's inferior status:

> With the elimination of midwifery, all women – not just those of the upper class – fell under the biological hegemony of the medical profession. In the same stroke women lost their last autonomous role as healers. The only roles left for women in the medical system were as employees, customers, or "material".
>
> (Ehrenreich and English 1979, p. 88)

With women confined to the margins, men's status as experts was confirmed, and it was middle-class men who were said to possess the expertise to transform conventional medicine into 'scientific' medicine (Ehrenreich and English 1979, p. 70). As a result, the medical profession became, as it arguably remains, primarily the reserve of the middle-class, white patriarch.

Because women have long been seen to 'occupy the world of private emotion and affections, whereas men are allocated to social roles emphasizing reason, instrumentality, and public responsibility' (Turner 1995, p. 95), science did not look kindly on them. Consequently, 'the very notion of the dispassionate scientist, whose mind transcended his body, defined science as a male pursuit. The *object* of scientific knowledge – that is nature – was female' (Hesse-Biber 1996, p. 19; emphasis added). If women were too weak and lacking in reason to be doctors, then they were perfectly positioned to be patients (Ehrenreich and English 1979, p. 92; see also Turner 1995, pp. 102–103). This subjugation served a dual purpose: Western culture has historically framed the female body in binaries: 'beautiful but unclean, alluring, but dangerous […] mysterious, duplicitous – a source of pleasure and nurturance, but also of destruction and evil' (Suleiman 1986, p. 1), therefore, by rendering women patients, male doctors were able to exert control over that which they were hitherto unable to understand. This has led scholars to describe the male scientific triumph over the female body in terms of colonisation (McGrath 2002, p. 30; Turner 1995, p. 28). As Roberta McGrath (2002, p. 30) suggests, 'maps and women's bodies both harboured and advanced fantasies and projections of future invasion'. That this 'invasion' of women's bodies occurred at the height of the European empires' projects of colonisation suggests a particular nervousness amid the otherwise secure patriarchy surrounding that which they did not know, or could not understand, both globally and in the domestic sphere.

Sander L. Gilman (1985) shows how apparent discoveries around female sexuality and racial difference both paralleled and informed one another. Drawing on Sigmund Freud's notion of adult female sexuality as 'the "dark continent" of psychology' (Gilman 1985, p. 238), as an unknown quantity, he argues:

> It is Freud's intent to explore this hidden "dark continent" and reveal the hidden truths about female sexuality, just as the anthropologist – explorers (such as Lombroso) were revealing the hidden truths about the nature of the black. Freud continues a discourse which relates the images of male discovery to the images of the female as object of discovery.
>
> (Ibid.)

It is instructive that the repression of women via medicine should occur at the backdrop of the nineteenth century *fin de siècle*. At a time when the New Woman was emerging, medicine was seeking to reinstate her in a traditional, unthreatening role via its deployment of Foucault's 'normalizing gaze' (Hesse-Biber 1991, p. 176). Creating an anatomy of the female body meant the patriarchy could contain that which it saw as a threat to its authority. Men's fear of femininity has been explored at length in the field of psychoanalysis, with Freud suggesting that 'the man is afraid of being weakened by the woman, infected with her femininity and of then showing himself incapable' ([1918] 1991, p. 271). As such, Mary Ann Doane aligns representations of women with those of disease: 'they are both socially devalued or undesirable, marginalized elements which constantly threaten to infiltrate and contaminate that which is more central, health or masculinity' (1985, p. 152). Nowhere is this elision of femininity and disease more pronounced than in the nineteenth century hystericisation of the female body.

Foucault describes hystericisation as 'a threefold process whereby the female body was analyzed – qualified and disqualified – as being thoroughly saturated with sexuality; whereby it was integrated into the sphere of medical practice' (1976, p. 104). By diagnosing women as hysterical, and therefore irrational, the patriarchy was able to reign with the backing of science. It was no coincidence, then, that as women demanded greater freedoms, patriarchal institutions sought to undermine them, bolstered as they were by science and the academy (Sayers cited in Hepworth 1999, p. 37). Hysteria can therefore be read as a patriarchal construct deployed in order to stymie women's emancipation – and for that matter physical movement – by literally sending them to their sickbeds. It would become the answer to everything, 'a catchall for the fantasies, not of the person who is or believes himself ill, but of the ignorant doctor who pretends to know why' (Foucault 1967, p. 138). In short, medicine was dominated by male practitioners who claimed more knowledge of women's bodies than women themselves, knowledge which ironically, contained more than a degree of fantasy (McGrath 2002, p. 30). This meant that women, having been expelled from the medical profession, were now being alienated from their own bodies.

The medicalisation of the female body in the nineteenth and twentieth centuries operated to reinforce and even idealise oppressive gender roles. During the Victorian period, agoraphobia, an illness that literally kept women indoors, was as common a diagnosis as hysteria. It became 'expressive of Victorian morality in which the good woman was a woman within a household' (Turner 1995, p. 106). The sick, house-bound female was reconstructed as aspirational, and not only for the middle-classes (Bordo [1993] 2003; Ehrenreich and English 1979; Michie 1987; Turner 1995). In other words, to be ill, was to be ideally feminine. For Bordo (1989) then, female disorders and 'normal' female practices operate on a continuum. She suggests that we might view female maladies as *exposing* normative femininity:

> In hysteria, agoraphobia, and anorexia, the woman's body may thus be viewed as a surface on which conventional constructions of femininity are exposed starkly to view, through their inscription in extreme or hyperliteral form.
>
> (Bordo 1989, p. 20)

This is a point I address throughout this book: the extent to which pro-ana online spaces expose not only medical authority but also hegemonic femininity. Ironically, the nineteenth-century medical gaze, which claimed to shed light upon darkness and uncover the secrets of the body, actually shrouded it further in mystery. Analysis of so-called female pathology then, reveals more about the cultural construction of gender than it does about the anatomy of the body. Furthermore, through close examination of 'normal' femininity, the blurred boundaries between that which is considered pathological and that which is considered normative are illuminated.

But how are such practices maintained? Feminist theorists of the body engage with a range of Foucauldian theory to account for the continued regulation of the female body, but *Discipline and Punish: The Birth of the Prison* (1979) where Foucault puts forward his theory of the disciplines has taken precedence. Here, he shows how 'discipline produces subjected and practised bodies, "docile" bodies' (Foucault 1979, p. 137), using the metaphor of the Panopticon to illustrate how 'the automatic functioning of power' is guaranteed (1979, p. 201). For Bordo (1989), 'through the pursuit of an ever-changing, homogenizing elusive ideal of femininity [...] female bodies become what Foucault calls "docile bodies"' (1989, p. 14; see also Bordo [1993] 2003). For Sandra Lee Bartky (1990), women internalise a Panoptical male gaze, which renders them self-surveilling subjects. Although Bartky's position has been criticised as 'needlessly reductionist' (Deveaux 1994, p. 226), her thesis has been influential in a contemporary reading of the male gaze, with Winch suggesting that in postfeminist 'girlfriend culture', women are complicit (2013, p. 6). Winch coins the 'girlfriend gaze' (2013), whereby women are seen to embrace their '*to-be-looked-at-ness*' (Mulvey 1975, p. 11, emphasis in original) on the understanding that it is in their best interests to invest in their body and self as a neoliberal project (Winch 2013, p. 21). Such discourses are embraced by the women's magazines, which I present in the next chapter.

Importantly, both Bartky and Bordo emphasise that for women to remain focussed on their pursuit of the ideal, it is necessary that compulsory participation in the 'fashion-beauty complex' is constructed as pleasurable (Bartky 1990); that a transformation takes place in which 'conditions that are "objectively" (and on one level, experientially) constraining, enslaving, and even murderous, come to be experienced as liberating, transforming, and life-giving' (Bordo 1989, p. 15). If the quest for the ideal is framed as enjoyable and even therapeutic, then conformity to its requirements is more readily guaranteed. However, at the same time, as pain is converted into pleasure, signifiers of health are redefined as illness, as Naomi Wolf (1991) explores at length in *The Beauty Myth*. In line with Bordo et al., Wolf draws comparisons between modern–day 'disorders' and those of the nineteenth century, to suggest that 'both the Victorian and the modern medical systems reclassify aspects of healthy femaleness into grotesque abnormality' (1991, p. 22). In sum, present-day notions of what is normal and healthy are paradoxical; by medicalising beauty and beautifying medicine, the medical and beauty industries collectively assure the self-regulation of the female body.

The apotheosis of the 'medico-beauty paradigm' (Jones 2008) is in cosmetic surgery culture, where breast augmentation, rhinoplasty and lip implants are depicted in the diction of medicine and beauty simultaneously. A sustained discussion of the politics of cosmetic surgery is more than can be undertaken in this book; however, it is imperative to point out here that simply because such procedures are constructed in this way, women should not be seen as passive dupes. Kathy Davis is adamant about this and emphasises the importance of individual decision-making, arguing that 'cosmetic surgery can be an informed choice, but it is always made in a context of limited options and circumstances that are not of the individual's making' (1995, p. 13). Contrary to Davis and in line with Bordo, my focus is not on whether such practices are empowering for the individuals who engage in them, rather I am interested in the 'complexly and densely institutionalized *system* of values and practices', which constructs them as necessary (Bordo [1993] 2003, p. 32; emphasis in original). As Meredith Jones argues, cosmetic surgery is 'too complicated a practice to be analysed in terms of agency or victimhood' (2008, p. 16). Anorexia and, to an extent, pro-anorexia have been subject to juxtaposing evaluations, which position them as either protest against or compliance with patriarchal structures – or both. Nonetheless, like Jones, I suggest that approaching practices in such a way oversimplifies them. I attend to this in detail throughout the book, but next, I turn to the history of anorexia.

Medicalising anorexia

Anorexia held cultural significance long before it became a medical category in the nineteenth century. A number of scholars locate it within a history of female piety, where the female saints of medieval Europe were said to engage in *anorexia mirabilis* or miraculous starvation (Bell 1985; Brumberg 1988; Bynum 1997; Hepworth 1999; Vandereycken and Van Deth 1994). However, Walter Vandereycken and Ron Van Deth (1994) point out that fasting was central to Western religion long before the medieval period, as well as being a practice which was undertaken by men. From the twelfth century onwards though, women had begun to participate more in religious life and as the female saints gained prominence, so did their eating practices. The self-starvation endured by these women was considered miraculous and 'the chronicles and hagiographies of the period tell numerous stories of women who ate almost nothing or claimed to be incapable of eating earthly fare' (Brumberg 1988, p. 41). Comparisons then between *anorexia nervosa* and *anorexia mirabilis* have been abundant, with Rudolph M. Bell (1985) proposing a direct correlation between the self-starving female saints of the middle-ages and present-day anorectics. Joan Jacobs Brumberg, however, disagrees with the parallels between these women, suggesting that 'to conflate the two is to ignore the cultural context and the distinction between sainthood and patienthood' (1988, p. 46). For instance, it has latterly been suggested that Catherine of Siena, the first and perhaps most famous 'holy anorexic', self-starved, not out of commitment to God, but because she was ill (Vandereycken and Van Deth 1994, p. 27). There is a danger here though, argues Caroline Walker Bynum, of simply suggesting that 'these medieval eating disorders are different from nineteenth- and twentieth-century ones only because medieval people "theologized" what we today "medicalize"' (Bynum 1997, p. 145). Equally, this places women who self-restrict within a dichotomous framework where if they are not 'normal' then they are saintly or sickly. Bynum's analysis is more nuanced: she suggests that the holy anorectic emerged because, 'In medieval Europe (as in many countries today) women are associated with food preparation and distribution rather than food consumption. The culture suggested that women cook and serve, men eat' (1997, p. 146). As such, women's non-participation in eating stemmed from their roles as servants, rather than self-imposed religious abstention:

> Chronicle accounts of medieval banquets, for example, indicate that the sexes were often segregated and that women were sometimes relegated to watching from the balconies while gorgeous foods were rolled out to please the eyes as well as the palates of men.
>
> (Bynum 1997, p. 146)

There are similarities here between women and food as passive objects of a male gaze. In this context, food is a metonym for traditional femininity: passive, beautiful and there for men's pleasure. During the medieval period then, women were central to food practices, yet paradoxically divorced from them, in the same way that during the nineteenth century they became synonymous with their bodies and simultaneously alienated from them. As such, the 'discovery' of *anorexia nervosa* in Europe in the nineteenth century provides insight, not only into the medical culture of the time, but also women's present-day estrangement from their bodies.

Julie Hepworth suggests that the advent of anorexia operated to reinforce women's inferior status (1999, p. 27), arguing that 'the early influence of this early classification has continued through to the late twentieth century and the categorization of *anorexia nervosa* within the *Diagnostic and Statistical Manual of Mental Disorders – IV Revised (DSM-R)*' (1999, p. 2). Published by the American Psychiatric Association, the *Diagnostic and Statistical Manual of Mental Disorders (DSM)* is a reference guide used to diagnose mental disorders. Since Hepworth was writing, *DSM-5* has been published and *anorexia nervosa* remains a listed mental disorder (American Psychiatric Association 2013, pp. 338–345). Although there is some discrepancy around the exact date, it is generally agreed that *anorexia nervosa* became a medical category in 1873, when eminent English physician Sir William Withey Gull, and synchronously in France, neurologist Dr Charles Lasègue assigned it as such (Brumberg 1988; Hepworth 1999; Heywood 1996). For these physicians, such a finding was a coup and as Hepworth wryly notes 'Drs W.W. Gull and E.C. Lasègue have been credited, and have credited themselves, with the "discovery" of anorexia nervosa' (1999, p. 27). Gull himself was insistent that he had discovered anorexia independently of Lasègue and that this should be recognised (ibid., pp. 30–31). The two men's diagnoses of anorexia did, however, differ. Gull's rested heavily upon a biomedical account of anorexia at the expense of psychological and cul-tural influences (Gremillion 1992; Hepworth 1999; O'Connor 1995). Lasègue, by contrast, focussed more on the psychological (Brumberg 1988, p. 199). Nonetheless, both doctors ultimately agreed on one thing: that women's inher-ent irrationality was the key explanation for anorexia (Hepworth 1999, p. 29).

The foundations upon which anorexia are built are decidedly shaky: if resting on erroneous notions of female unreason was not enough, the term *anorexia nervosa* itself is also misleading. The word anorexia derives from the Greek, '*an-* without + *orexis-* appetite' (Collins 2011, p. 36), literally trans-lating to 'without appetite'. However, as Bell points out, '"anorexia ner-vosa" (aversion to food due to some personality disorder) is something of a misnomer. Many of those who suffer from the disease do not report a "loss of appetite," although obviously they do not eat enough to be healthy' (1985, pp. 1–2). As authors of anorexia memoirs attest, it is not that anorectics do not have an appetite, but that they work obsessively to curb it (see, for example, Bowman 2007; Hornbacher 1999; Liu [1979] 2000). What is more, the suffix *nervosa* suggests that this lack of appetite is the consequence of a nervous disease, which Hepworth argues 'served to pathologise the condition, and reinforce the use of medical scientific and clinical discourses in its documentation and management' (1999, p. 32).[2] The history of *anorexia nervosa* is thus riddled with inaccuracies. Physicians in their immense authority were guided by the superficial signs of weight loss, and treatment centred upon returning the body to what they conceived as its proper visual representation of femininity via controlled feeding (O'Connor 1995, p. 543).[3] Hence, the 'cure' for anorexia was visual and one whereby health and gender identity were conflated: as long as a woman *appeared* as she should, all was ostensibly well. This is clearly problematic: a focus on the visual signs of anorexia further contributes to its stigma, yet it also risks discounting those who are struggling with anorexia because they appear to be a 'normal weight' (Rich 2006, p. 290). Despite this, anorexia's visual bias persists.

Megan Warin (2004) explores the privileging of the visual in her account of the media reception of her ethnography of anorexia: journalists insisted on accompanying her research with images of emaciated bodies, regardless of her refusal that her work, and for that matter her research subjects, should be pre-sented in this way. For Warin, visual media representations of anorexia reduce it to a primitivism which 'others' the anorectic (2004, p. 100). Pre-sent-day anorectics are thus deemed spectacles much as they were in the nineteenth century: their bodies are not only reduced to their surface value, they are rendered objects of intrigue and even awe. As I pointed out in the introduction to this book, thinness is highly valued in the modern West. Helen Gremillion, who argues that modern psychiatry, rather than providing a cure, informs and perpetuates anorexia, states that, 'anorexia cannot be "cured" in the traditional sense because it not only *embodies* the status quo, but also calls it into question' (1992, p. 58, emphasis in original). Gremillion's thesis expresses the inherent paradox of anorexia: as both conforming to and disrupting hegemonic gender identity. The desire to be thin and in control of bodily impulses is so deeply enmeshed in Western culture, that if anorexia is to be 'cured', then the culture in which it is situated must be treated also.

Despite this, medical discourse all too often displaces and erases cultural explanations, constructing women variously as at-risk or as harbingers of disease; prone to developing eating disorders but also holding the power to spread them. Hence, Burke (2006) argues that anorexia is presented by mainstream culture as 'contagion' between women rather than having any cultural cause. Contradictorily, this imbues the anorectic with the power 'to move vulnerable, female spectators to imitation' (Ferreday 2012, p. 143). Women are therefore helpless and threatening at the same time, as the media articles in the introduction to this book showed. They are constructed in such a way that they require protection from themselves, which has the effect of exonerating not only the medical profession, but also the media and beauty industry, of any blame for the culture of thinness. As Sharlene Hesse-Biber (1996) argues, by treating women's eating and weight-loss practices as a disease, the responsibility is placed upon the individual, any societal influence is elided, and a recovery market is generated. An individual-medical bias is, therefore, hindering a holistic understanding of anorexia and pro-anorexia, both of which are culturally constituted.

Anorexia and resistance

As Foucault argues, '[w]here there is power, there is resistance, and yet, or rather consequently, this resistance is never in a position of exteriority in relation to power' (1976, p. 95). It has therefore been claimed that the hunger strike may be the 'last weapon in a struggle for power of someone who feels desperate or powerless' (Vandereycken and Van Deth 1994, p. 74). Given women's inferior position in patriarchal society, anorexia is often read as a *protest* against the constraints of being a woman (Bordo [1993] 2003; Grosz 1994; Orbach 1986). Bynum locates women's self-starvation during the medieval period within a set of other religious practices which women endured not solely to show their commitment to God, but also to paradoxically resist patriarchal control (1997; see also Ash 1990, p. 95). Renowned female saints of the time, Catherine of Siena and Columba of Rieti, were said to have rebelled against their parents' plans to marry them off through their 'extreme food and sleep deprivation, their frenetic giving away of paternal resources, and their compulsive service of family members in what were not necessarily welcome ways' (Bynum 1997, pp. 147–148). Similarly, during the nineteenth century, some women used the 'sick role' as a means of evading their domestic obligations: if they were ill, they could not become pregnant or do housework (Ehrenreich and English 1979, p. 123). Rather than a form of acquiescence, religious and domestic practices could be utilised by women as a means of negotiating their subordinate status.

The commitment and suffering endured by anorectics in patriarchal society has led Susie Orbach to draw comparisons to the political hunger strikes of the suffragettes (1986, p. 27), much to the vexation of Brumberg who describes this as a 'well-intentioned but desperate attempt to dignify these all too-frequent disorders' (1988, p. 36). In fact, Brumberg takes issue with the cultural model of anorexia in general, suggesting that it 'denies the biomedical component of this destructive illness by obscuring the helplessness and desperation of those who suffer from it' (ibid.). Similarly, unconvinced by the protest paradigm, Tzachi Zamir describes those who self-starve as 'indifferent' and 'highly self-centered' (2012, p. 147; the author bases his evaluation on having read autobiographies of anorectics). Whilst it is difficult to argue persuasively that the plight of the anorectic is entirely politically motivated – indeed, doing so may conceal the very real distress of the individual's situation – to see their plight as wholly pathological or self-centred, as Zamir does, is equally reductive. In short, scholars cannot agree whether the anorexic – holy or contemporary – is self-sacrificing or self-absorbed; rebelling against the constraints of femininity or unhealthily reinforcing them. Fortunately, Bordo, in her elegant undoing of the protest/disease binary, urges us to recognise the possibility that anorexia can, and does, occupy both factions: the eating disordered individual may be deeply distressed but her pain '[communicates] an excruciating message about the gender politics that regulate our lives' ([1993] 2003, p. 65).

Whilst it is undeniable that women have always used their inferior roles as a means of resistance, this is not to say that *all women* have the resources to do so. Any reading of anorexia or other so-called female maladies requires consideration of social class dimensions. As chapter four explores in detail, anorexia has long been hailed an illness of high-achieving middle-class girls, despite research which consistently argues to the contrary. However, Lupton (1994) argues that those who defy medical authority (and anorexia is seen as a form of defiance) are invariably middle-class and educated, whereas those of lower socio-economic status may feel too intimidated to do so. Likewise, the women who were inserted into the sick role during the nineteenth century were not the poor or working class, but the privileged (Ehrenreich and English 1979, p. 104) – such women possessed the means to use the role to their advantage. Gremillion notes that many anorectics are 'amateur theorists' of their 'illness' (1992, p. 59): they have the resources and access to knowledge which enables them, to an extent, to challenge doctors' advice, even if this may be ultimately to their detriment. Such expertise is evidenced in the afore-mentioned anorexia memoires, with both Marya Hornbacher (1999) and Grace Bowman (2007) recalling that their entire identity rested upon their academic excellence and an extraordinary ability to self-starve. Of course, there are many anorexic women who do not fit this middle-class demographic and it is perhaps because of this that their stories remain unwritten.

By drawing on reservoirs of patriarchal knowledge, anorectics are able to appropriate medical thought and carve out opportunities for resistance. This is because although, 'discourse transmits and produces power [it] also undermines and exposes it, renders it fragile and makes it possible to thwart it' (Foucault 1976, p. 101). The creation of pro-ana online spaces and their co-opting of medical discourse exemplifies Foucault's (1976) 'reverse' discourse whereby terminology used to categorise and undermine marginalised groups is adopted by these groups for their own purposes. Foucault uses the example of homosexuality to show how a pathological category has been converted into an identity (1976, p. 101). Likewise, having been labelled as anorexic, those who engage with pro-ana culture are using the very language of their diagnosis as a means of resistance and empowerment. Their claims to being pro-anorexic constitute their demands to legitimacy and call into question the authority of medicine, all the while altering the meanings of the language they appropriate. Jack Halberstam points out that a 'reverse discourse is in no way the "same" as the discourse it reverses; indeed, its desire for a reversal is a desire for transformation' (2005, p. 53). The extent to which pro-ana online spaces transform discourse is a question I pose throughout this book, for, as Foucault (1976) warns us, power is both mobile and productive in nature, and consequently it cannot be claimed.

Even so, the Internet has provided numerous opportunities to resist medical authority: pro-ana culture is part of the wider phenomenon of the 'medicalization of cyberspace' wherein online spaces offer a wealth of health services and guidance as well as lay information at the click of a button (see Miah and Rich 2008). This ranges from support forums for chronic pain sufferers who can discuss their experiences alongside like-minded others without fear of being misunderstood (Becker 2013); to spaces for euthanasia advocates to plan activism and find an emotional outlet (McDorman 2001); to pro-suicide groups that provide detailed guidance on how to end one's life and an opportunity to talk over such plans in a non-judgemental space (Westerlund 2012). The endless possibilities for support, guidance and diagnosis have led Miah and Rich to liken the medicalisation of cyberspace to 'a novel medical discovery – not quite a cure for cancer, but in this trope, an artefact on to which profound expectations and imaginations are placed' (2008, p. 8). The Internet, and its imagined potential, can therefore be likened to the miraculous expectations endowed upon the doctors of old, albeit expectations that could not necessarily be fulfilled. However, it can also enable an individual to better understand and manage their illness, often resulting in what has been termed the 'expert patient' (Department of Health cited in Fox et al. 2005, p. 965). Nick Fox, Katie Ward and Alan O'Rourke (2005) argue that the expert patient pervades pro-ana online spaces: she may subvert the medical model of anorexia and in some cases be anti-recovery, but pro-ana online provides her with valuable coping tools. At the same time, the very existence of the pro-ana phenomenon indicates the extent to which anorexia is not a condition from which one simply recovers. As such, online spaces can provide a release for those who feel they are unable to speak openly about their illness, where they might 'construct stories that are not based on a "restitution narrative", but which instead focus on the disordered, painful and repressed feelings and experiences of illness' (Miah and Rich 2008, p. 62).

Pro-ana culture's counterhegemonic approach to eating disorders has led scholars to highlight its transformational possibilities. Pollack (2003, p. 249) suggests that 'the anorexic's reappropriation of the psychiatric label could signify an empowering reversal strategy', and Day and Keys (2008a) conclude that although these spaces demonstrate users' conformity to dominant ideals, pro-anorectics are actively creating new meanings around self-starvation (see also Ferreday 2003). Like Henry Jenkins' fans (2003), rather than consuming media in their original form, pro-ana users actively produce and consume their own artefacts (even if this involves appropriating existing sources), and as Jenkins points out, 'media conglomerates often respond to these new forms of participatory culture by seeking to shut them down or reigning in their free play with cultural material' (2003, p. 289). Unlike the *Star Wars* fans that Jenkins speaks to, pro-ana online spaces are subject to continual erasure, because as well as appropriating media objects, they demonstrate an irreverent attitude towards medicine – whilst using the tools of that very same authority. Because of this, they hold the potential to expose the requirements of mainstream thinness culture and, at the same time, critique contemporary understandings of anorexia. It is important to note though, as Bordo does, that 'the exposure of such mystifications, which should not be impeded by too facile a celebration of resistance, must remain central to a feminist politics of the body' (1993, p. 199). Ultimately, pro-ana online spaces are shaped by the medical gaze they disrupt, and they are constituted by the media images they appropriate. A key task for this book is to interrogate how these powers operate.

Conclusion

This first contextual chapter sought to interrogate the medical gaze in Western culture with the aim of providing an understanding of the landscape in which pro-ana online spaces are situated. First, I showed how the medical gaze came to be, outlining its emergence in the Enlightenment. It was during this period of scientific revolution that belief in God was replaced by faith in medicine and the patient became a passive object of the physician's normalising gaze. The effect of this hierarchy of knowledge was one where the 'patient' was distanced from their own body, making it further susceptible to colonisation by the medical authority. In the next section, I explored the detrimental effect of the patriarchal medical profession on women's position in society: drawing primarily on the work of Ehrenreich and English (1979), I showed how women were ejected from the profession and made objects of scientific study, the legacy of which remains to this day. I then looked to nineteenth century Europe and the emergence of the specifically female 'disorders': hysteria, agoraphobia and, of course, anorexia. It has been argued that such disorders can be read as exposing the requirements of ideal Victorian womanhood – pro-anorexia then, is an alarming comment on contemporary femininity.

In the third section, I attended to the history of anorexia itself, exploring how, in the medieval period, it was read as a miraculous practice enacted by female saints who were showing their devotion to God. Such a reading was problematised when anorexia was mandated as a medical category in the nineteenth century. I argued that the medicalisation of anorexia is rooted in gender inequality: its 'discovery' relied on understandings of women as irrational and its 'cure' centred on feeding diagnosed women until their bodies *looked* normatively feminine. Given that anorexia has been read as a protest against the constraints of normative femininity, as well as a misguided attempt to comply with its requirements, in the final section of this chapter I turned to the possibilities for resistance. From medieval saints to the nineteenth-century sick role, women have always found that 'where there is power, there is resistance' – and contemporary pro-ana culture is no different. Nonetheless, as I pointed out, not all women have access to the means of resistance; therefore, we must continually question the degree to which these modes are oppositional and who they serve.

All the same, the norms and practices perpetuated by the medical profession to ensure healthy citizens and those endorsed by [pro-]eating disordered individuals to maintain extreme thinness are on a continuum. Ultimately, the normal and the pathological are entwined to the extent that, in some cases, they are one and the same. This paradox has produced a culture where on the one hand, women are praised for losing weight, and on the other they are vilified for being *too thin*. I explore this further in the next chapter, which interrogates how thinness operates in popular culture, specifically women's magazines. These texts, like medical discourse, hold body-disciplining in high regard, the sum of which makes a culture of disordered eating inevitable.

Notes

1 Throughout this book, following scholars of Fat Studies, I place 'obesity' – and its variations – in inverted commas to indicate that it is a contested and problematic term (see, for instance, Rothblum and Solovay 2009).
2 Interestingly, the suffix 'nervosa' was favoured by Gull for its gender neutrality (Lasègue had wanted it to be known as 'l'anorexie hystérique' or hysterical anorexia, thus an illness which could only affect women): if it were a malady of the nervous system, anorexia could affect anyone regardless of gender, as Gull's had research shown (Brumberg 1988).
3 Erin O'Connor argues that the provenance of this visual bias towards anorexia diagnoses lies in Gull's 1873 talk on anorexia to the Clinical Society of London, during which he showed photographs of anorexic patients before and after treatment (1995, p. 536).

References

American Psychiatric Association. (2013) *Diagnostic and Statistical Manual of Mental Disorders*, 5th edn, (DSM-5). Washington, DC: APA.

Ash, J. (1990) 'The discursive construction of Christ's body in the later Middle Ages; resistance and autonomy', in Threadgold, T. and Cranny-Francis, A. (eds.) *Feminine-masculine and Representation*. Sydney: Allen & Unwin, pp. 75–105.

Bartky, S.L. (1990) *Femininity and Domination: Studies in the Phenomenology of Oppression*. New York: Routledge.

Becker, K.L. (2013) 'Cyberhugs: Creating a voice for chronic pain sufferers through technology', *Cyberpsychology, Behavior, and Social Networking*, 16(2), pp. 123–126.

Bell, M. (2009) '"@ the Doctor's Office": Pro-anorexia and the medical gaze', *Surveillance & Society*, 6(2), pp. 151–162.

Bell, R. M. (1985) *Holy Anorexia*. Chicago, IL: University of Chicago Press.

Bordo, S. (1989) 'The body and the reproduction of femininity: A feminist appropriation of Foucault', in Jaggar, A.M. and Bordo, S. (eds.) *Gender/Body/Knowledge: Feminist Reconstructions of Being and Knowing*. New Brunswick, NJ: Rutgers University Press, pp. 13–33.

———. (1993) 'Feminism, Foucault and the politics of the body', in Ramazanoglu, C. (ed.) *Up against Foucault: Explorations of Some Tensions between Foucault and Feminism*. Abingdon, OX: Routledge, pp. 179–202.

———. ([1993] 2003) *Unbearable Weight: Feminism, Western Culture and the Body*, 10th anniversary edition. Berkeley: University of California Press.

Bowman, G. (2007) *Thin*. London: Penguin.

Brumberg, J.J. (1988) *Fasting Girls: The History of Anorexia Nervosa*. Cambridge, MA: Harvard University Press.

Burke, E. (2006) 'Feminine visions: Anorexia and contagion in pop discourse', *Feminist Media Studies*, 6(3), pp. 315–330.

Bynum, C.W. (1997) 'Feast, fast, and flesh: The religious significance of food to medieval women', in Van Esterik, P. and Counihan, C. (eds.) *Food and Culture: A Reader*. London: Routledge, pp. 138–158.

Cogan, J.C. (1999) 'Re-evaluating the weight-centered approach toward health: The need for a paradigm shift', in Sobal, J. and Maurer, D. (eds.) *Interpreting Weight: The Social Management of Fatness and Thinness*. New York: Aldine de Gruyter, pp. 229–253.

Collins Dictionary and Thesaurus. (2011) 1st edn. Glasgow: HarperCollins.

Czerniawski, A.M. (2007) 'From average to ideal: The evolution of the height and weight table in the United States, 1836–1943', *Social Science History*, 31(2), pp. 273–296.

Davis, K. (1995) *Reshaping the Female Body*. New York and London: Routledge.

Day, K. and Keys, T. (2008a) 'Starving in cyberspace: A discourse analysis of pro-eating-disorder websites', *Journal of Gender Studies*, 17(1), pp. 1–15.

———. (2008b) 'Starving in cyberspace: The construction of identity on "pro-eating-disorder" websites', in Riley, S., Burns, M., Frith, H., Wiggins, S., and Markula, P. (eds.) *Critical Bodies: Representations, Identities and Practices of Weight and Body Management*. Basingstoke, Hampshire: Palgrave Macmillan, pp. 81–100.

———. (2009) 'Anorexia/bulimia as resistance and conformity in pro-Ana and pro-Mia virtual conversations', in Malson, H. and Burns, M. (eds.) *Critical Feminist Approaches to Eating Dis/orders*. London: Routledge, pp. 87–96.

Deveaux, M. (1994) 'Feminism and empowerment: A critical reading of Foucault', *Feminist Studies*, 20(2), pp. 223–247.

Doane, M.A. (1985) 'The clinical eye: Medical discourses in the "woman's film" of the 1940s', in Suleiman, S.R. (ed.) *The Female Body in Western Culture: Contemporary Perspectives*. Cambridge, MA: Harvard University Press, pp. 152–174.

Ehrenreich, B. and English, D. (1979) *For Her Own Good: 150 Years of Experts' Advice to Women*. London: Pluto Press.

Ferreday, D. (2003) 'Unspeakable bodies: Erasure, embodiment and the pro-ana community', *International Journal of Cultural Studies*, 6(3), pp. 277–295.

———. (2012) 'Anorexia and abjection: A review essay', *Body & Society*, 18(2), pp. 139–155.

Foucault, M. (1967) *Madness and Civilization: A History of Insanity in the Age of Reason*. Howard, R. (trans.). London: Routledge.

———. (1973) *The Birth of the Clinic: An Archaeology of Medical Perception*. Sheridan, A.M. (trans.). London: Routledge.

———. (1976) *The Will to Knowledge: The History of Sexuality Volume 1*. Hurley, R. (trans.). London: Penguin.

———. (1979) *Discipline and Punish: The Birth of the Prison*. Sheridan, A.M. (trans.). London: Penguin.

Fox, N., Ward, K., and O'Rourke, A. (2005) 'Pro-anorexia, weight-loss drugs and the Internet: An "anti-recovery" explanatory model of anorexia', *Sociology of Health & Illness*, 27(7), pp. 944–971.

Freud, S. ([1918] 1991) 'The taboo of virginity (contributions to the psychology of love III)', in Richards, A. (ed.) and Strachey, J. (trans.), *On Sexuality*. London: Penguin, pp. 261–283.

Gailey, J.A. (2009) '"Starving is the most fun a girl can have": The pro-ana subculture as edgework', *Critical Criminology*, 17, pp. 93–108.

Gilman, S.L. (1985) 'Black bodies, white bodies: Toward an iconography of female sexuality in late nineteenth-century art, medicine, and literature', *Critical Inquiry*, 12(1), pp. 204–242.

Gremillion, H. (1992) 'Psychiatry as social ordering: Anorexia nervosa, a paradigm', *Social Science & Medicine*, 35(1), pp. 57–71.

Grosz, E. (1994) *Volatile Bodies: Towards a Corporeal Feminism*. Bloomington: Indiana University Press.

Halberstam, J. (2005) *In a Queer Time & Place: Transgender Bodies, Subcultural Lives*. New York: New York University Press.

Hartley, C. (2001) 'Letting ourselves go: Making room for the fat body in feminist scholarship', in Braziel, J.E. and LeBesco, K. (eds.) *Bodies Out of Bounds: Fatness and Transgression*. Berkeley: University of California Press, pp. 60–73.

Haworth-Hoeppner, S. (1999) 'Medical discourse on body image: Reconceptualizing the differences between women with and without eating disorders', in Sobal, J. and Maurer, D. (eds.) *Interpreting Weight: The Social Management of Fatness and Thinness*. New York: Aldine de Gruyter, pp. 89–112.

Hepworth, J. (1999) *The Social Construction of Anorexia Nervosa*. Sage Knowledge. Available at: http://knowledge.sagepub.com/view/the-social-construction-of-anorexia-nervosa/SAGE.xml (Accessed: 9 November 2015).

Hesse-Biber, S. (1991) 'Women, weight and eating disorders: A socio-cultural and political-economic analysis', *Women's Studies International Forum*, 14(3), pp. 173–191.

———. (1996) *Am I Thin Enough Yet? The Cult of Thinness and the Commercialization of Identity*. New York: Oxford University Press.

Hewitt, M. (1983) 'Bio-politics and social policy: Foucault's account of welfare', in Featherstone, M., Hepworth, M., and Turner, B.S. (eds.) *The Body: Social Process and Cultural Theory*. London: Sage, pp. 225–255.

Heywood, L. (1996) *Dedication to Hunger: The Anorexic Aesthetic in Modern Culture.* Berkeley: University of California Press.

Hornbacher, M. (1999) *Wasted: A Memoir of Anorexia and Bulimia.* London: Flamingo.

Jenkins, H. (2003) 'Quentin Tarantino's Star Wars? Digital cinema, media convergence, and participatory culture', in Thorburn, D. and Jenkins, H. (eds.) *Rethinking Media Change: The Aesthetics of Transition.* Cambridge, MA: MIT Press, pp. 281–312.

Jones, M. (2008) *Skintight: An Anatomy of Cosmetic Surgery.* Oxford: Berg.

LeBesco, K. (2004) *Revolting Bodies? The Struggle to Redefine Fat Identity.* Amherst: University of Massachusetts Press.

Liu, A. ([1979] 2000) *Solitaire.* Lincoln, Nebraska: iUniverse.com.

Lupton, D. (1994) *Medicine as Culture: Illness, Disease and the Body in Western Societies.* London: Sage.

Malson, H. (2008) 'Deconstructing un/healthy body-weight and weight management', in Riley, S., Burns, M., Frith, H., Wiggins, S., and Markula, P. (eds.) *Critical Bodies: Representations, Identities and Practices of Weight and Body Management.* Basingstoke, Hampshire: Palgrave Macmillan, pp. 27–42.

———. (2009) 'Appearing to disappear: Postmodern femininities and self-starved sub-jectivities', in Malson, H. and Burns, M. (eds.) *Critical Feminist Approaches to Eating Dis/orders.* London: Routledge, pp. 135–145.

McDorman, T.F. (2001) 'Crafting a virtual counterpublic: Right-to-die advocates on the Internet', in Asen, R. and Brouwer, D.C. (eds.) *Counterpublics and the State.* New York: SUNY Press, pp. 187–209.

McGrath, R. (2002) *Seeing Her Sex: Medical Archives and the Female Body.* Manchester: Manchester University Press.

Miah, A. and Rich, E. (2008) *The Medicalization of Cyberspace.* Abingdon, OX: Routledge.

Michie, H. (1987) *The Flesh Made Word: Female Figures and Women's Bodies.* New York: Oxford University Press.

Mulvey, L. (1975) 'Visual pleasure and narrative cinema', *Screen*, 16(3), pp. 6–18.

O'Connor, E. (1995) 'Pictures of health: Medical photography and the emergence of anorexia nervosa', *Journal of the History of Sexuality*, 5(4), pp. 535–572.

Orbach, S. (1986) *Hunger Strike: The Anorectic's Struggle as a Metaphor for Our Age.* London: Faber and Faber Limited.

Pollack, D. (2003) 'III. Pro-eating disorder websites: What should be the feminist response?', *Feminism & Psychology*, 13(2), pp. 246–251.

Rich, E. (2006) 'Anorexic dis(connection): Managing anorexia as an illness and an identity', *Sociology of Health & Illness*, 28(3), pp. 284–305.

Rothblum, E.D. and Solovay, S. (eds.). (2009) *The Fat Studies Reader.* New York: New York University Press.

Suleiman, S.R. (1986) 'Introduction', in Suleiman, S.R. (ed.) *The Female Body in Western Culture: Contemporary Perspectives.* Cambridge, MA: Harvard University Press, pp. 1–4.

Turner, B.S. (1982) 'The discourse of diet', in Featherstone, M., Hepworth, M., and Turner, B.S. (eds.) *The Body: Social Process and Cultural Theory.* London: Sage, pp. 157–169.

———. (1992) *Regulating Bodies: Essays in Medical Sociology.* London: Routledge.

———. (1995) *Medical Power and Social Knowledge*, 2nd edn. London: Sage.

———. (1996) *The Body and Society*, 2nd edn. London: Sage.

Vandereycken, W. and Van Deth, R. (1994) *From Fasting Saints to Anorexic Girls: The History of Self-Starvation*. London: Athlone Press.

Warin, M. (2004) 'Primitivising anorexia: The irresistible spectacle of not eating', *The Australian Journal of Anthropology*, 15(1), pp. 95–104.

Westerlund, M. (2012) 'The production of pro-suicide content on the Internet: A counter-discourse activity', *New Media & Society*, 14(5), pp. 764–780.

Williams, S.J. (2003) *Medicine and the Body*. London: Sage.

Winch, A. (2013) *Girlfriends and Postfeminist Sisterhood*. Basingstoke, Hampshire: Palgrave Macmillan.

Wolf, N. (1991) *The Beauty Myth: How Images of Beauty Are Used against Women*. New York: Harper Perennial.

Zamir, T. (2012) 'The theatricalization of death', *Journal of Medical Humanities*, 33, pp. 141–159.

2 'Lose weight without dieting'

Disciplining the body in women's magazines

Lose weight without dieting: [...] putting ice-cubes in your drink forces your body to heat itself up, burning calories [...] If you get a food craving, chew gum or clean your teeth instead.

(Cosmopolitan 2010, p. 195)

Pro-ana tips and tricks: Brush your teeth, chew sugar-free gum or mints. Instead of bingeing, eat crushed ice.

(*Foreverproana*)

This chapter identifies the ways women are invited to police the female body – whether their own or the bodies of others – through discourses which disguise such calls to discipline. Drawing upon a set of ubiquitous cultural texts – women's magazines – it shows how women are taught to evaluate, measure, regulate and castigate female bodies in order to fulfil femininity proper. Understanding this call to become a self-surveilling subject is imperative if we are to appreciate the motivations behind pro-ana online spaces, the discourses employed by pro-ana enthusiasts and the processes of cultural appropriation that these users engage in when constructing their digital spaces and maintaining their online identities. As the two quotations at the head of this chapter illustrate, the cultural boundaries between 'acceptable' and 'pathological' engagements with the female body are blurred. Whilst the former quotation is from a women's lifestyle magazine, supported by advertising and available in all good newsagents, the latter is from a user-generated online space, a site of controversy and the subject of moral panic for promoting eating disorders. What *Cosmopolitan* describes as a means of losing weight without dieting is classified by *Foreverproana* as one way of maintaining anorexia. Although the content of the advice is virtually identical, its presentation could not be more different: *Cosmopolitan* denies that its recommendations are about dieting, whereas *Foreverproana* frames the same advice as a method of self-starvation.

In July 2014, the tacit relationship between pro-ana culture and the mainstream was brought to the fore: 'Thinspiration! Three new celeb diets for you to try', exclaimed the headline on the front cover of *Reveal* magazine (Reveal 2014). After public outrage, the magazine's editor-in-chief quickly released a statement defending the magazine's decision to use the term thin-spiration, denying that it was promoting eating disorders: 'It is hard to understand why we are now being accused of being "pro-anorexia" just because we have used a word, which some people associate with pro-anorexia sites' (Ennis 2014). The statement was brief and *Reveal* primarily sought to provide its own definition of the term: 'The word "Thinspiration" on the cover this week was used to describe the way in which three celebrities have dieted and exercised to lose unwanted pounds' (ibid.). For *Reveal*, thinspiration was simply about weight loss and it strongly denied it had anything to do with anorexia. This example is important for two reasons: firstly, it shows how the language of 'reverse' discourse can be re-appropriated by dominant discourses and thus utilised to reinforce the status quo. Secondly, it demonstrates the extent to which the culture of compulsory thinness operates around denial and disguise. Taking the blurred boundaries between normative and non-normative diet practices as a starting point, this chapter explores how mainstream texts (as opposed to marginal pro-ana texts) simultaneously deploy and denounce compulsory body disciplining.

As I outlined in the introductory chapter, this book is underpinned by a postfeminist neoliberal understanding of femininity. The simplest way to demonstrate how this postfeminist neoliberal voice speaks to women is through analysing a set of mainstream texts before attending to the ostensibly marginal texts that constitute pro-ana online in the next chapter. Undoubtedly, a wealth of examples from popular culture could serve this purpose, such as make-over television programmes and weight-loss forums to name but a few. However, it is in women's magazines that pro-ana and weight-loss discourses are at once utilised and undermined. Consequently, this chapter critically examines the postfeminist texts in which pro-ana finds not only its precedent but its appropriation and repudiation. It is divided into four sections. The first section profiles each of the magazines, attending to the way they have changed over time. The second and third sections explore the texts' repudiation of fatness and thinness, respectively, demonstrating that whilst bodies which are considered fat are denounced by the magazines, so are bodies which are deemed *too* thin. Mindful of the magazines' criticisms of fatness and thinness, the final section presents their seeming rejection of diet culture and accompanying insistence that the reader should love her body.

Profiling the magazines: 1999–2018

After consulting the UK National Readership Survey's data on print magazines, four of the most popular magazines – whose primary readership is women aged 15–34 – were selected for analysis (National Readership Survey 2017).[1] This comprised weekly magazines, *heat* and *Reveal*, both of which are archetypal celebrity gossip magazines; and monthly publications, *Cosmopolitan* and *Glamour*, which are more broadly lifestyle magazines. Given that the first pro-anorexia websites emerged in the late 1990s, the titles gathered are from the period 1999 to 2018. By focusing on this stretch of time, we are able to see how body disciplining is constructed in the magazines during the advent of pro-anorexia in the margins, through to its arrival in mainstream culture.

Joke Hermes argues that women's magazines are enjoyable because they are 'easily put down' (1995, p. 32), what is more, they are just as easy to pick up: their audience extends beyond readers who part with their money, taking up subscriptions or occasionally buying a magazine for a train journey. Despite their ubiquity, creating a comprehensive archive is a challenge and during the research process I was often confronted with magazines having gone missing from archives or simply never having been available. Andrea McDonnell tackled similar issues in her research into celebrity gossip magazines, noting that these texts 'become a kind of cultural ephemera as soon as they are produced; they do not have an archival home' (2014, p. 17). This illustrates the low cultural value afforded to such publications (Hermes 1995; Holmes 2005): had I chosen to examine *Vogue* magazine, for example, I would have been presented with bound and catalogued copies, in other words, an archival home. The transience of these texts and the difficulties I had comprehensively gathering them adumbrates the challenges I would face collecting data from pro-ana online spaces. At the same time, it reflects wider cultural assumptions that women's collections are not as important as those of men (see Pearce 1995). Nonetheless, I was ultimately able to collate a total of forty-two issues across the four titles from randomly selected weeks and months for analysis. Each magazine was read from cover to cover, taking the female body as the main point of interrogation; from there I identified the recurring themes which I explore in the subsequent sections below.

Although each title has its own unique style and format, all four magazines are united by a disciplinary gaze that extends beyond body size: every aspect of the reader's life is subject to regulatory surveillance and potential transformation. This appears, for example, in the form of advice on how to lead a balanced life: 'How to have love and a career' (Glamour 2013, front cover) or via revelations as to what men *really* think: 'Men talk: Love, sex, break-ups and bad behaviour' (Cosmopolitan 2013, front cover). The reader is urged to look after her skin by following 'the tan commandments' (Reveal 2013, pp. 58–59) and consider questions such as, 'Does it matter if you earn more than your bloke?' (heat 2015, p. 25). We are told that the latter was put to a vote on heat's corresponding website *heatworld*, and that the answer was a resounding 'no' (ibid.). Websites and social media are used by all four publications to feed the print content and *vice versa*. For *Glamour* though digital media ultimately prevailed and by the end of 2017, it moved to 'digital first' format, only publishing print editions twice per year (BBC 2017).

Despite the unwavering approach to the reader's life as a project which must be appraised and can always be improved, within the twenty-year period explored, the magazines' disciplinary gaze adopts different guises. The calls to 'lose weight without dieting' as the quote at the start of this chapter urges, become ever more cloaked in discourses of health and of body confidence. In 2014, *Cosmopolitan* introduced a regular feature entitled, 'My body's amazing because…'. Here, readers who do not conform to hegemonic standards of thinness recount their personal narratives, from body shame to body confidence, accompanied by their naked (but carefully covered) portraits. Equally, *Glamour* who in 2001 told readers, 'why stress makes [them] fat (and how to beat it)' (pp. 182–184), changes tack in later years. Instead, articles such as '10 secrets of healthy people' (Abrahams 2016, pp.235-241) and an exposé of the clean eating movement (White 2017, pp. 152–156) replace the more direct promotion of the thin ideal. *heat* too has undergone numerous changes since its inception in 1999: the earlier issues feature longer articles, analysis of film and television, and coverage of male celebrities, whereas a few years after the launch it becomes more centred on female celebrities and in turn more focussed on the body. According to Holmes (2005), *heat* initially struggled to sell copies and it was only when its editor 'shap[ed] it into a "true celebrity magazine," with an equally clearer address to a female audience' that its success soared (p. 23). Although the regular features, 'Circle of Shame' and 'Hoop of Horror' which highlighted predominantly female celebrities' apparent imperfections – from cellulite to sweat patches – were dropped in 2011 (Plunkett 2013), the magazine maintains a watchful eye over women's bodies. Diet and exercise plans are regular features and celebrities' body size is monitored. However, in the latter years, this is relayed through the diction of happiness and confidence and by 2018, *heat* is using plus size models in its fashion spreads.

Of the four titles, *Reveal* is most critical of women's bodies, particularly those of reality television stars. In the latter years, in line with the other titles, it ostensibly critiques the pressures on women to conform to the thin ideal. However, such critiques always fall short: for instance, in a spread exposing very thin celebrities with large, surgically enhanced breasts, *Reveal* seeks to temper such pressures, but it does so by finding out 'what normal blokes think' (2013, front cover). Instead of challenging female bodily ideals, this reinforces the longstanding heteronormative worldview of women's magazines (Ballaster et al. 1991; McCracken 1993; Winship 1987), asserting that men's opinions of women's bodies are what really matter. Despite this, feminists have long warned against an outright rejection of women's magazines (Gill 2007; Hermes 1995; McRobbie 1997; Winship 1987; Wolf 1991). As Ballaster et al point out, 'Women's magazines contain, within single issues and between different titles, many competing and contradictory notions of femininity' (1991, p. 22). In so doing, the magazines both avoid political comment and express a 'pluralism of opinions' (Winship 1987, p. 100). For example, in 2018, *Reveal* hails 'The *Love Island* body backlash', criticising the predominance of very thin women on the reality TV show (pp. 20–21). Their columnist Gabby Allen is quoted saying she '[hopes] they bring some curvy and edgy girls in soon' (Reveal 2018, p. 20), twenty pages later, however, is Allen's column, 'Gabby's beach body countdown', where she advises meditating to lose weight and urges exercising on holiday, because that way, 'you're killing two birds with stone – burning fat and tanning!' (ibid., p. 40). Such inconsistencies may seem confusing, but they allow the magazines to appeal to a range of readers' viewpoints simultaneously whilst evading alliance with any particular political standpoint.

Compulsory self-surveillance has long pervaded women's media, however, Gill argues that in postfeminist culture it has developed threefold:

> first the dramatically increased intensity of self surveillance, indicating the intensity of the regulation of women (*alongside the disavowal of such regulation*); secondly, the extensiveness of surveillance over entirely new spheres of life and intimate conduct; and thirdly the focus upon the psychological – upon the requirements to transform oneself and remodel one's interior life.
>
> (2007, p. 261; emphases added)

The 'disavowal of such regulation' permeates the magazines increasingly over the twenty-year period: a denial and disguise of the promotion of self-surveillance which pro-ana online spaces have adopted in order to evade censorship. More specifically, calls to regulate are veiled through the rhetoric of choice and personal freedom. Choice, and an assumed freedom that comes through choice, is visible throughout the sample, with *Cosmopolitan* and *Glamour* emphasising personal choice and individuality more. Features with headlines and pull quotes such as 'Your top-to-toe life, love and looks makeover' (Cosmopolitan 2002, front cover) and '... if you don't come from one of those enviably close families – you have the rest of your life to build your own' (Glamour 2008, p. 45) articulate this focus whilst implicitly stating that the responsibility for the perfect life rests with the individual. In the same vein, *Cosmopolitan* features an article on transgender activist and journalist Paris Lees, addressing Lees' 'fight to be recognised for who she is' (2014, p. 184). Whilst trans-inclusive coverage is welcome progress, Lees' story is depicted as one of individual triumph rather than an opportunity to critique wider power structures. As Janice Winship argues, 'by constantly affirming individual success, *Cosmo* obscures the fact that in the class society we live in, for every woman who "wins", there are many "losers"' (1987, p. 120). Thus, the focus on certain women's success stories (and perceived failings) operates 'to convert continued gender inequality from a structural problem into an individual affair' (Rottenberg 2014, p. 420).

As such, the autonomy and sexual freedom advanced by second-wave feminism is personalised, reneged, or repackaged as a consumer product. The postfeminist subject is able to choose from hundreds of different high street styles (Glamour 2013, front cover) and even her friendships are instrumentalised in articles such as, 'The five friends every woman needs', which includes for example: 'Pal #1 The Party Planner' and 'Pal #4 The Soul Sister' (Cosmopolitan 1999, pp. 119–120). Although the importance of female friendship is continually laboured, any real solidarity amongst women in these texts is limited and friends are presented as yet another product the reader should consume in order to achieve femininity proper. Hence, checklists and rules are plentiful across all four titles, with an emphasis on both ease and necessity. Whether it's the '7 Gospels of the Beauty Bible' (Glamour 2001, pp. 256–260); 'Ten things you need to look like ... Kendall Jenner' (heat 2014, p. 63); or '16 easy hair updates' (Reveal 2016, p. 47), the magazines show readers how to live and they outline the simple ways such a lifestyle can be purchased. In short, over the twenty-year period, the magazines begin to embrace diverse bodies and adopt feminist rhetoric more, but they remain wedded to compulsory self-surveillance even if it is cloaked in discourses of self-acceptance.

'Toxic fat'

The magazines maintain a watchful eye over women's body size and eating practices – whether readers or celebrities – and although self-regulation is always encouraged, certain forms of fat are permissible, whether in bodily or food form; others, however, are subject to, often cruel, castigation. Arbitrary boundaries are thus established between good and bad bodies, and good and bad foods. These demarcations invariably correlate with social class divisions: the bodies and food choices of middle-class women are coded as respectable whilst those of lower-class women are derided.

During the two decades examined, reporting on reality TV stars increased, particularly in the cheaper weekly magazines, *heat* and *Reveal*. For the most part, the reality TV star is framed as undeserving of their latterly acquired fame and fortune and is thus a subject of scorn. As Imogen Tyler and Bruce Bennett point out, despite its apparent absence in neoliberalism, social class is paramount in celebrity culture and the 'celebrity is an increasingly significant means by which reactionary class attitudes, allegiances and judgements are communicated' (2010, p. 376; see also Williamson 2010). Hence, celebrities (and not limited to those from reality TV) are convenient mediums through which wider prejudices around the female body can be channelled. *Reveal*'s year on year coverage of the body of Frankie Essex from British reality TV show, *The Only Way is Essex*, epitomises both the castigation of the reality TV star and the disavowal of such judgements. In 2012 Essex, is pictured as part of a spread on 'shocking weight gains' alongside American singer-songwriter, Lady Gaga. Both women are criticised for their larger bodies: Gaga is described 'puffy and bloated' (Reveal 2012, p. 8) and Essex's weight gain is even more extensively derided. Her 'successful slimming' in the past is said to have enabled her to 'finally bag her ideal man' (Reveal 2012, p. 4), thus conflating a slender body with the acquirement of a heterosexual relationship. Candid paparazzo images depict the star eating fast food and the accompanying text is scathing, alluding to the star's exposed stomach flesh as a 'muffin top bulging' (ibid., p. 4). As well as suggesting that an unhealthy diet prompted her weight gain, the coupling of visible body fat and of fast food mid-mastication operate as signifiers of class and taste (see Bourdieu

1984; Lupton 1996). Put differently, whilst the images of Essex eating fast food appear to explain her 'bulging' stomach, they also clearly position her as lower class and a legitimate object of disdain, regardless of her fame. As Winch argues:

> the working class body is configured as pathological through its associ-ation with excessive sexuality, which itself is marked on the body through fat; exploiting the fear of fat is a strategy of class exploitation in an aspirational popular culture.
>
> (2013, pp. 13–14)

Hence, Essex, representing the working-class body through her culturally devalued status as a reality TV star, is a vehicle through which *Reveal* can reasonably express anxiety around fat, excessive sexuality and class prejudice. Through 'successful slimming' though, Essex's sexuality can be regulated, and her social status temporarily raised.

This adumbrates a *Reveal* article some years later where a set of reality TV stars – Essex included – are derided for wearing bikinis which are 'too teeny' (2016, p. 7). Both Essex and women from British reality TV show *Geordie Shore* are unfavourably compared to Hollywood actress Jessica Alba who 'wore a succession of gorgeous bikinis which covered her modesty' (ibid., p. 7). Alba here connotes respectable femininity not only through her 'better-fitting bikini' (ibid., p. 7), but also through her career as an established actress as opposed to a reality TV star. On the contrary, Essex's bikini is described as 'the fashion equivalent of stuffing all your shopping into one bag to avoid paying an extra 5p' (ibid., p. 7). Essex then is coded as both cheap and excessive. This is because the rise to fame and subsequent weight struggles of women like Essex serve as clear warnings over 'the difficulty and undesirability of transgressing class boundaries' (Tyler and Bennett 2010, p. 389). Such women may acquire vast financial capital, but they 'are symbolically denied social mobility because their nouveau riche spending patterns are seen as distasteful and vulgar' (Bullen 2014, p. 185). Whilst there are some exceptions, such as Victoria Beckham (Edwards 2013) and Cheryl Tweedy (Woods 2014), the majority remain objects of scorn. As Efrat Tseëlon (1995, p. 77) argues 'woman is simultan-eously constructed and condemned as deceitful artifice', and for the reality TV star, her condemnation can be brutal.

Reveal may mock the fat body, but it also portrays it as pathological and potentially fatal. This is communicated in a range of ways: from a grave report on Britain's fattest teen who 'can't stop eating [herself] to death' (2010, pp. 28–29) to a celebratory article on a woman who lost ten stone: 'I was morbidly obese – now I'm a model!' (2016, front cover). Such statements serve to emphasise the link between 'obesity' and morbidity, thus reinforcing long-held, albeit contested understandings, that the former leads to the latter (see Cogan 1999). As a result, articles on weight loss across all titles are invariably told as both life-changing and life-saving narratives. British reality TV star, Scarlett Moffatt, for example, recounts breaking down in the doctor's surgery after being told she was 'obese' (heat 2017, p. 13). When *heat* asks her how her life has changed since losing weight, she responds with an anecdote: 'I was throwing out my old bras and my little sister — she's only ten — could fit her whole head in one cup!' (ibid., p. 13). Shortly after, she likens her previous size to carrying a child: 'I've lost 3st 4lb, and that's roughly what my three-year old cousin Noah weighs. It's like I've been piggy backing Noah for years and I've just dropped him off at school' (ibid., p. 13). By describing her former weight uncannily as the equivalent of a ten-year old's head or a three-year old's body, Moffatt reinforces the life-changing nature of weight loss; as a figurative shedding of unwanted flesh and subsequent renewal. With a few exceptions, weight loss and weight gain for these magazines are literally a matter of life and death, respectively.

Expert opinion is invoked to further substantiate the texts' condemnation of fat and this is particularly prominent in the coverage of cellulite. The summer issues of the magazines examined are generally replete with advice on how to eradicate it, and the lexis is invariably medical. *Reveal*'s four-page spread on cellulite describes it as something Britney, Pink and Lily Allen all '*suffer*' from (2008, pp. 12, 14, emphasis added) and Martine McCutcheon is deemed 'not *immune* to cellulite' (ibid., p. 13, emphasis added). Readers are then provided with an anti-cellulite diet that will not only rid them of the affliction that 'shocked onlookers' when they saw it on Kim Cattrall (ibid., p. 14), but can also help them to 'drop up to 10lb' (ibid., p. 15). The overriding assertion is that weight loss is key to curing this ill. *Glamour* corroborates such a claim, consulting the expertise of a medical doctor who concedes, 'The worst case of cellulite I ever saw was on someone who wasn't overweight [...] However cellulite can look worse on overweight women; slimming to a healthy weight will probably improve your appearance' (2005, p. 348). Cellulite is conceived as a medical problem, a 'case' to be dealt with, and the optimum way to do so is to diet. Even if the cellulite remains, being slimmer is presented as akin, not only to being healthy, but also to being attractive.

By couching cellulite in medical rhetoric, the magazines pathologise it, despite the fact that it is simply 'healthy adult female flesh', which has been fallaciously cast as a disorder (Wolf 1991, p. 227). Even *Cosmopolitan* — who insist ever more over the twenty-year period that readers should love their bodies — struggle to accept cellulite. In the same issue that urges readers to follow 'body-confidence queens' on Instagram (Cosmopolitan 2015, p. 65) and say, 'Bye Bye body hang-ups' (ibid., p. 189), is a spread on 'affordable' beauty treatments including a £250 'Cellulite buster' (ibid., p. 147) — the affordability of which is disputable. As Wolf points out, cellulite is 'an invented "condition" that was imported into the United States by Vogue in 1973; they refer to this texture as "disfiguring", "unsightly", "polluted with toxins"' (1991, p. 227). This narrative is replicated in a *Glamour* article on 'toxic fat', a term to describe fat caused by stress, which the magazine both coins and prescribes time-consuming and costly regimes to treat (2003, pp. 182–184). In short, the magazines fabricate problems to which they then provide solutions (Winship 1987, p. 101).

They thus operate as experts who know the reader better than she knows herself: as one *Cosmopolitan* article insists, 'get your body baby ready (even if you don't want one … yet)' (2005, p. 241). The addition of the adverb 'yet' here assumes that all women's biological destiny is motherhood, therefore excluding those who do not want, or cannot have, children. It then warns the reader against the many obstacles that could prevent her from conceiving, from smoking to stress, to body weight and sexually transmitted diseases (ibid., pp. 241–242). Underpinning this article is the understanding that if the reader does not heed such advice, she has only herself to blame if she does not ultimately reproduce. This is because postfeminist culture charges women with new time frames during which key life events must be achieved (McRobbie 2009; Negra 2009). Consequently, rituals such as marriage and pregnancy, rather than being a choice have become commodified and as Diane Negra argues, motherhood itself is now a form of 'social currency' (2009, p. 68). As a result, the magazines have stipulations on how pregnancy should be managed. A lengthy feature in *heat* warns of the dangers of over exercising when pregnant; criticising those who do (2008, pp. 90–96), whilst praising the appetites of actresses Kate Hudson and Milla Jovovich who are 'Not too scared to eat cake!' (ibid., p. 96). As McDonnell points out, 'the tone of the pregnancy narrative depends on the degree to which the expectant celebrity adheres to the moral standard set out by the magazine' (2014, p. 94). Perhaps unsurprisingly, *Reveal* has few qualms about criticising pregnant women and in articles such as 'Pregnancy obsessions' (2016, front cover) and 'Pregnant and panicking' (2011, pp. 34–35), the subjects are portrayed as irrational and out of control. In the latter article, the magazine uses before and after photographs to encourage the reader to recoil at the growing pregnant body of singer Jessica Simpson who is reportedly 'stressed, bloated and turning to junkfood' (Reveal 2011, p. 35). The caption beneath the two contrasting images reads: 'Her sexy look made her a star, but now she feels like a beached whale' (ibid.). Simpson's body is no longer associated with the sexiness her petite denim shorts denote in the 'before' picture, and she is now likened to a vast animal. Over the twenty years examined, the pregnant body is thus increasingly constructed as interchangeable with the fat body. The weight gain often experienced during pregnancy is presented as an inconvenience which must be dealt with as soon as possible. For D. Lynn O'Brien Hallstein (2011), the pressures on women to lose their pregnancy weight represent a backlash against second-wave feminism, which reasserts motherhood and beauty as paramount for women.

Following the birth of her first child, American model and reality TV star, Kim Kardashian reportedly 'hates how "saggy" her boobs have become' and has been upset 'about her mum-tum' (heat 2013, p. 9). *heat* reassuringly responds to Kardashian's self-criticism: 'We think she should give herself a break' (ibid.) – its friendly copy is seemingly supportive. However, as Myra Macdonald highlights, 'These features remind us that the magazine is our trusted friend […] Turn to the back pages, though, and advertisements for clinics offering cosmetic surgery or liposuction predominate' (1995, p. 208). Sure enough, some pages later is an advertisement by cosmetic surgery company, Transform (2013) for post-natal breast augmentation. It features a testimonial from a satisfied customer who has undergone the procedure: 'I'm back to my old self and thrilled with the results' (Transform 2013, p. 63). The combination of Kardashian's upset and the advert for cosmetic surgery imply that the post-pregnancy body is a flaw that can be corrected, rather than a natural part of motherhood. *heat* conceding that Kardashian 'should give herself a break' whilst endorsing post-natal cosmetic surgery renders it the archetypal contradictory postfeminist text: it acknowledges that the pressure to lose baby weight is a problem yet endorses the practice at the same time. By the same token, an article on British reality TV star Ferne McCann begins by pointing out that for celebrities, 'the pressure to slim down and shape up before the baby's even left the birth canal plays heavily on the stars' minds' (*heat* 2018, p. 21). In spite of this, *heat* applauds McCann's post-partum body transformation and promotes her new project: a gym for single mothers, which provides childcare, so they too can exercise and manicure their bodies like McCann. Articles such as this briefly offer a critique of the culture of compulsory thinness, only to ultimately reinforce it, with *heat* (via McCann) proposing a concept which means no-one has an excuse for not losing weight, including single mothers. The magazines thus promote and denounce weight-loss practices in turn, and celebrities who are lauded for losing weight in one issue, all too often are reprimanded for taking it too far in the next.

'Did she push her weight loss too far?'

The motif of the *too* thin woman appears across all four titles: it ranges from coverage of celebrities who are said to have pursued their weight loss to an extreme, to articles on everyday women who have endured and overcome eating disorders. By marking a select few women as direly thin, the texts are able to maintain the bifurcation between 'thinness that is healthy and thinness that is not healthy' which has the effect of further stigmatizing disordered eating and reinforcing thinness as a signifier of health (McKinley 1999, p. 98; see also Ferreday 2009, p. 202). As Jones argues of the famous women who take cosmetic surgery 'too far': 'they are necessary for the practice's integration and normalisation; they are the "unnatural" measuring sticks against which the "new natural" can be measured, accepted and condoned' (2008, p. 107). In the same way, the woman who is too thin is an asset to the culture of compulsory thinness.

The *too* thin woman in the magazines is subjected to the same scrutiny as the woman who has gained weight or left her cellulite 'untreated', for example. *Reveal* profiles 'Diet winners & sinners' (2011 front cover) where some women are applauded for their weight loss whilst others, such as Nicola Roberts from British band Girls Aloud, are chastised for being too thin and told to eat carbohydrates (ibid., pp. 12–13). Equally, British comedian Dawn French is reprimanded for having saggy skin on her face caused by a four-stone weight loss (ibid., p. 20). Achieving the correct level of thinness endorsed by the magazines is an endless quest and even Frankie Essex who has been constantly derided by *Reveal* for her weight gain, is pictured in the self-same publication, ribs jutting, accompanied by the caption: 'Frankie in July: Did she push her weight loss too far?' (2017, p. 7) There is no acknowledgement that the magazine had, six years earlier, criticised her for having a 'muffin top bulging' (Reveal 2012, p. 4).

Moreover, when a celebrity is said to have become *too* thin, it is invariably explained by a personal crisis. *heat* describes singer Miley Cyrus's weight loss thus: 'As the star's personal troubles pile up, the pounds are dropping off ...' (2013 p. 10). By portraying the star's skinny frame as the result of inner turmoil, *heat* evade political comment. As Eva Chen argues of such neoliberal discourses, 'Social, structural problems still exist, but the responsibility or blame now shifts from society to the individual' (2013, p. 446). Similarly, when a *Cosmopolitan* article about celebrities' extreme weight loss reports that female celebrities are competing with one another to be thinner (2005, pp. 107–108), the phenomenon is explained at the individual level. The magazine draws on the expertise of a psychotherapist who argues that

> this sense of distorted body image is a frequent phenomenon when girls get together. "Girls are brought up to be competitive with each other," she says. "Men generally still define themselves by what they've achieved and what they own, but women do so by how they look".
>
> (Ibid., p. 108)

Explaining phenomena through psychology (albeit popular psychology) is a common device across all four titles: because psychological discourse focuses on the individual, structural commentary is more easily avoided. In this instance, the psychotherapist acknowledges that diet culture is a result of socialisation but no less reinforces such practices as 'contagion' between women, which 'sustains a patriarchal approach to female relations by foregrounding the body rather than the broader socio-cultural critiques of gender/power relations favoured by feminist interpretations' (Burke 2006, p. 317). In this same issue *Cosmopolitan* shows the reader how to find their 'diet personality' (2005 pp. 231–238), thereby reinforcing the centrality of women's appearance the psychotherapist highlights.

This contradictory pattern recurs in 2007 when the magazine undertakes an exposé of 'LA's size-0 boot camps', investigating the gruelling regimes celebrities undergo to achieve a size zero dress size (Cosmopolitan 2007, pp. 106–109). However, at the end of the article is a set of tips on how to '[get] skinny the A-list way' (ibid., 109). Consequently, even when extreme dieting is condemned, there is the tendency to investigate exactly how it is executed and detail it to their readers. A spread in *heat* entitled 'When skinny gets skinnier' scrutinises before and after images of celebrities' weight loss (heat 2013, pp. 10–11), asking leading questions including: 'Has [reality TV star Millie Mackintosh's] wedding diet gone too far? (ibid., p. 11). Despite the implied answer being affirmative, the article specifies the seven diet initiatives Mackintosh is said to be following, such as: 'A six-week sugar ban [and a] Three-day cleanse with Honestly Healthy' (ibid.), therefore functioning more as weight-loss guidance than a warning against extreme dieting. As Gill argues, irony and knowingness pervade postfeminist media and have 'become a way of "having it both ways"' (2007, p. 266).

One way the magazines are able to hold opposing worldviews at the same time is by distancing themselves from the media at large: they position thinness culture as a phenomenon which is perpetuated *elsewhere*, commenting on it as objective observers. An early issue of *heat* reports 'How some stars are taking stick thin to a frightening extreme' (1999, pp. 36–37). The featured celebrities are mockingly diagnosed with 'Lollipop syndrome' because their bodies are so thin their heads look disproportionately large and thus resemble lollipops (ibid.). In what seems a cynical turn, *heat* blames the media and celebrity culture for the women's skinny frames, asking 'with intense pressure from both the industry and press for female stars to become pin thin, is it any wonder British and American celebrities are getting distorted perceptions of their bodies?' (ibid., p. 37). By criticising 'the industry and press', *heat* positions itself as a knowing spectator, when ironically it is part of the culture it criticises. Although Rebecca Feasey (2006) considers the possibility that *heat* could be an empowering postfeminist text because it deconstructs the celebrity body, the title nonetheless continually criticises women's bodies. Consequently, for Jo Littler, 'the magazine's ironic distance from celebrity culture offers an example of a discourse which is channelled straight back in to feeding it – reselling fame for contemporary popular consumption' (cited in Holmes 2005, p. 36). As I argue later, these contradictions are mirrored in the narrative of pro-ana online spaces: the phenomenon may subvert hegemonic understandings of anorexia, but it ultimately reinforces compulsory thinness. Within both pro-ana online and the magazines explored in this chapter there is potential for political engagement, but it is never quite realised.

All four magazine titles feature coverage of disordered eating, but they confine it to individual women and even use it as a means of exonerating the magazines from their role in thinness culture. When *Reveal* believes Victoria Beckham has taken her weight loss 'too far' (2009, pp. 6–7) it summons expert opinion to corroborate its claims, including a doctor from an eating disorder clinic who muses, 'It's no wonder we have an epidemic of eating disorders in this country when young women see pictures like this and think this is how they should look' (ibid., p. 6) This statement draws on the 'girls in danger' discourse identified in the introductory chapter and it serves the magazines twofold: on the one hand, it presents women as passive dupes (Chen 2013) incapable of critique and therefore in need of protection; on the other, it positions Beckham's emaciated body as the cause of such duping. This allows *Reveal* to continue valorising thinness because it is presented as a concern for individual women rather than a cultural problem.

Similarly, in a *Reveal* article on British actress Gemma Oaten's struggle with anorexia, she is quoted stating, 'anorexia has the highest mortality rate of all mental illnesses. And that's not because girls with anorexia look in a magazine and want to be a model, believe me' (2015, p. 28). Whilst it is true that anorexia is not caused by the media *per se*, such a statement in a magazine whose primary focus is women's body size appears, at best, biased and, at worst, cynical on the part of the publication. At the same time, anorexia here functions to signify thinness that has been taken too far, which in turn legitimises thinness in any other form. In an article on Hollywood actress Portia de Rossi's history of anorexia, legitimate thinness is communicated through before and after photographs. In the before image, de Rossi is shown with her bones protruding, captioned by the statement: 'her weight plummeted to just 5st 12lb' (Reveal 2010, p. 19). In the caption on the after image, she is still thin, but less so and no mention is made of her weight, just that she is 'much healthier, happier' (ibid.). Health and happiness – in the magazines and pro-ana online spaces alike – have come to replace ideal thinness and symbolise it simultaneously. At the same time, anorexia allows for a binary between thinness that is desirable and thinness that is not, and in turn an evasion of the gendered power structures that constitute it.

'Skip the fad diets and focus on a happy, healthy you'

Despite the magazines' repudiation of fat and condemnation of certain thin bodies, readers and celebrities alike are compelled to announce their body satisfaction and refrain from dieting. This is primarily enacted thus: through interviews with celebrities who claim to enjoy food and never diet; coverage of readers who assert to love their bodies; and finally, through the *food swap*. The food swap purports to be a rejection of the conventional diet and instead comprises exchanging a higher calorie food for a lower (or zero) calorie option. In short, compulsory thinness haunts the magazines but is obfuscated by new modes of self-regulation and 'the Panglossian contention that "you are more beautiful than you think"' (Gill and Orgad 2015, p. 338).

Diet and exercise, rather than being framed as methods of weight loss, are reconstructed as confidence-building practices: an exclusive spread in *heat* on a new exercise trend is referred to as a 'method of empowerment' with the emphasis on strength and enjoyment as opposed to slimming (2016, p. 69), and a feature on finding the right swimwear to suit your body mentions 'confidence' four times with *heat*'s style editor appeasing the reader: 'don't worry, I've got the tips and tricks that will have you feeling confident and looking good, whatever your shape or size' (2018, p. 11). Across all four titles, compulsory confidence is yet another yardstick against which women are urged to measure themselves. Ironically, this continued pressure to be confident is recognised by *Cosmopolitan*'s own beauty director, Ingeborg van Lotringen, who admits, 'I feel bad about my thighs. I know that's the wrong thing to say.

In this age of politically correct body-positivity, I should rock my cellulite with womanly pride' (2018, p. 92). Lotringen demonstrates, albeit tacitly, the extent to which body-positivity has become another device which functions to make women feel guilty or inadequate. For Rosalind Gill and Shani Orgad, '[Love your body] discourses are affectively powerful precisely because they offer some recognition of the cultural injuries inflicted on women in a patriarchal society, but [...] this must be only momentarily acknowledged before it is overcome, triumphed over' (2015, p. 338). As such, visible fat – when it is not being criticised – is portrayed as an act of courage. In *heat*, 'curvy girls' are praised for 'prov[ing] you don't have to be stick-thin to strut your stuff in the sun' (2008, pp. 6–7) and *Reveal* applauds supermodel Cindy Crawford when a photograph is 'leaked' showing her, 'completely untouched, Cindy's natural tummy can be seen and a hint of cellulite is visible at the tops of her thighs' (2015, p. 27). Neither *Reveal* nor women's magazine *Marie Claire* (who, according to *Reveal*, took the photograph and are quoted praising the image) point out that magazines themselves retouch such images. As a result, they evade acknowledging their role in the culture of compulsory thinness and disguise it through the rhetoric of self-acceptance.

The magazines then, are intent on telling readers that it is okay – honourable even – to be fat and enjoy eating, but this often comes with caveats or hidden sleights. When *Cosmopolitan* puts fat actress Rebel Wilson on its cover in January 2016, it commends her confidence, even if it is marred somewhat by her disclosure that she uses food as a coping mechanism: 'Rebel is defiant about her size and her love of food. By her own admission, she is an emotional eater' (2016, p. 82). Further, when Frankie Essex appears in a *Reveal* spread on 'bikini body confidence', she is lauded for 'proudly embrac[ing] her curves' (2017, p. 6). However, the article closes with a statement of paradoxical self-acceptance from Essex: 'I'll always have a saggy belly, but I accept that now. I can wear Spanx or a swimsuit' (ibid., p. 7). Whilst Essex may claim to 'accept' her 'saggy belly', she does so under the condition that she can wear clothing which covers it, therefore tempering her 'confident outing' cited by *Reveal* (2017, p. 6). Women who are considered fat are not only called upon to be confident but also to explain their size in ways that slender women are not. Welsh singer, Charlotte Church is quoted in a *Glamour* interview saying 'I've never dieted in my life. I do love a good curry and a bacon fry-up. I'm a natural fat girl!' (2005, p. 65). Church claims here to be unaffected by thinness culture and to embrace the label 'fat girl', thereby reinforcing the imperative to self-acceptance. In a report entitled, 'The life and times of a size 18 bunny' (Cosmopolitan 2017, pp. 124–125), a *Cosmopolitan* editor works on location at a Playboy casino in order to show readers how it feels 'to be the biggest Bunny on the casino floor' (ibid., p. 125). The focus of the article is the editor's size because she is said to be comparatively larger than the other women working at the casino. Nonetheless, she is presented as happy with her body and poses in full Playboy bunny attire, thus exhibiting rather than concealing her body in a statement of self-love.

Over the two decades analysed, *Cosmopolitan* and *Glamour* in particular increasingly urge the reader to make use of digital media for body positivity and self-acceptance. In June 2014, *Cosmopolitan* devotes a 30-page special section to Instagram, focusing mainly on 'swimwear to make you feel fabulous' (p. 149). It implores readers to follow body positivity accounts on the social media platform, as it does again the year after, stressing the importance of 'the body-confidence queens you *need* to follow on Instagram' (Cosmopolitan 2015, p. 65; emphasis in original). In April 2016, *Glamour* too praises the platform declaring, 'Reason #786 to be hooked on Instagram? It's the perfect platform to discover new designers' (p. 34). A year later though, in a special issue devoted to Instagram, this earlier description is revised: 'Instagram, the place you once used for poring over shoes and hot people is becoming a platform for grassroots activism and *real* change' (O'Donoghue 2017, p. 47; emphasis in original). According to *Glamour*, 'hashtags are changing the world' (ibid., p. 46) – social media then becomes a catalyst for social change and self-acceptance.

Despite increasing exhortations to body positivity, the reader is nonetheless urged, as the quote in the header states, to lose weight without dieting. When *Glamour* tells readers to 'skip the fad diets and focus on a happy, healthy you' (2014, pp. 183–185), further interrogation simply reveals dieting by another name, namely the *food swap*. *Glamour* hail the food swap as one of the secrets of healthy people (2016, p. 240). It is lauded for its simplicity and the promise that you can still enjoy food by merely 'replac[ing] butter with sweet potatoes' when making brownies (Cosmopolitan 2015, p. 191) or engaging in '[meditative] breath[ing] instead of stress snacking' (ibid.), for instance. In reality, readers are impelled to regulate their eating practices in such a way that dieting is disguised. In keeping with its light-hearted register, *heat* takes a humorous approach to the food swap: 'if you're still trying to fit your buns in that bikini, why not try swapping your floury bap for an avocado? [...] A messy feast, sure, but just think of the Instagram followers' (2016, p. 73). *heat* may be mocking the ubiquity of food photos, especially avocados, on social media (see Holland 2015), but it no less endorses eating this relatively expensive food instead of the much cheaper alternative, bread. Rather than forgoing food entirely, the food swap is about making the 'right' choice, and as these publications continually show, there are penalties for those who make the wrong choice.

In an interview with 'reality TV's most successful fitness queen Charlotte Crosby' (2017, pp. 4–8), *heat* questions her about her recent weight loss. Throughout the interview, Crosby's method of dieting is presented as one in which she has her cake and eats it, or, as *heat* says, '[proves] that it's possible to lose weight without having to sit in a cupboard munching chia seeds while your mates go out on the lash' (2017, p. 4). At the end of the interview, Crosby's food swaps are listed in detail: exchanging beer and wine for vodka and tonic; eating popcorn instead of crisps and a 'big lettuce leaf' in place of a tortilla wrap (ibid., p. 8). Crosby may be cutting out a plethora of foods, but she does not refer to the food swap as a diet, claims never to weigh herself and insists she is still enjoying life. The food swap then is a swap itself: a substitute language for talking about dieting without mentioning it by name or risking accusations of promoting thinness. Whilst contemporary pro-ana online spaces are disguising advice around maintaining anorexia in the language of dieting, the magazines are one step ahead, concealing dieting through the food swap – although as I will show, older incarnations of pro-ana online were more open and direct about their aims (and therefore continually removed by Internet moderators).

Deception thus permeates both mainstream and marginal manifestations of weight-loss culture. This is encapsulated through the recurrent 'tips and tricks' which feature in both the magazines and pro-ana online spaces and constitute advice which is on some level misleading: whether on the part of the individual enacting it, those witnessing it, or both. For example, in pro-ana online spaces, tips and tricks guide users on how to self-starve whilst simultaneously signalling to others that they are simply health-conscious (chapter three attends to this in detail). For the magazines, the reverse is true: tips and tricks are presented as techniques to help the reader eat healthily, yet they disguise their true aim, of food restriction and subsequent weight loss. In the article on Charlotte Crosby, her tips and tricks are enumerated beneath the heading, 'Eat, drink & still shrink: Charlotte's rules for slimming down while still having a life' (heat 2017, p. 7). Tips and tricks then are presented to the reader as shortcuts; rather than making life easier though, they amount to yet another way in which women are cajoled into 'having it all' in neoliberal culture (Genz 2010).

By 2016, heat introduced a regular 'Life hacks' feature, comprising travel, food and fitness guidance which it claims will '[help] you win at life' (2016, p. 69). 'Life hacking', according to Evgeny Morozov (2013) is presented as a way of managing one's life more efficiently, but instead increases workload because so much time must be spent on life hacking itself. heat is no different and winning at life requires utilising loyalty schemes to be upgraded to first class travel on airlines (2016, p. 75); undertaking High Impact Intensity Training workouts to lose weight after Christmas (2017, pp. 69–72); and consuming chia seed drinks to prevent the urge to snack (2018, p. 75). Although they are under the umbrella of life hacking, ironically all the suggested practices require time commitments and disposable income in order to reap their rewards. Furnished with this information, the neoliberal citizen has no reason not to make full use of it. When *Glamour* makes it imperative that readers 'Eat out guilt free', listing 'the healthier options at [their] favourite restaurant chains' complete with calorific breakdowns of all the dishes (2008, p. 61), the implication is that if readers do not make the healthier choice, they are guilty of yielding to temptation and have therefore failed to fulfil the requirements of ideal femininity set out by the magazine. The journey to fulfilling such an ideal is paradoxical: saving time requires spending time; loving one's body requires continually improving it; and losing weight must be achieved without dieting.

Conclusion

The contemporary UK women's magazine offers insight into the ways compulsory thinness is negotiated in the mainstream. In cultural contexts where feminism has had many gains, it is no longer acceptable to promote thinness as an ideal – yet there remains a sizeable market for it. As a result, the magazines are fraught with contradiction as they simultaneously embrace and disavow diet culture. Over the twenty-year period from which the publications were selected, obligatory weight loss is increasingly disguised so as to suggest that the magazines no longer endorse such practices, and readers are urged to be happy and confident as they are. However, happiness and confidence come with stipulations.

Fat, as I have argued, is denounced in a number of different ways: at times it is subjected to light-hearted mockery, at others, it is portrayed as pathological and potentially fatal. Cellulite for instance, is described – albeit erroneously – not only as unwanted fat, but in rhetoric to suggest it is a medical condition which must be treated. Women's bodies are therefore framed as problems for which the magazine has solutions. This is further prominent in the coverage of the post-partum body, which is entreated to return to its prior state as soon as possible after giving birth. Hence, as the analysis suggests, fatness and pregnancy are increasingly elided. The repudiation of fat in the magazines, however, is complicated by a disapproval of women who are said to have taken their weight loss *too* far. The *too* thin woman's appearance is often cruelly disparaged, and at times, she is blamed for perpetuating thinness culture and even eating disorders. The motif of the *too* thin woman in all four titles operates to suggest that extreme weight loss is an individual, personal problem, rather than a cultural, political one. At the same time, as I sought to show, by focusing on the practices and bodies of specific women – at any size – the magazines strive to assert a critical distance.

Such distance is reinforced by labouring the importance of loving your body. Body positivity is particularly apparent in the publications from the latter years where the reader is urged to be confident and happy and abandon dieting. Nonetheless, as I have argued, the diet merely assumes a new form, and the reader is regaled with tips and tricks on food swaps, such as substituting crisps for popcorn and snacking for meditating. In so doing, she is told she can *have it all*: to lose weight without dieting. By disguising dieting in this way, the magazines attempt to reconcile the demands of hegemonic femininity with those of feminism. In practice, such reconciliation only results in contradiction; for example, a celebrity who is praised in one issue for embracing her curves is castigated in another for gaining weight. As my analysis showed, this is most glaring in *Reveal*'s coverage of Frankie Essex who is treated as the embodiment of flawed femininity. From the outset, Essex is derided for putting on weight, yet latterly, she is criticised for taking weight loss too far. Ultimately, this suggests that women *cannot have it all.*

Above all, these texts adopt discourses that are startlingly similar to those in pro-ana online spaces. If *Cosmopolitan* tells the reader to 'keep snacks somewhere unreachable and you'll eat less of them' (2010, p. 195), then pro-ana site *Ethereal Anas* suggests users might resist cravings by 'put[ting] [their] favourite foods in the freezer'. Whilst *Cosmopolitan*'s tips and tricks are framed as legitimate modes of dieting, *Ethereal Anas* has long since been taken offline because it suggests such advice can help to maintain anorexia. When the focus is on the extreme, the so-called norm is spared criticism, until of course *Reveal* directly used the lexis of pro-ana in 2014. This was a watershed moment in thinness culture because the magazine's use of 'thinspiration' to promote celebrity diets unwittingly exposes the arbitrary line between legitimate and illegitimate exhortations to weight loss. Nevertheless, *Reveal* was able to recover from accusations of promoting anorexia by repudiating pro-anorexia. As I have argued, the woman who is *too* thin is a useful device in thinness culture – equally useful is the phenomenon of pro-anorexia because it signals the point at which dieting has gone *too* far. Tips on how to slim down for summer can be read as benign when compared to guidance that has the express aim of upholding an eating disorder.

In the next chapter, I investigate the pro-anorexia landscape in detail, examining how these spaces operate under the continued threat of censorship and erasure, whilst borrowing from and contributing towards hegemonic culture. Given that they are unhampered by advertising and antithetical to the mainstream medicalising of anorexia, I ask if pro-ana online spaces might offer the critique of compulsory thinness culture that the magazines continually fail to fulfil.

Note

1 It is important to point out that the magazines examined in this chapter derive from a UK context, whereas pro-ana online has a global dimension. Nonetheless, whilst this analysis is culturally specific, the discourses in these texts are reflected in pro-ana culture at large, as I demonstrate in later chapters.

References

Abrahams, A. (2016) '10 secrets of healthy people', *Glamour*, pp. 235–241.

Ballaster, R., Beetham, M., Frazer, E., and Hebron, S. (1991) *Women's Worlds: Ideology, Femininity and the Woman's Magazine*. Basingstoke, Hampshire: The Macmillan Press Ltd.

BBC. (2017) 'Glamour magazine goes "digital first" and cuts back print editions', *BBC*, 6 October. Available at: www.bbc.co.uk/news/entertainment-arts-41527740 (Accessed 10 August 2018).

Bourdieu, P. (1984) *Distinction: A Social Critique of the Judgement of Taste*. Nice, R. (trans.). New York: Routledge.

Bullen, J. (2014) *Media Representations of Footballers' Wives: A Wag's Life*. Basingstoke, Hampshire: Palgrave Macmillan.

Burke, E. (2006) 'Feminine visions: Anorexia and contagion in pop discourse', *Feminist Media Studies*, 6(3), pp. 315–330.

Chen, E. (2013) 'Neoliberalism and popular women's culture: Rethinking choice, freedom and agency', *European Journal of Cultural Studies*, 16(4), pp. 440–452.

Cobb, G. (2017) '"This is not pro-ana": Denial and disguise in pro-anorexia online spaces', *Fat Studies*, 6(2), pp. 189–205.

Cogan, J.C. (1999) 'Re-evaluating the weight-centered approach toward health: The need for a paradigm shift', in Sobal, J. and Maurer, D. (eds.) *Interpreting Weight: The Social Management of Fatness and Thinness*. New York: Aldine de Gruyter, pp. 229–253.

Cosmopolitan. (1999) National Magazine Company, April.

———. (2002) National Magazine Company, January.

———. (2005) National Magazine Company, September.

———. (2007) National Magazine Company, January.

———. (2010) National Magazine Company, January.

———. (2013) Hearst Magazines, July.

———. (2014) Hearst Magazines, June.

———. (2015) Hearst Magazines, June.

———. (2016) Hearst Magazines, January.

———. (2017) Hearst Magazines, August.

———. (2018) Hearst Magazines, July.

Edwards, T. (2013) 'Medusa's stare: Celebrity, subjectivity and gender', *Celebrity Studies*, 4(2), pp. 155–168.

Ennis, J. (2014) 'Reveal's response to this week's magazine cover', *Reveal*, 3 July. Available at: www.reveal.co.uk/lifestyle/news/a581999/reveals-response-to-this-weeks-magazine-cover.html (Accessed 6 May 2016).

Feasey, R. (2006) 'Get a famous body: Star styles and celebrity gossip in *Heat* magazine', in Holmes, S. and Redmond, S. (eds.) *Framing Celebrity: New Directions in Celebrity Culture*. London: Routledge, pp. 177–194.

Ferreday, D. (2009) *Online Belongings: Fantasy, Affect and Web Communities*. Oxford: Peter Lang.

Genz, S. (2010) 'Singled out: Postfeminism's "new woman" and the dilemma of having it all', *The Journal of Popular Culture*, 43(1), pp. 97–119.

Gill, R. (2007) *Gender and the Media*. Cambridge: Polity.

Gill, R. and Orgad, S. (2015) 'The confidence cult(ure)', *Australian Feminist Studies*, 30(86), pp. 324–344.

Glamour. (2001) Condé Nast, April.

———. (2003) Condé Nast, February.

———. (2005) Condé Nast, June.

———. (2008) Condé Nast, September.

———. (2013) Condé Nast, July.

———. (2014) Condé Nast, June.

———. (2016) Condé Nast, April.

heat. (1999) Emap, 9–25 August.

———. (2008) Bauer Media, 17–23 May.

———. (2013) Bauer Media, 6–12 July.

———. (2014) Bauer Media, 24–30 May.

———. (2015) Bauer Media, 20–26 June.

———. (2016) Bauer Media, 20–26 August.

———. (2017) Bauer Media, 7–13 January.

———. (2018) Bauer Media, 16–22 June.

Hermes, J. (1995) *Reading Women's Magazines: An Analysis of Everyday Media Use*. Cambridge: Polity Press.

Holland, M. (2015) 'The truth about why we're all obsessed with avocados', *Stylist*, Available at: www.stylist.co.uk/life/the-truth-about-why-were-all-obsessed-with-avocados/60762 (Accessed 21 December 2018).

Holmes, S. (2005) '"Off-guard, unkempt, unready"?: Deconstructing contemporary celebrity in Heat magazine', *Continuum: Journal of Media and Cultural Studies*, 19(1), pp. 21–38.

Jones, M. (2008) *Skintight: An Anatomy of Cosmetic Surgery*. Oxford: Berg.

Lupton, D. (1996) *Food, the Body and the Self*. London: Sage.

Macdonald, M. (1995) *Representing Women: Myths of Femininity in the Popular Media*. London: Edward Arnold.

McCracken, E. (1993) *Decoding Women's Magazines: From Mademoiselle to Ms*. Basingstoke, Hampshire: The Macmillan Press Ltd.

McDonnell, A. (2014) *Reading Celebrity Gossip Magazines*. Cambridge, UK: Polity Press.

McKinley, N.M. (1999) 'Ideal weight/ideal women: Society constructs the female', in Sobal, J. and Maurer, D. (eds.) *Weighty Issues: Fatness and Thinness as Social Problems*. New York: Aldine de Gruyter, pp. 97–115.

McRobbie, A. (1997) '*More!* New sexualities in girls' and women's magazines', in McRobbie, A. (ed.) *Back to Reality? Social Experience and Cultural Studies*. Manchester: Manchester University Press, pp. 190–209.

———. (2009) *The Aftermath of Feminism: Gender, Culture and Social Change*. London: Sage Publications Ltd.

Morozov, E. (2013) 'Down with lifehacking!' *Slate*, 29 July. Available at: www.slate.com/articles/technology/future_tense/2013/07/lifehacking_is_just_another_way_to_make_us_work_more.html (Accessed 10 August 2018).

National Readership Survey (2017) 'Women's magazines', *Results*, Available at: www.nrs.co.uk/latest-results/nrs-print-results/womens-magazines-nrsprintresults/ (Accessed 5 October 2018).

Negra, D. (2009) *What a Girl Wants? Fantasizing the Reclamation of Self in Postfeminism*. London: Routledge.

O'Brien Hallstein, D.L. (2011) 'She gives birth, she's wearing a bikini: Mobilizing the postpregnant celebrity mom body to manage the post–second wave crisis in femininity', *Women's Studies in Communication*, 34(2), pp. 111–138.

O'Donoghue, C. (2017) 'How hashtags are changing the world', *Glamour*, pp. 46–49.

Pearce, S.M. (1995) *On Collecting: An Investigation into Collecting in the European Tradition*. London: Routledge.

Plunkett, J. (2013) 'Interview: Heat magazine's Lucie Cave: "It's about being cheeky, funny, not mean"', *The Guardian*, 31 March. Available at: www.theguardian.com/media/2013/mar/31/heat-magazine-lucie-cave-celebrities (Accessed 5 November 2018).

Reveal. (2008) National Magazine Company, 31 May–6 June.

———. (2009) National Magazine Company, 7–13 March.

———. (2010) National Magazine Company, 13–19 November.

———. (2011) Hearst Magazines, 3–9 December.

———. (2012) Hearst Magazines, 29 September–5 October.

———. (2013) Hearst Magazines, 6–12 July.

———. (2014) Hearst Magazines, 5–11 July.

———. (2015), Hearst Magazines, 28 February–6 March.

———. (2016) Hearst Magazines, 2–8 April.

————. (2017) Hearst Magazines, 2–8 September.

————. (2018) Hearst Magazines, 16–22 June.

Rottenberg, C. (2014) 'The rise of neoliberal feminism', *Cultural Studies*, 28(3), pp. 418–437.

Transform (2013) *We can't say that cosmetic surgery changed her life. But Becky can* [Advertisement in *heat*], 6–12 July, p. 63.

Tseëlon, E. (1995) *The Masque of Femininity*. London: Sage.

Tyler, I. and Bennett, B. (2010) '"Celebrity chav": Fame, femininity and social class', *European Journal of Cultural Studies*, 13(3), pp. 375–393.

White, S.K. (2017) '#cleaneating? No thanks', *Glamour*, pp. 152–156.

Williamson, M. (2010) 'Female celebrities in the media: The gendered denigration of the "ordinary" celebrity', *Celebrity Studies*, 1(1), pp. 118–120.

Winch, A. (2013) *Girlfriends and Postfeminist Sisterhood*. Basingstoke, Hampshire: Palgrave Macmillan.

Winship, J. (1987) *Inside Women's Magazines*. London: Pandora Press.

Wolf, N. (1991) *The Beauty Myth: How Images of Beauty Are Used Against Women*. New York: Harper Perennial.

Woods, F. (2014) 'Classed femininity, performativity, and camp in British structured reality programming', *Television & New Media*, 15(3), pp. 197–214.

3 Normalising pro-anorexia

This chapter charts the changes and developments in pro-ana culture since its inception in the late twentieth century. I propose that what began as both a community and a subversive 'movement' has become individualised and normalised. When Internet moderators block and remove pro-ana content, users respond by carving out creative ways to circumvent censorship and evade deletion, such as disguising spaces in discourses of health or beauty, coining obscure hashtags or denying that content promotes anorexia through disclaimers. In negating such claims, however, users not only avoid censorship, but they are also able to espouse views that would otherwise be considered pro-ana. As such, through their denial and disguise of pro-ana content, users are ultimately blurring the boundaries between pro-ana and mainstream thinness culture.

This chapter is divided into two main sections. The first looks at the history of pro-ana online and considers what remains of the original forums and websites that one might categorise as 'pro-ana' – the majority of which were deleted during the process of writing this book. The second section attends to the current pro-ana landscape, which operates primarily across a raft of social media platforms rather than forums and static websites; it is split into four subsections. To begin with, I explore the practices of censorship social media platforms enact in attempts to suppress pro-ana content, emphasising their arbitrary delineation of posts that are acceptable and posts that are not. The subsequent three subsections examine how such censorship practices have influenced pro-anorexic expression. First, I look to the lexical developments in pro-ana culture as users create a new vocabulary to circumvent censorship. Next, responding to the way many of the bodies which adorn the image boards borrow from pornography, I show how the eroticising of the anorexic body is blurring the line between what constitutes #proana and what constitutes #sexy. Finally, I explore the marketisation of pro-ana and the coining of 'healthy thinspo', illustrating how the diet industry and pro-ana culture borrow from one another. I argue that all such developments are ultimately contributing to the normalisation of pro-anorexia.

The original landscape and its remains

Pro-ana online spaces have altered significantly since their inception for two main reasons: first, as a result of the Internet-wide 'transformation from networked communication to "platformed" sociality' (Van Dijck 2013, pp. 4–5), which has seen users migrate from websites and forums to social media, and second, because of censorship and castigation, which has meant they must continually adapt in order to remain online. These changes have had an impact on the sense of community the spaces were originally understood to possess. Numerous scholars (myself included) have approached research into pro-anorexia as an exploration of a 'community' (see for example: Boero and Pascoe 2012; Brotsky and Giles 2007; Day and Keys 2008a, 2008b, 2009; Ferreday 2003, 2009; Giles and Newbold 2011; Polak 2010; Stommel and Koole 2010; Yeshua-Katz and Martins 2013). Pro-ana culture in such work is understood in line with Malcolm R. Parks' (2011) definition of a virtual community in that it promotes a sense of identity and togetherness against the odds. It was Howard Rheingold (1993), however, who first theorised virtual communities, suggesting that they emerged 'in part [as] a response to the hunger for community that has followed the disintegration of traditional communities around the world' (p. 62). Vincent Miller has since suggested the Internet-wide 'movement from blogging, to social networking, to microblogging demonstrates the simultaneous movements away from communities, narratives, substantive communication, and towards networks, databases and phatic communion' (2008, p. 398). Thus, it can be argued that virtual communities are increasingly rare. Although scholars such as Boero and Pascoe read pro-ana not 'as *virtual* communities, but as *real* communities based on real human interaction convening in a virtual space' (2012, p. 34; emphases in original), I suggest that such a sense of community in pro-ana culture – whether virtual or real – has since disintegrated also, thereby leaving the hunger for community identified by Rheingold once again unsated. When I began this project, I set out to find the communities to which the aforementioned scholars refer, yet I was confronted with what I can only describe as a pro-ana graveyard. This consisted of numerous spaces, formerly having been active and thriving with conversation, now sitting silently, invariably not having been updated for years. In some cases, authors had fled to new platforms and renamed their sites, whereas others had explicitly changed their *pro*-anorexia stance to one dedicated to recovery. Other sites and forums simply remain abandoned, frozen in time.

The 'about' section of pro-ana site and forum, *Anamia Universe*, provides a comprehensive overview of the various guises a pro-ana space such as this has assumed because of being closed down continually by Internet moderators:

> Anamia Universe is now on version four. We didn't start out as pro-ana, just an ED support forum. We got bigger and bigger and that was when all the attention got us shut down. I was distraught. I had to cobble together

version two. And then guess what? That got shut down too! So here we are with what I hope will be the final version of Anamia Universe. It's not a pro-ana site. Even still, who knows how long this will last?

(*Anamia Universe*)

The author's hopes were not met and at the time *Anamia Universe* was accessed, the site had been frozen. Likewise, *Thinspo HQ* recounts undergoing similar changes after deletion. On the landing page, the author concludes that the forum has now changed from 'hard-core pro-ana to a unique support forum', adding 'Big changes are afoot − pro-ana is evolving' (*Thinspo HQ*). Nonetheless, clicking the links to access the forum for both *Anamia Universe* and *Thinspo HQ* simply yields: 'page cannot be displayed'. Pro-ana forum, *Beauty of Ana* has also undergone several changes, stating that its original site is now functioning as an archive and it has a partner site, *Beauty of Ana 2*, which requires users to log in to view and submit content. It explains that it has changed for the following reasons:

I know we've said constantly that we're not pro-ana (even though we respect those who want to make pro-ana about support instead of harm), however, this doesn't mean we are now pro-recovery. Rather, in *Beauty of Ana 2* we are saying no to underwear pics and no to supporting unhealthy diets.

(*Beauty of Ana*)

The statement is contradictory which makes it, perhaps intentionally, difficult to ascertain whether the site is pro-ana or not − and moreover what it actually means to be 'pro-ana'. *Beauty of Ana* is keen to shed the pro-ana label which has become synonymous with harm, yet seeks to retain its supportive elements. The site also strives to dissociate itself from the 'underwear pics' which seem to be ubiquitous across the contemporary thinspo spaces discussed below. This space may be grappling with its own identity but, what it does make clear, is that there is a need for it to exist.

Where some closed forums and sites have been able to post their own explanations to users, others have to contend with automated messages from their hosts, such as those on webs.com (2014) which read 'We're sorry this website is frozen', or Yahoo! (2014): 'You have reached the cached page for [...]' and beneath this statement in smaller text: 'Yahoo! is not responsible for the content of this page'. One such cached site hosted by Yahoo!, *Living pro-ana*, displays an emblem, 'Anorexia is a lifestyle, not a disease'. Other spaces though, hold no explanation for their demise. *Anything for Thin*, for instance, ceased updating in July 2013 with commenting having terminated roughly around the same time. There is no indication why, thus suggesting either that the site was frozen, or the community was warned independently that its leader would move to a new space. Nonetheless, the statistics counter at the bottom of the page carries on regardless: 'Welcome visitor no. 02086750' (*Anything for Thin*), but there is no-one there to greet.

A plethora of these older spaces draw on religious rhetoric and rituals of the Judeo-Christian tradition in their quest for thinness (Bell 2009; Day and Keys 2008a, 2008b, 2009; Lelwica et al. 2009; Mulveen and Hepworth 2006; Nash 2006; Norris et al. 2006). Links to these kinds of sites were generated by my searches but appeared to have been abandoned for newer platforms and beliefs. Many centred around being an 'angel' of Ana, constructing Ana as a leader the users worship and in whose presence they are always inferior. Eda R. Uca (2004) explores the phenomenon in its early, more devout form, quoting verbatim the 'Ana Creed' and the 'Ana Psalm' which details the beliefs of followers of Ana such as, 'I believe in calorie counters as the inspired word of god, and memorize them accordingly [...] 'Strict is my diet. I must not want' (p. 44 and p. 46). Today, many pro-ana online spaces have moved away from such manifestly pious language and have gravitated instead towards a more 'self-help' style of communication, using motivational and inspirational slogans and rhetoric, which I explore in detail below.

Despite their evangelical tone and media claims that pro-ana online spaces are 'recruiting grounds for eating disorders' (Boero and Pascoe 2012, p. 28), the spaces examined in this study do not proselytise and the older sites and forums in particular frequently display their own warnings about the content viewers will access if they click through. This also serves to filter out what users call 'wannarexics': 'people who want to take part in the community but whose credibility as eating disordered is in doubt' (Boero and Pascoe 2012, p. 39). On their landing page, *World of Pro-ana*, for example, states: 'NO wannarexics. Only post if you have a genuine ED. We are encouraging and supportive here but we do not promote EDs'. Thus, rather than seeking to persuade new members to join, pro-ana online spaces often deploy mechanisms to keep the disingenuous out. However, because they are located in a culture where thinness is valued, their attempts to create a boundary between those who are anorexic and those who want to be thin, are often in vain.

Others insert warnings denouncing responsibility for the content on the sites, such as *Kneeling to Ana* which asserts: 'Anas and Mias only. If you have any kind of ED or are in recovery, please do not enter this site'. *Ethereal Anas* appeals to the potential viewer's compassion: 'You are entering a pro-ana site. Please understand that we made the choice to be like this. We are tired of being judged and misunderstood. Haters have no place here'. *Guide to Ana* is more explicit about who should enter, declaring, 'This site is not for anyone who is underage or easily influenced. Entering this space means you are of legal age and are therefore responsible for any consequences that may arise from viewing this content'. Other spaces address potential viewers more emotively: 'Anorexia is NOT cool. If you can access help, please do. This is not a diet site. Anorexia is hell and you cannot choose to have it' (*Fallen Ana*). This statement is then followed by hundreds of photographs of glamorously-dressed, skinny celebrities. Spaces such as these therefore create their own filtering mechanisms in attempts to protect the vulnerable girls that cause so much concern for the media. However, in current pro-ana spaces, these user-led warnings have been replaced with the platforms' own public service announcements, as spaces such as Tumblr, Instagram and Pinterest seek to exert control over the pro-ana landscape as I will now explain.

The current landscape

In recent years, whilst many of the pro-ana discussion forums discussed above have become harder to find or have been taken offline, thinspo image boards on sites including Instagram, Tumblr and Pinterest have increased. Despite platforms such as Tumblr declaring in 2012 that they would remove all pro-ana blogs (Ostroff and Taylor 2012) and Instagram continually striving to make pro-ana and thinspiration hashtags unsearchable (BBC Trending 2018), thousands of images are posted every day which are identifiable as pro-ana. However, these images tend to conform to mainstream beauty ideals and/or eroticise the anorexic body. Furthermore, new ways of identifying, or rather obscuring, pro-anorexia content have emerged including hashtags such as #thynspoo or #ana; spaces claiming to promote 'healthy thinspo'; and others bearing disclaimers to deny that they are pro-ana.

There is a range of important research on the impact of censoring pro-ana hashtags (Chancellor et al. 2016; Gerrard 2018; Moreno et al. 2016); however, it does not address how pro-ana users' attempts to circumvent censorship are normalising the phenomenon. Although Debbie Ging and Sarah Garvey (2018) recognise the mainstreaming of pro-ana, they suggest it is a positive development which 'invite[s] more holistic and contextualised understandings' (p. 1197). Whilst I agree that pro-ana texts are better visible than suppressed, I contend that the current postfeminist neoliberal context in which they are situated means that their mainstreaming is further entrenching thinness as an ideal, rather than providing a meaningful critique. Additionally, although there are still some forums to be found, pro-ana exists primarily on social media platforms where it is text-light and image-heavy which makes it harder to identify as pro-ana content. Images have always been important to pro-ana users, but even where contemporary platforms allow for text and discussion, it is minimal, and the existing pro-ana 'community' is predominantly composed of hashtags and images. This is not only because of the architecture of the social networks in which pro-ana culture sits, but also because of its controversial status, subsequent censorship and the neoliberal climate which is characterised by a shift from community to individual.

'Everything okay?': modes of censorship

Each of the social media platforms examined in this book have policies around removing content they consider harmful, of which disordered eating is a part. However, the point at which a platform considers content harmful or benign often appears arbitrary. Tumblr is a microblogging platform where users post multimedia content and have the option to follow others' blogs. In its community guidelines, which were consulted during the research period, it stated: 'We aim for Tumblr to be a place that facilitates awareness, support and recovery, and we will remove only those posts or blogs that cross the line into active promotion or glorification of self-harm' (Tumblr 2014a). Despite this, a wealth of content which promotes self-starvation and self-laceration was yielded by my searches. The question remains whether this is because it is untraceable by Tumblr or because 'the line' to which they refer is ever blurred. As it does today, a search for pro-ana or thinspo on Tumblr would generate a public service announcement as follows:

> Everything okay? If you or someone you know is struggling with an eating disorder NEDA [National Eating Disorders Association] is here to help […] And, if you could do with some inspiration and comfort in your dashboard, go ahead and follow NEDA on Tumblr.
>
> (Tumblr 2014b)

It does, however, at the bottom of the page provide a link to 'view search results', therefore, even though Tumblr frames pro-ana content as problematic, it gives users the option to proceed, having duly presented support resources. Schott and Langan (2015, p. 1171) are sceptical about the relationship between the NEDA and Tumblr, suggesting that the two organisations profit from such an association: the NEDA receives direct advertising, and Tumblr puts forth the appearance of protecting its users. Therefore, the relationship between controversial content and platforms such as Tumblr is not necessarily fraught with tension. As Katrin Tiidenberg and Edgar Gómez Cruz (2015, p. 89) note in their research into 'NSFW'[1] selfies on Tumblr, those who post the images may not have the same visual culture as the mainstream, but their images are nonetheless a commodity which contributes to the platform's profit.

Pinterest is a social media platform where users post images or 'pins' to create a collection or 'board' centred on a particular topic and like Tumblr, users may follow one another's content. Unlike Tumblr, during the research period, Pinterest was more explicit about the types of posts it allowed and its 'Acceptable Use Policy' provided examples of permissible content. One such example was an image of a slim woman with a toned stomach; emblazoned over which was a motivational platitude: 'Remember, Rome wasn't built in a day. Work hard, good results will come' (Pinterest 2014a). The language is typically neoliberal, framing the body as a project to be worked upon which Pinterest deems legitimate, as the caption confirms: 'In this context this image is promoting fitness, not self-harm' (ibid. 2014a). However, that the platform considered it necessary to provide an example and to assert that the image is acceptable *in this context* is tacit acknowledgement of how easily such boundaries are blurred. If Pinterest believed content was promoting self-harm, it would generate warnings similar to those of Tumblr, providing contact information for the National Centre for Eating Disorders,[2] advising users as follows: 'Eating disorders are not lifestyle choices, they are mental disorders that if left untreated can cause serious health problems or could even be life-threatening' (2014b). Pinterest's disclaimer focuses on refuting pro-ana culture's claims to lifestyle choice and places anorexia in a paradigm of pathology, the same paradigm used by medicine, the media, and society at large. In what seems a contradictory move though, the page would show the results immediately without the need for further navigating, although the results generated for these hashtags were frozen and no longer updated. Now however, Pinterest has updated its policy and the example image is no longer included, furthermore, a search for pro-ana or thinspo, or any of its derivatives simply states that the content cannot be found, as Instagram has suggested for a long time.

Like Tumblr and Pinterest, Instagram is a social media platform where users may share multimedia content and follow one another's accounts. In its community guidelines it warned that 'any account found encouraging or urging users to embrace anorexia, bulimia, or other eating disorders; or to cut, harm themselves, or commit suicide will result in a disabled account without warning' (Instagram 2014). It did not indicate how it defines encouragement of eating disorders, but a hashtag search for 'pro-ana' or 'thinspo' on Instagram, both during the research period and to this day, returns the result, 'Not found'. In the world of Instagram, these words simply do not exist, but contrary to the platform's declaration that they will delete self-harm accounts, at the time of writing these terms still generate user-account results, thus evidencing the challenges in censoring such content.

The architecture of Reddit differs greatly from that of Tumblr, Pinterest and Instagram and in turn so does its handling of pro-ana content. Reddit is an online bulletin board that divides areas of interest into sections called subreddits. Users vote to increase or decrease the popularity of posts within a subreddit and those which receive the most 'upvotes' increase in visibility – on both Reddit and the Internet at large. My search engine queries thus gave rise to the popular subreddit, *thinspirationpics*. Although to access the subreddit, users had to confirm they were over the age of eighteen, during the research period it was publicly available. A subreddit devoted to pro-ana also existed, but it had a protected page and users had to be approved to view content, therefore I did not investigate this space. However, it is illuminating that on Reddit, pro-ana was private, but thinspo was public: this suggests that the former is problematic, but the latter is not, thereby echoing the views of *Reveal* magazine discussed in chapter two. Like *Reveal*, *thinspirationpics* denies associations with pro-anorexia, firmly telling users on its landing page: 'Important: this is not a pro-ana subreddit. Users posting pro-ana content will be banned' (*thinspirationpics*). It is worth noting that subreddits are created and moderated by users rather than by Reddit employees and that during the research period Reddit had no specific policy around self-harm content in the way the other platforms did. As such, *thinspirationpics* users were self-censoring their space from the outset, as opposed to taking the lead from the platform. With restrictions such as these in place from users and platforms alike, pro-ana advocates have carved out creative methods in order that their content appears online.

#thynspooo: circumventing censorship

The current pro-ana landscape comprises both a denial of pro-ana status and a disguising of pro-ana lexicon. Because of censorship, users have adapted their vocabulary in order to survive: they deploy obscure hashtags – such as '#thynspooo' and '#proanna' – to evade deletion, as well as more innocuous hashtags – such as '#blithe' and '#sexy' – which do not immediately appear to be of a pro-ana nature. In so doing, users effectively exclude outsiders, parents, or those with censorial privilege, whilst simultaneously signalling to fellow pro-anas that such content can be found therein. Over time, as new words are coined they become further detached from their roots to the extent that their meaning is indecipherable to those outside of pro-ana networks. For instance, the term 'bonespo' indicates images of bodies thin to the point their bones are revealed. Ostensibly this term, a portmanteau of the words bone and inspiration, the latter contracted to 'spo', does not necessarily signal pro-ana content, unless the viewer has prior knowledge. Through ellipsis and hybridising words, their original meanings are obfuscated and content is safeguarded, at least until it catches the attention of moderators and the chase starts anew.

The tactics deployed by pro-ana users are both creative and resistant and echo the offline linguistic strategies of other marginalised groups who seek to construct identities which dominant groups may perceive as deviant. For instance, in her study into the ludic activity of Moroccan immigrant children in Spain, Inmaculada M. García-Sánchez (2010) found that the children engaged in codeswitching to act out desired feminine identities disapproved of by their parents. By switching from Moroccan Arabic to Spanish, they were able to play with this identity without falling under the censure of caregivers. Thus, adopting different languages depending on context can be an empowering and subversive device. Boellstorff (2003) explores how creating new vocabularies allows subaltern groups to carve out their own identities. He shows how lesbian and gay Indonesians establish their subjectivities as *lesbi* and *gay*, as opposed to adopting already assigned Western or Indonesian terms (2003, emphases in original). He nonetheless points out that, 'they cannot compose any script they please; their bricolage remains shaped by a discourse originating in the "West" and filtered through a nationalistic lens' (Boellstorff 2003, p. 237). Therefore, when marginalised groups appropriate language, they remain beholden to its rules. By the same token, pro-ana users may subvert medical authority, but they use its language to do so.

Despite this, such tactics disrupt common sense meanings and therefore contain radical potential. In her research into women's self-imaging practices on Instagram, Magdalena Olszanowski (2014) suggests that users' innovative flouting of the rules of social media sites can have the effect of undermining the authority of these platforms. The consequence of pro-ana users' circumvention of censorship, however, is double-edged: on the one hand, they problematise what it means to be anorexic and on the other, they normalise it. This can be seen in a post produced by a search for #thin where the author describes her guilt over missing a workout. She applies numerous hashtags to her post, which range from the banal: '#exercise', '#squats', '#weight', '#fitness', '#motivation', to the obscure: '#thynspooo', '#thigh_gap', '#thynspiration'. The latter terms render pro-anorexic the pivotal hashtags which she also applies: '#thin', '#slim', and '#fit'. Such a post then, reveals the fine line between normative body disciplining and anorexia, therefore demonstrating how language can be either legitimate or pathological depending upon context (cf. Ferreday 2003, p. 285). In other words, such posts expose the extent to which so-called disordered body practices and everyday body disciplining are on a continuum, thus rendering successful censorship by Internet moderators impossible.

With the hashtags '#pro-anorexia' and '#pro-ana' having been frozen out on many platforms, '#ana' in these spaces would often be used to indicate pro-anorexic content, even though it is divorced from its prefix 'pro'. This may successfully elude those for whom it is not intended, but it also makes anorexic and pro-anorexic content one and the same. The material generated by the term ana is generally *pro*-anorexic in nature, in that it espouses thinness at any cost, but it does also include some recovery content. Nonetheless, which mindset the poster endorses is not always apparent: one post yielded by a #ana search features a photograph of a plate of noodles, but only by reading the hashtags '#edrecovery, #fuckana and #strongnotskinny', can we see that this post is about the user's struggle to recover from anorexia, rather than her desire to maintain it. Without hashtags, this image could be the user documenting their meals or even expressing disgust over a certain food. It is the hashtags that provide context and meaning.

The relationship between image and text on social media then reflects how image and text relate to one another in other media. Roland Barthes famously argued that images hold multiple meanings and, 'in every society various techniques are developed intended to *fix* the floating chain of signifieds in such a way as to counter the terror of uncertain signs' (1977, p. 39, emphasis in original). Text, in the form of a caption, for example, seeks to fix the meaning of the image, through what Barthes calls 'anchorage' (ibid., p. 38). Divorced from their hashtags, many pro-ana images could be rightly interpreted as diet advice, fashion promotion, celebrity fan images, or simply a banal photograph. By using hashtags, pro-ana users anchor the meaning of the images they post. However, as Stuart Hall ([1980] 2009) points out, there is always space for alternative negotiated or oppositional readings. The ambiguity of the image, even when accompanied by a caption or hashtag, works to the benefit of pro-ana users. If an image has any number of possible meanings, then it cannot be unequivocally a pro-ana post, and as a result, it can more readily evade censorship.

For instance, another post generated by #ana endorses self-starvation rather than recovery: it features a photograph of a can of Red Bull and a bottle of Coca Cola which on the outset appear mundane and could be merely indicating a user's keenness for caffeine drinks. However, the user's name, 'hollow girl', a reference to emptiness, and the accompanying hashtags: '#ana #mia #ednos #blithe #fasting' 'anchor' the post to pro-ana rather than recovery as did the #ana image of the plate of noodles discussed above. Thus, we can infer that caffeine drinks here are being used as weight-loss supplements. However, anchoring here relies on the reader's understanding of pro-ana lexis. '#blithe' in this context does not indicate carefree happiness, but a lack of concern, seemingly for one's well-being, as posts tagged with this word signpost self-harm (see also Moreno et al. 2016, p. 80). This can be inferred by clicking the hyperlinked hashtag and seeing thousands of other posts which feature 'blithe' alongside hashtags referencing self-harm and images of emaciated bodies or razor blades. By playing with image and text in such a way, users behave like creators of subcultural spaces. In his seminal work on subcultures, Dick Hebdige (1991) argues that everyday objects, such as safety pins and Vaseline used by punks

> are open to a double inflection: to "illegitimate" as well as "legitimate" uses. These "humble objects" can be magically appropriated; "stolen" by subordinate groups and made to carry "secret" meanings: meanings which express, in code, a form of resistance to the order which guarantees their continued subordination.
>
> (p. 18)

Pro-ana users then 'steal' certain objects – such as caffeine drinks – and furnish them with meanings specific to their culture. At the same time, they alter the meanings of existing words, thereby contributing to the polysemy of language, as well as demonstrating a lack of regard for authority. The choice of the term 'blithe' is instructive as it implies a lack of concern not only for oneself, but also for the arbiters of meaning. Blithe is also effective because of its seeming innocuousness: unlike terms such as 'cutting' or 'starve', its meaning is not immediately identifiable as 'harmful', therefore the images it accompanies can be hidden in plain sight.

Even without censorship, the architecture of the social media platforms discussed in this book is more conducive to diminishing the pro-ana voice than that of forums, for example. The latter centre primarily on discussion and the written word, but the former do not encourage layers of conversation in the same way. As danah boyd concedes, 'networked publics' affordances do not dictate participants' behavior, but they do configure the environment in a way that shapes participants' engagement' (2011, p. 39). The architecture of social media platforms encourages users to communicate in symbolic form, rather than engage in lengthy discussions. They post images which other users may 'like' (Instagram and Tumblr), 'reblog' (Tumblr), 're-pin' (Pinterest), or 'upvote' or 'downvote' (Reddit). Users can comment and have discussions on all these platforms, but in the data examined, these tended to be minimal. Dialogue on Instagram especially tends to be composed of hashtags as a post resulting from a search for #thynspiration demonstrates.

The post features an image of a slender woman wearing underwear and a cropped t-shirt. She is recumbent which emphasises a flat stomach and, with one leg raised slightly, she highlights the gap between her thighs. A thigh gap, where the tops of thighs do not meet, is coveted in these spaces as it indicates extreme thinness – although it is not clear if the image depicts the poster herself. The accompanying caption suggests that the poster is unhappy: 'I wish I had never been born'. The first commenter responds, 'F4f?', the abbreviated form of 'follow for follow' where a user suggests they will follow those who follow them in return. The second commenter simply confirms they like the original post and the third and final commenter offers some solace to the original poster, telling her, 'you were meant to be born' accompanied by heart emojis. In the six hours since the original post was made the user acquires numerous 'likes' but no substantial dialogue is established. The opportunity to comment then may present the appearance of interactivity and collaboration, but it is ultimately un-participatory (see Dean 2005). Comments by their very nature do not necessarily require a response, and as Miller suggests they are 'phatic' (2008, p. 398). In the platforms discussed, layers of comments accompany images without forming substantial dialogue and at times they exist independently of one another. This is not to say that communication is only worthwhile when lexical; on the contrary, communicating through images and/or minimal text can be incredibly powerful, as the visual arts and poetry attest. Thus, the image-dominant nature of these platforms means that photographs and their attendant hashtags are a substitute for language. In this #thynspiration image, aside from the caption, 'I wish I had never been born', it is the attendant hashtags, such as '#wishtobeskinny', '#cutting', and '#depressed' that indicate the user's misery stems from her body image. Although Brooke Wendt proposes that 'when one reads an image's hashtags, it diverts one from discovering visual nuances since hashtags place all words and phrases on an equal level' (2014, p. 33), I argue that hashtags, in a pro-ana setting at least, can provide further ambiguity and even complicate the meaning of an image. The tags, '#skinny' and '#thynspiration' as well as '#fat' and '#whale' that accompany the image of this slender woman, leave to interpretation whether the individual in the photograph is being framed as thinspirational and therefore ideally thin, or overweight and in need of thinspiration. In short, the current pro-ana landscape is image-heavy and text-light in such a way that its meanings are ambiguous. This serves its users well because, if it is unclear whether a post is promoting anorexia or endorsing caffeine drinks for example, then its content becomes more difficult to police.

'Sexy shots': eroticising the pro-anorexic body

Savvy users ensure that an abundance of pro-ana content remains online because reading it as such relies on prior knowledge and understanding of their ever-changing culture. Users continually play with language and images, altering meanings as they see fit. As well as these more tangible disruptions to meaning, users also disguise their spaces by borrowing from gendered discourses of health and beauty which value women for their physical attractiveness above all else – a device which renders moderation all the more challenging.

Anorexia has long been theorised as contradictory in that it simultaneously rejects a sexualised female body and conforms to hegemonic standards of femininity (Bordo [1993] 2003; Hesse-Biber 1996; Heywood 1996; Malson 2009; Turner 1996). By the same token, pro-ana online spaces have been conceived as both espousing female beauty ideals and critiquing their unattainability (Day and Keys 2008a, 2008b, 2009; Ferreday 2003). However, the pro-ana culture explored in this book promotes hegemonic beauty as a means of legitimising its texts. The bodies adorning these spaces are often in various stages of undress: in bikinis, workout clothing, or underwear. Characteristic of postfeminism, the women featured often adopt eroticised poses 'closely resembling the heterosexual male fantasy found in pornography' (Gill 2007, p. 258). In other words, these spaces have been increasingly co-opted by a postfeminist celebration of sexual freedom, which on the one hand allows them to evade censorship, but on the other, normalises anorexia.

This is at its starkest in *thinspirationpics*, the subreddit devoted to thinspiration. This space is keen to create a separation not only between pro-ana and thinspo, but an even more arbitrary division between being thinspo and looking at thinspo: 'This is not about *being* thinspo but appreciating the beauty of thinspo' (emphasis added). This contradictory statement implies that an admiration of thinspo is acceptable, provided it is on an aesthetic level. Reddit's interpretation of thinspo is illuminated when considered in the context of the gender demographics of the spaces examined in this study. Research has suggested that Pinterest users are predominantly women, as are those on Instagram but to a lesser extent, whereas Tumblr is populated by almost the same number of men and women (Duggan and Brenner 2013). Reddit, however, is dominated by men (Duggan and Smith 2013) or rather, as Adrienne Massanari (2017) has shown, it is populated by toxic masculinity and is a breeding ground for misogyny. Hence, it is instructive that this space is more concerned with the notion of *looking at* thinspo than it is with 'being thinspo', entertaining as it does an implicitly heterosexist male audience.

thinspirationpics labours the rhetoric of beauty, fitness and an appreciation of the female body: 'We welcome images of skinny, slim, petite, athletic, beautiful women. Artistic shots, sexy shots, self-portraits and nudes. As long as it's thinspirational – slender, artistic, beautiful'. Pro-ana is thus placed within discourses of beauty and sensuality. As Foucault (1976) argues of sex and sexuality in 'The Repressive Hypothesis', it can only be discussed in language which has been subjected to censorship. By using adjectives such as 'sexy' and 'artistic', *thinspirationpics* reframes the objectionable elements of extreme thinness, thereby 'rendering it morally acceptable and technically useful' (Foucault 1976, p. 21). Thinspo here is constructed as both acceptable and useful because it operates to shore up patriarchal understandings of the female body as an object to be admired and evaluated. As Bordo argues of the expressly female pathologies, anorexia and hysteria: 'one source of potential for resistance and rebellion is pressed into the service of maintaining the established order' (1989, p. 22). Such disorders then, instead of enacting a protest against restrictive gender norms, ultimately come to support them.

Although *thinspirationpics* stresses the 'artistic' requirements of images submitted to the space, every post is tagged as 'NSFW'. The majority of images feature nude or partially nude women in eroticised poses with their faces obscured. They consequently adopt what Attwood terms 'Porn *style*' (2009, xiv emphasis in original), a look which originates in porn but has now become mainstream (see also Gill 2009). The women of *thinspirationpics* therefore epitomise Winch's (2013) postfeminist girlfriend gaze: rather than being passive receivers of the male gaze, they actively exhibit their bodies. Posts range from images of models and celebrities, reposts from other subreddits that users have deemed thinspo-worthy, through to selfies with requests for feedback and validation. In line with the other social media platforms examined, users of *thinspirationpics* do not engage in substantial dialogue with one another, rather they post phatic statements praising or deriding women's bodies. One user eliciting feedback on her body posts an image of herself and asks: 'Everyone says I'm too thin, what do you guys think?' (*thinspirationpics*). This prompts supportive comments such as 'You're perfect. They're just jealous they don't look like you' (ibid.). The suggestion here is that this user embodies the perfection her (implicitly female) peers are lacking. Such dialogue reflects the way in which postfeminist empowerment is 'tied to possession of a slim and alluring young body, whose power is the ability to attract male attention and sometimes female envy' (Gill 2009, p. 103). This Reddit user is reassured repeatedly by commenters that she has such power. Comments either focus on her capacity to thinspire: 'perfection! you're my new inspiration', or her sexual desirability: 'You're gorgeous. I would worship you like the goddess you are and f*** you like a whore' (*thinspirationpics*). In its aggressive appreciation of the original poster's body, the latter comment demonstrates the extent to which thinspiration spaces have become centred on conforming to heteronormative ideals, rather than offering a critique of hegemonic understandings of anorexia.

The images in *thinspirationpics* serve not only as thinspiration, but also as a form of erotic titillation. A male-presenting user posts an image of a model, captioning it, 'Wow'. The woman pictured has a visible ribcage, and unusually for a woman so thin: full breasts. This prompts comments such as: 'Wow. She's got it all: skinny with boobies [...] Doesn't get better than this' (*thinspirationpics*). The use of the term 'boobies', a slang term for women's breasts, connotes a classed perception of femininity, and one that is at odds with the middle-class, de-sexualised image of the anorectic. In addition, the synthesis of emaciation and womanly curves here is indicative of the postfeminist motif of 'having it all' (Genz 2010): a woman whose ribs are jutting but breasts are full demonstrates mastery over her body, as indicated by the visible ribcage, but, at the same time, she maintains archetypal womanliness as signified by her breasts. Reddit's thinspo subject then, comes to embody the contradictory requirements of twenty-first-century femininity, as well as demonstrating the extent to which pro-ana culture has been absorbed into the mainstream.

The marketisation of pro-ana and 'healthy thinspo'

thinspirationpics' reframing of pro-ana culture shows how a phenomenon once composed of dissident voices is being recuperated by the hegemony. As Hebdige (1991) argues of subcultures, they are always susceptible to incorporation and he describes two modes through which this takes place:

1) the conversion of subcultural signs (dress, music, etc.) into mass-produced objects (i.e. the commodity form);
2) the 'labelling' and re-definition of deviant behaviour by dominant groups – the police, the media, the judiciary (i.e. the ideological form).

(p. 94)

Both modes occur in pro-ana culture: it has been subject to commodification by the diet industry (via pro-ana marketing sites) and, it is being re-defined by the media (as *Reveal*'s use of the term thinspiration in chapter two shows).

The marketing sites yielded as a result of search engine queries for 'pro-ana' and 'thinspo' illustrate the stealthy appropriation of pro-ana rhetoric and discourses by the diet industry. Even user-led site, *A1 Thinspo* advertises a paid, graded membership plan, and although it does not make clear what membership entails, users receive 'free' weight-loss supplements ranging from appetite suppressing lollypops to fat-burning pills. Other sites such as *30 Days to Thin* (2014), *Pro Ana Tips* (2014), *Prothinspiration Diet* (2014), and *Thinspiration Pro Ana Tips* (2014), advertise weight-loss programmes requiring the purchase of guidebooks. These spaces all draw on 'testimonials' from young women who describe a life of loneliness and misery before this book and its diet guidance provided them with salvation. A testimonial on *Thinspiration Pro Ana Tips* features a young woman called Jenny describing the bullying she experienced as a result of being fat: 'when I entered college, and heard someone say "fatty Jenny" pointing at me one day and then the next day, I heard someone say "rolly Jenny", followed by "humpty Jenny"' (2014). Likewise, the author of the book *30 Days to Thin: Get the Body you Deserve* (Clark 2012), which a number of these marketing sites promote, claims she used to weigh over 200 lbs., adding, 'There is no other way to describe this period of my life than absolutely horrible. I did not have any friends and I went straight home after school' (Prothinspiration Diet 2014*)*. As well as suggesting that the individual is wholly responsible for their body size, these spaces conflate a fat body with social exclusion, implying that, 'a fat person's only shot at citizenship comes if he or she gratefully consumes the panoply of diet and fitness products made available by industry and government' (LeBesco 2004, p. 57). In each of these examples, the women find social approval after successfully following the '30 Days Thin' diet plan, thus underlining that thinness 'promises the rewards of cultural acceptance' (Hesse-Biber 1996, p. 68).

Pro-ana marketing sites have the explicit aim of selling weight-loss products, and they use pro-ana to do so. As David Harvey points out, neoliberalism '[assumes] that individual freedoms are guaranteed by freedom of the market and of trade' (2005, p. 7). This logic requires new markets to open continually, even if it amounts to exploiting disordered eating for financial gain. Despite this, the mainstream media do not seek to differentiate between 'pro-ana' spaces which have been co-opted by marketing and those that may offer genuine support. An article in *The Huffington Post* incites panic over pro-ana sites purportedly selling merchandise such as bracelets and appetite suppressants (Sherriff 2014). One of the spaces it references is the now-deleted *Tangerine Monday*, which the journalist defines as a pro-ana site. Although this site adopts pro-ana lexicon and describes itself as, 'Weight Loss Anorexia Tips and Blog', it centres wholly on the promotion of a weight-loss drug, offering free samples and requesting customers' credit card details (Tangerine Monday 2014). These 'pro-ana' spaces have emerged to capitalise on the phenomenon and in so doing they are perpetuating its vilification.

At the same time as pro-ana rhetoric has entered the mainstream, pro-ana users are disguising their spaces as weight-loss motivation blogs and drawing on discourses of health to legitimise them. This reinforces spurious cultural understandings that good health can only be achieved through weight loss (Cogan 1999, p. 246; see also Malson 2008, p. 35). By conflating healthy eating with losing weight, thinness becomes synonymous with healthiness and in turn, fatness with being 'sloppy, careless, and self-indulgent' (Hartley 2001, p. 65). This is particularly prevalent in the individual blogs which were indexed on the first pages of my search engine queries. The blogs vary in the ways they repudiate pro-ana: from statements of denial, through to interspersing images of bony torsos with healthy recipe ideas and exercise plans. The women featured in these spaces have, without exception, long flowing hair, they are predominantly white, often tanned, and where their faces are shown, they wear makeup. Hence, these blogs pay homage to normative femininity and reinforce the notion that a slim, attractive body is 'a healthy, normal body' (Lupton 1996, p. 137; see also Malson 2008).

All such blogs feature the term thinspo in either their blog title or tagline, a number of which also have disclaimers denouncing pro-anorexia. The blog, *Land of Skinny* is replete with images of thin and semi-naked women on beaches, by swimming pools, or mid-workout in the gym. They are depicted actively manicuring their bodies and such images are interspersed with others of nutritious salads and plates of fruit. This, however, is at odds with the diet advised by the blogger which is composed of water, eggs and celery. Put simply, this blog is not about health, but thinness, and the meagre diet it advises reinforces the thin body as 'an indicator of health and beauty/femininity, regardless of what means are used to secure or maintain it' (Parsons 2015, p. 111). Despite this, at the top of the *Land of Skinny*'s homepage is the statement: 'Disclaimer: you are entering a healthy thinspo blog. I do not promote eating disorders. I provide motivation for people to lose weight in a healthy way'. Denial of pro-ana is enacted by the repetition of the adjective 'healthy' which serves to pre-empt accusations of the damaging behaviour associated with eating disorders, and 'motivate' furnishes the blogs with a sense of activity and enthusiasm which is inconsistent with the apparent passive misery of anorexia.

This upbeat tone and depiction of weight loss as a positive development is echoed by *Heartthinspo* which describes itself as 'a healthy thinspo and progress blog', and promises to help users 'stay motivated, healthy and thin with tips, tricks, pics and recipes'. The reference to 'progress' precludes the possibility that this blog is fostering dangerous practices, or that its author is retreating to disordered eating, instead it claims to endorse health and motivation. Such discourses resonate with Maxine Woolhouse et al.'s (2011) findings on young women's talk around food: neoliberal rhetoric around choice is deployed to construct weight-loss practices as normal, healthy eating. For example, when the author of *Howtothinspo* − a blog which combines images of fresh fruit and vegetables, women mid-work-out, and motivational guidance on weight loss − is reprimanded by a poster claiming to be a mother whose daughter has become addicted to thinspo sites, she replies: 'Hey, I'm just promoting healthy-eating and exercise − that's not harmful. I'm sorry that your daughter is struggling though'. By situating thinspo within neoliberal discourses of health, users seek to justify their claims, and in turn, thinspo is reframed as a normal, healthy practice and an informed choice.

Pro-ana culture adopts the 'apparently neutral' vocabulary espoused by postfeminism and neoliberalism (Wilkes 2015, p. 30) and this operates to legitimise it. These spaces cheerfully tell their viewers that giving up is not an option with reminders such as: 'if you want it, work for it!' (*Workingforthin*) and 'Sore or sorry. You pick' (*Howtothinspo*). However, the current pro-ana landscape is contradictory and at times its users appear undecided as to whether they are pro-ana or not. This is demonstrated by one blogger who describes herself as 'Ana, Mia, thinspo addict'. She adds immediately after, 'This is *not* pro-ana' (*Beach Thinspiration*). She self-identifies as anorexic and bulimic with an addiction to thinspo, whilst simultaneously denying that her blog is pro-ana. This may be indicative of her struggle for recovery as well as her attempts to legitimise her blog, but it also shows the extent to which the path to successful femininity is loaded with contradictions that impede a young woman's sense of identity (Budgeon 2011, p. 289). Western culture tells her she must be thin, but she must also look healthy. As a consequence, such bloggers, perhaps inadvertently, seek to create a distinction between pro-ana and thinspo as a means of defending their desire to be thin.

The tendency towards 'healthy thinspo' has also given rise to the coinage, 'fitspo', a portmanteau of fit and inspiration. The aim of fitspo is to inspire individuals to focus on fitness, rather than thinness, through images, recipes and exercise advice. However, users often combine #thinspo and #fitspo in posts and blogs, implying that there is little difference between the two. Indeed, research has shown that fitspo content often leads users to thinspo content (Ghaznavi and Taylor 2015) and that the two adopt similar discourses (Boepple and Thompson 2016) which can negatively impact upon body image (Lewallen and Behm-Morawitz 2016; Tiggemann and Zaccardo 2015). Yet, in the mainstream, fitspo persists as the healthy form of thinspiration and *The Huffington Post*, which has condemned pro-ana and even featured an article drawing on Tiggemann and Zaccardo's research in order to criticise fitspo culture (Adams 2015), also has a section on its website devoted to it. 'Huff-Post Fitspiration' provides not only weight-loss and exercise guidance, it also draws on fitness inspiration which it takes directly from Instagram (HuffPost Fit-spiration 2016); ironically profiting from that which it criticises.

Nonetheless, fitspo is afforded more legitimacy than thinspo, even though the difference between the two is merely nominal. The blog, *Workingforthin* describes itself as both 'fitspo & thinspo'. The author tells her 'story' of an obsession with weight loss which led to disordered eating, however she declares that she has now regained control and all she wants is to be, 'healthy happy and fit'. This echoes the weight-loss discourses presented by the women's magazines in the previous chapter, wherein dieting is repudiated and replaced with the imperative to be happy, healthy and confident instead. The author of *Workingforthin* differentiates between an eating disordered past and a healthy present composed of thinspo and fitspo. In so doing, she seeks to assert a boundary between deviant and normal weight-loss practices.

Thinspo and fitspo occupy a liminal space, and as a result, they can be read as legitimate in ways that pro-ana cannot. This may mean they are less susceptible to censorship, but it also means they are more vulnerable to incorporation by the mainstream. Users draw upon postfeminist neoliberal rhetoric to deny that their content is pro-anorexic, and in turn suggest it is simply about motivating people to lose weight healthily. However, these discourses of denial and disguise are blurring the boundaries between what is anorexic, pro-anorexic, thinspo, or fitspo, which results in such content being more pervasive than ever. Hidden in plain sight, pro-ana online spaces have not disappeared, instead they have been normalised.

Conclusion

This chapter has argued that pro-ana online culture has altered drastically since its inception in the late twentieth century. What began as a communicative discussion-based phenomenon has become image-led and individualised. This is both a consequence of censorship and the developments in social media architecture, which have facilitated phatic expression more than discursive communication. Pro-ana online spaces in their current incarnation reflect the contemporary postfeminist neoliberal climate which shifts the focus from the community to the individual and encourages women to engage in an unending project of self-improvement. The pro-ana phenomenon has always been steeped in contradictions, but the former landscape was at least easy to identify with its prayers to Ana and landing pages signalling its content. By collating mainstream weight-loss advice and photographs of skinny celebrities, the pro-ana phenomenon holds the potential to critique the oppressive culture of compulsory thinness. The act of labelling such advice and images as pro-anorexic or thinspirational raises important questions about how 'healthy' and 'normal' it is be, for example, constantly suppressing one's appetite in the hope of achieving a celebrity body.

However, as I have shown, censorship has seen users finding creative ways of ensuring their content stays online. In some cases, they coin obscure hashtags (such as 'thynspooo'), in others they adopt innocuous ones (such as 'fitness'). Both such methods mean pro-ana content is more difficult to police: either because its rhetoric is indecipherable and thus untraceable, or it is commonplace enough that its texts can hide in plain sight. Furthermore, users are denying outright that their spaces are pro-ana and drawing on the language of health and beauty as a means of disguise. This may allow their texts remain online, but it also means that they are merging with the mainstream. All the while, pro-ana diction is being appropriated to sell weight-loss supplements.

With its motivational platitudes and erotic shots, contemporary pro-ana culture demonstrates 'one way in which potential resistance is not merely undercut, but *utilized* in the maintenance and reproduction of existing power relations' (Bordo 1989, p. 15; emphasis in original). I am not suggesting that the pro-ana spaces of old were harmless, nor am I refuting the positive effects of healthy eating and regular exercise. What I am contesting is the extent to which these practices contribute towards the perpetuation of oppressive cultural norms. Ironically, pro-ana online spaces, which have been met with such outrage, have been co-opted by those who sought to critique them. At the same time, these spaces disguise themselves with the language of their censors, thus becoming unwitting handmaidens to postfeminist neoliberalism. The increasing focus on images and corresponding decrease in words has blurred the boundaries between what is pro-anorexic and what is 'normal' weight loss; what constitutes an anorexic body and what is 'sexy' and 'slim', to borrow the lexis of *thinspirationpics*. Indeed, were they not accompanied by the term thinspo, many images would not be identifiable as such. Consequently, censoring such spaces as many social media platforms do, calls that they improve their Content Advisory warnings (Moreno et al. 2016, p. 83) and recommendations that media literacy programmes warn users about social network media (Tiggemann and Zaccardo 2015, p. 66) are futile. This ignores the fact that these spaces, whether they are pro-ana, fitspo or healthy weight-loss blogs, are by-products of a culture which equates a slim body with being healthy and normal (Lupton 1996).

Notes

1 NSFW is the acronym for not safe for work, a tag which usually connotes nudity or violence.
2 It is worth noting that all the public service announcements led to support organisations based in the USA. This appears to be the default message if one has not set up an account indicating location. If location is indicated in one's profile then the suggested support organisation is local.

References

30 Days to Thin. (2014) *Homepage*. Available at: http://30daysthin.com/ (Accessed June 2014).

Adams, R. (2015) 'The major downside of all those #Fitspiration photos', *The Huffington Post*, 24 August. Available at: www.huffingtonpost.com/entry/fitspiration-making-you-feel-bad-about-your-body_us_55d5f549e4b055a6dab32b57 (Accessed May 2016).

Attwood, F. (2009) 'Introduction', In Attwood, F. (ed.) *Mainstreaming Sex: The Sexualisation of Western Culture*. London: I.B. Tauris & Co. Ltd, pp. xiii–xxiv.

Barthes, R. (1977) *Image Music Text*. London: Fontana Press.

BBC Trending. (2018) *BBC*. Available at: www.bbc.co.uk/news/blogs-trending-46505704 (Accessed January 2018).

Bell, M. (2009) '"@ the Doctor's Office': Pro-anorexia and the medical gaze", *Surveillance & Society*, 6(2), pp. 151–162.

Boellstorff, T. (2003) 'Dubbing culture: Indonesian *gay* and *lesbi* subjectivities and ethnography in an already globalized world', *American Ethnologist*, 30(2), pp. 225–242.

Boepple, L. and Thompson, K.J. (2016) 'A content analytic comparison of fitspiration and thinspiration websites', *International Journal of Eating Disorders*, 49(1), pp. 98–101.

Boero, N. and Pascoe, C.J. (2012) 'Pro-anorexia communities and online interaction: Bringing the pro-ana body online', *Body & Society*, 18, pp. 27–57.

Bordo, S. (1989) 'The body and the reproduction of femininity: A feminist appropriation of Foucault', In Jaggar, A.M. and Bordo, S. (eds.) *Gender/Body/Knowledge: Feminist Reconstructions of Being and Knowing*. New Brunswick, NJ: Rutgers University Press, pp. 13–33.

———. ([1993] 2003) *Unbearable Weight: Feminism, Western Culture and the Body*, 10th anniversary edition. Berkeley: University of California Press.

boyd, d. (2011) 'Social network sites as networked publics: Affordances, dynamics, and implications', in Papacharissi, Z. (ed.) *A Networked Self: Identity, Community, and Culture on Social Network Sites*. New York: Routledge, pp. 39–58.

Brotsky, S.R. and Giles, D. (2007) 'Inside the "pro-ana" community: A covert online participant observation', *Eating Disorders: The Journal of Treatment & Prevention*, 15(2), pp. 93–109.

Budgeon, S. (2011) 'The contradictions of successful femininity: Third-wave feminism, postfeminism and "new" femininities', in Gill, R. and Scharff, C. (eds.) *New Femininities: Postfeminism, Neoliberalism and Subjectivity*. London: Palgrave Macmillan, pp. 279–292.

Chancellor, S., Pater, J., Clear, T., Gilbert, E., and Choudhury, M.D. (2016) '#thyghgapp: Instagram content moderation and lexical variation in pro-eating disorder communities', *CSCW*, Proceedings of the 19th ACM Conference on Computer-Supported Cooperative Work & Social Computing, pp. 1201–1213.

Clark, C. (2012). *30 Days to Thin: Get the Body You Deserve.* No publisher. Available at: http://30daysthin.com/ (Accessed June 2014).

Cobb, G. (2017) '"This is not pro-ana": Denial and disguise in pro-anorexia online spaces', *Fat Studies*, 6(2), pp. 189–205.

Cogan, J.C. (1999) 'Re-evaluating the weight-centered approach toward health: The need for a paradigm shift', in Sobal, J. and Maurer, D. (eds.) *Interpreting Weight: The Social Management of Fatness and Thinness.* New York: Aldine de Gruyter, pp. 229–253.

Day, K. and Keys, T. (2008a) 'Starving in cyberspace: A discourse analysis of pro-eating-disorder websites', *Journal of Gender Studies*, 17(1), pp. 1–15.

———. (2008b) 'Starving in cyberspace: The construction of identity on "pro-eating-disorder websites"', in Riley, S., Burns, M., Frith, H., Wiggins, S., and Markula, P. (eds.) *Critical Bodies: Representations, Identities and Practices of Weight and Body Management.* Basingstoke, Hampshire: Palgrave Macmillan, pp. 81–100.

———. (2009) 'Anorexia/bulimia as resistance and conformity in pro-ana and pro-mia virtual conversations', in Malson, H. and Burns, M. (eds.) *Critical Feminist Approaches to Eating Dis/orders.* London: Routledge, pp. 87–96.

Dean, J. (2005) 'Communicative capitalism: Circulation and the foreclosure of politics', *Cultural Politics*, 1(1), pp. 51–74.

Duggan, M. and Brenner, J. (2013) *The Demographics of Social Media Users – 2012.* Available at: www.pewinternet.org/2013/02/14/the-demographics-of-social-media-users-2012/ (Accessed August 2016).

Duggan, M. and Smith, A. (2013) *6% of Online Adults Are Reddit Users.* Available at: www.pewinternet.org/2013/07/03/6-of-online-adults-are-reddit-users/#fn-55-1 (Accessed August 2016).

Ferreday, D. (2003) 'Unspeakable bodies: Erasure, embodiment and the pro-ana community', *International Journal of Cultural Studies*, 6(3), pp. 277–295.

———. (2009) *Online Belongings: Fantasy, Affect and Web Communities.* Oxford: Peter Lang.

Foucault, M. (1976) *The Will to Knowledge: The History of Sexuality Volume 1.* Hurley, R. (trans.) London: Penguin.

García-Sánchez, I.M. (2010) 'Serious games. Code-switching and gendered identities in Moroccan immigrant girls' pretend play', *Pragmatics*, 20(4), pp. 523–555.

Genz, S. (2010) 'Singled out: Postfeminism's "new woman" and the dilemma of having it all', *The Journal of Popular Culture*, 43(1), pp. 97–119.

Gerrard, Y. (2018) 'Beyond the hashtag: Circumventing content moderation on social media', *New Media & Society*, 20(12), pp. 4492–4511.

Ghaznavi, J. and Taylor, L.D. (2015) 'Bones, body parts, and sex appeal: An analysis of #thinspiration images on popular social media', *Body Image*, 14, pp. 54–61.

Giles, D.C. and Newbold, J. (2011) 'Self- and other-diagnosis in user-led mental health online communities', *Qualitative Health Research*, 21(3), pp. 419–428.

Gill, R. (2007) *Gender and the Media.* Cambridge: Polity.

———. (2009) 'Supersexualise me! Advertising and the "midriffs"', in Attwood, F. (ed.) *Mainstreaming Sex: The Sexualisation of Western Culture.* London: I.B. Tauris & Co. Ltd, pp. 93–109.

Ging, D. and Garvey, S. (2018) '"Written in these scars are the stories I can't explain": A content analysis of pro-ana and thinspiration image sharing on Instagram', *New Media & Society*, 20(3), pp. 1181–1200.

Hall, S. ([1980] 2009) 'Encoding/decoding', in Thornham, S. Bassett, C., and Marris, P. (eds.) *Media Studies: A Reader*. 2nd edn. New York: New York University Press, pp. 57–64.

Hartley, C. (2001) 'Letting ourselves go: Making room for the fat body in feminist scholarship', in Braziel, J.E. and LeBesco, K. (eds.) *Bodies Out of Bounds: Fatness and Transgression*. Berkeley: University of California Press, pp. 60–73.

Harvey, D. (2005) *A Brief History of Neoliberalism*. Oxford: Oxford University Press.

Hebdige, D. (1991) *Subculture: The Meaning of Style*. London: Routledge.

Hesse-Biber, S. (1996) *Am I Thin Enough Yet? The Cult of Thinness and the Commercialization of Identity*. New York: Oxford University Press.

Heywood, L. (1996) *Dedication to Hunger: The Anorexic Aesthetic in Modern Culture*. Berkeley: University of California Press.

HuffPost Fitspiration. (2016) *The Huffington Post*. Available at: www.huffingtonpost.co.uk/news/fitspiration/ (Accessed May 2016).

Instagram. (2014) *Community Guidelines*. Available at: https://help.instagram.com/477434105621119/ (Accessed June 2014).

LeBesco, K. (2004) *Revolting Bodies? The Struggle to Redefine Fat Identity*. Amherst: University of Massachusetts Press.

Lelwica, M., Hoglund, E., and McNallie, J. (2009) 'Spreading the religion of thinness from California to Calcutta: A critical feminist postcolonial analysis', *Journal of Feminist Studies in Religion*, 25(1), pp. 19–41.

Lewallen, J. and Behm-Morawitz, E. (2016) 'Pinterest or thinterest?: Social comparison and body image on social media', *Social Media + Society*, 2(1), pp. 1–9.

Lupton, D. (1996) *Food, the Body and the Self*. London: Sage.

Malson, H. (2008) 'Deconstructing un/healthy body-weight and weight management', in Riley, S Burns, M., Frith, H., Wiggins, S., and Markula, P. (eds.) *Critical Bodies: Representations, Identities and Practices of Weight and Body Management*. Basingstoke, Hampshire: Palgrave Macmillan, pp. 27–42.

———. (2009) 'Appearing to disappear: Postmodern femininities and self-starved subjectivities', in Malson, H. and Burns. M. (eds.) *Critical Feminist Approaches to Eating Dis/orders*. London: Routledge, pp. 135–145.

Massanari, A. (2017) '# Gamergate and the fappening: How Reddit's algorithm, governance, and culture support toxic technocultures', *New Media & Society*, 19(3), pp. 329–346.

Miller, V. (2008) 'New media, networking and phatic culture', *Convergence*, 14, pp. 387–400.

Moreno, M.A., Ton, A., Selkie, E., and Evans, Y. (2016) 'Secret society 123: Understanding the language of self-harm on Instagram', *Journal of Adolescent Health*, 58, pp. 78–84.

Mulveen, R. and Hepworth, J. (2006) 'An interpretative phenomenological analysis of participation in a pro-anorexia Internet site and its relationship with disordered eating', *Journal of Health Psychology*, 11(2), pp. 283–296.

Nash, J. (2006) 'Mutant spiritualties in a secular age: The 'fasting body' and the hunger for pure immanence', *Journal of Religion and Health*, 45(3), pp. 310–327.

Norris, M.L., Boydell, K.M., Pinhas, L., and Katzman, D.K. (2006) 'Ana and the Internet: A review of pro-anorexia websites', *International Journal of Eating Disorders*, 39, pp. 443–447.

Olszanowski, M. (2014) 'Feminist self-imaging and Instagram: Tactics of circumventing sensorship', *Visual Communication Quarterly*, 21(2), pp. 83–95.

Ostroff, N. and Taylor, J. (2012) 'Tumblr to ban self-harm and eating disorder blogs', *BBC Newsbeat*, 26 March. Available at: www.bbc.co.uk/newsbeat/17195865 (Accessed May 2012).

Parks, M.R. (2011) 'Social network sites as virtual communities', in Papacharissi, Z. (ed.) *A Networked Self: Identity, Community, and Culture on Social Network Sites.* New York: Routledge, pp. 105–123.

Parsons, J.M. (2015) *Gender, Class and Food: Families, Bodies and Health.* Basingstoke, Hampshire: Palgrave Macmillan.

Pinterest. (2014a) *Acceptable Use Policy.* Available at: https://about.pinterest.com/en/ acceptable-use-policy (Accessed June 2014).

———. (2014b) Available at www.pinterest.com (Accessed July 2014).

Polak, M. (2010) '"I think we must be normal ... there are too many of us for this to be abnormal!!!": Girls creating identity and forming community in pro-ana/mia websites', in Weber, S. and Dixon, S. (eds.) *Growing Up Online: Young People and Digital Technologies.* 2nd edn. New York: Palgrave Macmillan, pp. 83–96.

Pro Ana Tips. (2014) *Homepage.* Available at: http://proanatips.org (Accessed June 2014).

Prothinspiration Diet. (2014) *Homepage.* Available at: http://pro-thinspiration.com/ index.html (Accessed June 2014).

Reddit. (2014) Available at: www.reddit.com/ (Accessed July 2014).

Rheingold, H. (1993) *The Virtual Community: Homesteading on the Electronic Frontier.* New York: Addison Wesley.

Schott, N.D. and Langan, D. (2015) 'Pro-anorexia/bulimia censorship and public service announcements: The price of controlling women', *Media, Culture & Society*, 37(8), pp. 1158–1175.

Sherriff, S. (2014) 'Pro-anorexia sites selling merchandise, and even bracelets, to promote eating disorders', *The Huffington Post*, 26 March. Available at: www.huffington post.co.uk/2014/03/25/proanorexia-sites-selling-bracelet-merchandise_n_5026254. html (Accessed March 2014).

Stommel, W. and Koole, T. (2010) 'The online support group as a community: A micro-analysis of the interaction with a new member', *Discourse Studies*, 12(3), pp. 357–378.

Tangerine Monday. (2014) *Homepage.* Available at: http://tangerinemonday.com/ (Accessed March 2014).

Thinspiration Pro Ana Tips. (2014) *Homepage.* Available at: http://thinspirationproana. com/(Accessed June 2014).

Tiggemann, M. and Zaccardo, M. (2015) '"Exercise to be fit, not skinny": The effect of fitspiration imagery on women's body image', *Body Image*, 15, pp. 61–67.

Tiidenberg, K. and Gómez Cruz, E. (2015) 'Selfies, image and the re-making of the body', *Body & Society*, 21(4), pp. 77–102.

Tumblr. (2014a) *Community Guidelines.* Available at: www.tumblr.com/policy/en/com munity (Accessed June 2014).

———. (2014b) *Public Service Announcement.* Available at: www.tumblr.com/psa/search/ pro-ana (Accessed June 2014).

Turner, B.S. (1996) *The Body and Society.* 2nd edn. London: Sage.

Uca, E.R. (2004) *Ana's Girls.* Bloomington, IN: Author House.

Van Dijck, J. (2013) *The Culture of Connectivity: A Critical History of Social Media.* Oxford: Oxford University Press.

Webs.com. (2014) Available at: www.webs.com/ (Accessed July 2014).

Webstagram. (2014) Available at: www.web.stagram.com (Accessed July 2014).

Wendt, B. (2014) 'The allure of the selfie: Instagram and the new self-portrait', *Network Notebooks*. Vol. 8. Amsterdam: Institute of Network Cultures, pp. 1–50.

Wilkes, K. (2015) 'Colluding with neo-liberalism: Post-feminist subjectivities, whiteness and expressions of entitlement', *Feminist Review*, 110, pp. 18–33.

Winch, A. (2013) *Girlfriends and Postfeminist Sisterhood*. Basingstoke, Hampshire: Palgrave Macmillan.

Woolhouse, M., Day, K., Rickett, B., and Milnes, K. (2011) '"Cos girls aren't supposed to eat like pigs are they?" Young women negotiating gendered discursive constructions of food and eating', *Journal of Health Psychology*, 17(1), pp. 46–56.

Yahoo!. (2014) Available at: www.yahoo.com (Accessed July 2014).

Yeshua-Katz, D. and Martins, N. (2013) 'Communicating stigma: The pro-ana paradox', *Health Communication*, 2(5), pp. 499–508.

4 Intersectional privilege in pro-anorexia online spaces

Feminists have long refuted common sense understandings of the anorexic as a young, white, Western, middle-class girl striving for perfection (Bordo 2009; Malson and Burns 2009; Nasser and Malson 2009; Saukko 2009) but for pro-ana enthusiasts such an image remains central (see also Holmes 2015, p. 107). The spaces examined in this study reinforce white heterofemininity, collating as they do hegemonic representations of thinness and drawing on normative weight-loss discourses. Users venerate bodies which resonate with those idealised in mainstream culture and repudiate those which do not fulfil such ideals. This is not to say that all pro-ana users are white, middle-class heterofeminine teens, or that their spaces are borne out of uncritical consumption of media images of thin bodies. Rather, they appropriate hegemonic discourses for their own ends and in so doing reveal the extent to which the culture of compulsory thinness operates around privileged social categories. As such, this chapter takes a focussed look at the production of the thin ideal in pro-ana online spaces, interrogating the phenomenon through the critical paradigm of intersectionality. The pro-ana subject is not homogeneous and as this chapter will show, at times she optimistically embraces life with a love of raw food and exercise, whilst at others she is a self-hating advocate of grunge, or a cynical hipster. Consequently, I argue that this ostensibly marginalised space is shoring up intersectional privilege.

I approach this chapter in three sections: I begin discussing the key literature on intersectionality, before turning to analysis of pro-ana online spaces themselves. The first analysis section attends to how pro-ana culture discursively produces the thin ideal as white, whilst marginalising bodies of colour. I build on these claims to show how cultivated food choices in these spaces not only reinforce the centrality of white, middle-class privilege, but are also deployed by users as a means of disguising their eating disorder. The next analysis section explores two different forms of pro-ana subjecthood communicated in these spaces: first, the upbeat individual who cajoles fellow users into manicuring their bodies in service of compulsory heterosexuality, and second, the depressed proponent of grunge whose desire for thinness is characterised by self-hatred and despair. I suggest that both these forms of pro-ana identity are underpinned by neoliberal understandings of the self which do not sit well with intersectionality.

An intersectional approach

For Pierre Bourdieu, 'the body is the most indisputable materialization of class taste' (1984, p. 190). He suggests that social class emanates through the presentation and treatment of the body, from the clothes we wear, to the food we eat. Bourdieu's theories are a valuable starting point for a study of the body but, as Skeggs points out, his lack of attention towards gender ultimately means that his 'analysis is performative of the categories it seeks to critique (2004a, p. 27). Skeggs' approach is more holistic: she builds on Bourdieu's interrogation of class to suggest that 'bodies are the physical sites where the relations of class, gender, race, sexuality and age come together and are em-bodied and practised' (1997, p. 82). For Skeggs (1997), the body manifests (and also seeks to mask) a set of identities which overlap with one another. Therefore, it would be false to claim, for instance, that an individual's identity is constituted only by class, to suggest that neither race nor gender play a part. As Jasbir Puar says, 'identities cannot so easily be cleaved' (2014, p. 337) – it is for this reason that an intersectional approach to a study of the body is essential.

The term 'intersectionality' was coined by Kimberlé Crenshaw in 1989 to tackle the need to address the multiple categories which result in the oppression of an individual or group. Originally, Crenshaw deployed the concept to expose the invisibility of black women under the law, using these intersections of marginalisation as a springboard for further analysis (1989, p. 40). Crucially, the multiple ways in which an individual or group is oppressed may not be immediately obvious, hence intersectionality illuminates the terms of marginalisation, critiquing any notion that oppression is singular. An intersectional approach then does not privilege any social category (Carbado 2013; Villa 2011) or overlook identities which do not fit in to the main categories, barring them with 'the kind of magical "etcetera"' (Villa 2011, p. 177). It is important to note, however, as does Patricia Hill Collins, that '*all* women occupy the category of devalued Other that gives meaning to *all* masculinities' (2004, p. 187; emphases in original), however, 'within hierarchies of femininity, social categories of race, age, and sexual orientation also intersect to produce comparable categories of hegemonic, marginalized, and subordinated femininities' (ibid.). These 'comparable categories' mean that certain versions of femininity – and as I will argue, certain versions of embodied thinness – are valued over others.

Theorists have applauded the ambiguity of intersectional theory (Davis 2008; Lykke 2010). Davis, in particular, argues that 'paradoxically, precisely the vagueness and open-endedness of "intersectionality" may be the very secret to its success' (2008, p. 69). Nevertheless, it has not passed without criticism: Jennifer C. Nash suggests that it fails to address the way in which oppression and privilege traverse one another (2008, pp. 11–12) and Paula-Irene Villa argues that 'on the level of embodiment, intersectionality is only partly helpful' (2011, p. 183). Other critics have called for identities to be examined more collectively: as coalitions (Carastathis 2013) or assemblages (Puar 2014). However, Barbara Tomlinson points out that scholars are hasty to find fault with intersectionality in their rush to publish, and that they may 'exaggerate criticisms to draw on the prestige of the appearance of novelty and innovation in ways that are destructive rather than constructive and competitive rather than contributive' (2013, p. 997). If intersectionality is being critiqued merely in a quest for personal achievement, then a grave concern is its depoliticising by neoliberalism (Mohanty 2013; Tomlinson 2013, p. 999), as well as its co-opting by white feminism (Bilge 2013).

Importantly then, this chapter does not seek to disavow the racial history of intersectionality, or to appropriate it in order to make sense of white women's experiences. Instead, it employs intersectionality to expose the privileging of white, middle-class heterofemininity. I argue that the neoliberal logic of pro-ana culture obscures the extent to which the ideal body is situated at a privileged intersection of race, class and gender, amongst other identities. By approaching these spaces from an intersectional standpoint, I seek to show how the seeming neutrality of postfeminist neoliberalism renders 'the privileged white female an ally of the neoliberal project' (Wilkes 2015, p. 30).

'Black thinspiration' and the performance of whiteness

It is only relatively recently that whiteness has been interrogated in terms of race and thus understood as a social construct (see Dyer 1997; Gilman 1985). Gilman (1985) articulates the construction of whiteness as a privileged social category by showing how scientific thought sought to render people of colour inferior in order to shore up whiteness. He says: 'If their sexual parts could be shown to be inherently different, this would be a sufficient sign that the blacks were a separate (and, needless to say, lower) race, as different from the European as the proverbial orangutan' (Gilman 1985, p. 216). The genitalia under examination were predominantly those of women, hence Gilman shows how black femininity came to be repudiated through the elision of racial and sexual difference which secures hegemonic whiteness (see also Shaw 2005).

Across both the earlier and more recent incarnations of pro-ana online examined in this study, users assert the centrality of white femininity. The bodies in these spaces may be [fake-] tanned, but they are predominantly white, suggesting firstly, the non-white body, by its very absence is not thinspirational, and secondly, anorexia is only a concern for white women. The white body here is not deliberately pervasive, rather it prevails because, as Richard Dyer argues, 'it is not seen as whiteness, but as normal' (1997, p. 10). As a result, references to bodies which are not white, but are deemed thinspirational, are marked (see also Schott 2017). This is particularly prominent in *A1 Thinspo*, a website so vast and sprawling it claims to cover any type of thinspo one may desire: this ranges from categories on individually named celebrities, through to 'ballet thinspo', 'YouTube thinspiration' and pertinent to this discussion, sections devoted to thinspiration based on (non-white) ethnicity. Separate 'Black', 'Asian', and 'Latina' thinspiration pages ensure that bodies which are not read as white are defined entirely by ethnicity. This echoes the classificatory devices used in online porn spaces: sites such as PornHub offer a number of categories based on race and ethnicity, including (and not limited to) 'Asian'; 'Interracial'; 'Japanese'; 'Latina' (2014). Non-white porn and non-white thinspiration must be specifically sought, whilst white porn and white thinspo are simply seen as normal (cf. Dyer 1997, p. 10). What is more, whilst a number of the sub-links on *A1 Thinspo* for Black, Asian and Latina thinspo were broken, those still functioning provided only catwalk model and magazine images, thus tacitly suggesting that the thinspirational woman of colour is an exception.

Perhaps the most pronounced manifestation of whiteness on *A1 Thinspo* – and indeed in pro-ana culture at large – is the site's invocation of the Holocaust: flanked by links to images of models is a page entitled, 'Concentration Camp Chic'. The suffixing of 'chic' to a term not typically associated with elegance or style intertextually echoes the 1990s 'heroin chic' phenomenon whereby images of pale, emaciated bodies in the throes of drug-addiction became fashionable. Rebecca Arnold (2001, p. 52) argues that 'heroin chic' destabilises our desire to see images of an ideal self for instead we are 'given only images of human frailty, which is profoundly jarring and unsettling'. The invoking of 'Concentration Camp' chic in *A1 Thinspo* works in the same way, and yet it almost mocks the viewer, suggesting that if they really want to see images of severely emaciated individuals, they should look to the Holocaust. At the same time, it provides important insight into thinness culture. Unsurprisingly, this link was not functioning during the research period, and instead it directed the viewer to the preceding section. Nonetheless, that such a link once existed, and that images of persecuted individuals in concentration camps could be deemed thinspirational, suggests the extent to which context is disregarded in the pursuit for thinness. This indifference to cultural context is an archetypal trait of the self-serving postmodern subject who is so entrenched in constructing themselves as a 'work of art' that they fall short of showing due diligence to the cultural objects they plunder (Kinzey 2012; McGee 2005). Presumably, the Holocaust has been utilised here for thinspiration because of the correlation between the bodies of individuals in the final stages of anorexia and the extreme states of emaciation concentration camp victims were forced to endure. However, this parallel runs deeper: pro-ana online spaces venerate a white, slender body which is closely tied to depictions of the blonde, blue-eyed Aryan figure described by Dyer (1997, p. 118). Specifically, Michelle Lelwica, Emma Hoglund and Jenna McNallie argue that pro-ana websites represent an extreme version of the obsession with the thin body – an ideal which is 'constructed through and associated with racial–class–cultural privilege' (2009, p. 22). By drawing inspiration from the Holocaust, pro-ana users, albeit unwittingly, demonstrate that implicit in perfect thinness is whiteness, and a corresponding repudiation of bodies which do not fulfil this ideal.

The spaces examined in this study echo the castigation of the fat body that takes place in the magazines explored in chapter two. Nonetheless, such criticism manifests in more direct language. For instance, a number of the older pro-ana spaces utilise the fat body as motivation not to eat. *Guide to Ana* states that 'Only fat girls get hungry ... fat girls are weak. Do YOU want to be a fat girl?'. Here, being fat is presented as a consequence of a lack of self-discipline and therefore as a moral failing (Bordo [1993] 2003, p. 192; LeBesco 2004, p. 55). It is also deserving of punishment with *Ethereal Anas* advising users: 'Slap your body fat and watch it wobble [...] Look at fat people'. Suggesting users gaze upon 'fat people' as a means of fulfilling their weight loss is dehumanising and recalls the appalling exhibition during the nineteenth century of black South African, Sarah Baartman – more commonly known as the Hottentot Venus. Caged like a zoo animal, Baartman was displayed across Europe so that people could look at (and even touch) her large, protruding buttocks (Collins 2004; Gilman 1985). The objectification of Baartman's body was such that fatness and blackness were elided. As Andrea Shaw points out, 'Eurocentric ideals of feminine beauty have caused fatness and blackness to display an uncanny coincidence of boundaries as they are both physical attributes that immediately displaces some women from the Western beauty arena' (2005, p. 143). These ideals are evident in pro-ana online spaces where whiteness and thinness are coveted, and fatness and blackness are, at best, overlooked and, at worst, vilified.

This is not to say that injuries against people of colour are necessarily intentional on the part of users; nor is it to excuse such injuries, rather, the culture of compulsory thinness from which pro-ana users draw has historically disavowed the fat-*cum*-black body. Kathleen LeBesco suggests that large bodies 'provoke racist anxieties in the white modern West because of their imagined resemblance to those of maligned, ethnic and racial Others' (2004, p. 56). To be thin, then, is to fit in; but it is also, as Skeggs found in her ethnography of working-class white women from the north-west of England, a form of mobility (1997, p. 83). Schott argues along similar lines in her research into 'black girl thinspiration', proposing that 'black women's decision to join thinspiration is not an attempt to become Caucasian, but an act of survival in a social climate that valorizes a Eurocentric thin feminine beauty ideal' (2017, p. 1030). Indeed, the author of *Ethereal Anas* declares that if she is thin, 'people will look up to me, I will be respected'. It can therefore be argued that pro-ana online spaces shed light on the racial politics of mainstream thinness culture.

It is worth noting that whilst many pro-ana spaces – especially the older sites and forums – are critical of curves: 'breasts are just pointless fat' (*Ethereal Anas*); 'I hate curves. I want a body like an 11-year-old' (*Foreverproana*), a growing number of them endorse full breasts and buttocks, provided that is, the woman's body is otherwise slender (as per the *thinspirationpics* post, 'Wow', explored in chapter three). The venerating of such a body, as I pointed out in the previous chapter, encapsulates the postfeminist culture of having-it-all, but it also has the effect of excluding and denigrating black femininity. *thinspirationpics* aside, this body is particularly prevalent in the thinspo blogs indexed in the first pages of my search engine queries: *Heartthinspo, Howtothinspo, Land of Skinny, Beach Thinspiration, Workingforthin,* and *Your thinspo.* The bodies in these spaces, whilst very slim, have rounded breasts and buttocks and are depicted in poses to emphasise these features – important to this line of discussion, every one of them is white.

In her research into young black women's desire for the 'slim-thick' look – a small waist with full hips and large buttocks, Katherine Appleford (2016) argues that this 'bring[s] black women closer to notions of respectability and appropriateness, and encourage[s] black women to perform femininity in legitimized ways' (p. 208). What then, does such a look signify when it is enacted by *white* women such as those featured in pro-ana online spaces? I suggest that it highlights the extent to which particular body shapes are not questioned when co-opted by certain women, who are usually middle-class and white, but are marked when embraced by others, namely lower-class and women of colour. In white racist discourse, the black woman's rear has been framed as indicative of her untrammelled sexuality and thus looked upon with both awe and revulsion, as the aforementioned narrative of Sarah Baartman attests (Collins 2004; Gilman 1985). However, in recent years, an accentuated rear has become fashionable amongst women who are not black. Most notably, a large bottom has been popularised by two women whose ethnicity is constructed as ambiguous: singer and actress, Jennifer Lopez (Collins 2004; Molina-Guzman 2010) and celebrity, Kim Kardashian (Sastre 2014). That neither woman is of African descent is irrelevant to 'Western imaginations [which] have long filled in the color, moving women from Black to White and back again depending on the needs of the situation' (Collins 2004, p. 29). Such a paradox persists in pro-ana culture. For example, as I have argued elsewhere (Cobb 2016), the body of Kendall Jenner – Kardashian's younger, lighter-skinned, slender half-sister – is valorised in thinspiration spaces, yet it is also presented as a source of anxiety because of its proximity to her older, darker-skinned sisters.

Women's bodies are always at risk of being coded as excessively sexual, particularly if they are read as lower class (see Brown 2005; Skeggs 2004b) or black (see Collins 2004). In the above-mentioned thinspo blogs, large breasts and accentuated buttocks are coveted on selected (white) women: they evoke the erotic via minimal clothing such as underwear, bikinis or gym wear, whilst others appear to be naked – albeit posing strategically. This is not unusual for pro-ana culture: many thinspiration images depict women in stages of undress in order to show the extent of their thinness. However, these women are able to mitigate against feminine excess not only because of their slenderness, but also because of their middle-class, white status. As such, pro-ana online spaces show that successful embodiment of the thin ideal is contingent on race and class.

Middle-class whiteness pervades the bodies pro-ana users deem thinspirational, but it is also apparent in the (little) food they consume. A desire for 'purity' thus pervades these spaces. In a motivational monologue on *A1 Thinspo*, the author writes: 'Do you want to be pure? Eat fresh vegetables, drink cold water. Eat tainted food no more. And you will be pure. You are powerful, bold and in complete control of your body. You are Ana'. As though she is responding to this call, an Instagram user in a #bonespo search declares: 'I WILL achieve my goals. I will be pure and thin and perfect by the time I step off the plane'. Here, purity, thinness, and perfection are understood as interchangeable. Similarly, members of *Foreverproana* discuss feeling 'clean and pure and great' when fasting. Such statements recall the correlations between white as a skin colour and purity and cleanliness (Dyer 1997, p. 76). In their desire to be pure and clean then, users are also coveting whiteness.

Users post motivational phrases and images to encourage themselves and others in their quest for thinness. A thinspiration search on Pinterest yields numerous posts urging the viewer never to give up, including an image of a slender blonde-haired white woman accompanied by the warning: 'Eat junk, look like junk. Eat clean, look lean'. This post conflates junk food with a fat body and clean food with a lean body, thereby reinforcing the correlation between fatness and an ignorance of healthy eating (see LeBesco 2004, p. 112). This disregards the resources required to access such 'clean' food and instead attributes blame to the individual who ignorantly consumes unhealthy produce. Posts such as this one suggest that there is no excuse for being overweight because, within the logic of individualism which pro-ana culture embraces wholesale, '"failed" and "defective" forms of selfhood – childhood, illness, disability, or aged infirmity no longer find a safe haven' (McGee 2005, p. 174). The fat body under neoliberalism cannot be justified and it is up to the individual to rectify this 'defect' by whatever means. Therefore, intersectional privilege in these spaces is assumed, rather than questioned, and those who lack the resources to achieve the ideal body are simply not tolerated.

Spaces abound with 'tips and tricks' on how to hide an eating disorder, such as through performing a middle-class lifestyle. The author of *Kneeling to Ana* advises:

> Get into animal rights or develop an interest in organic food – go on to everyone about how bad chemicals are in food. Basically, get into anything that means you eat less but looks like it's about health and well-being. It works perfectly!

Here, an ethically aware persona can be appropriated to disguise anorexia. As Lupton notes, making these kinds of informed choices around food is indicative of a 'civilised' individual (1996, p. 93); in advising that such behaviour can be adopted to mask and maintain anorexia, this user paradoxically reinforces healthy *and* disordered eating as markers of a privileged subject. At the same time that this is a performance of middle-class values, it is also a performance of femininity, given that both healthy eating (Parsons 2015, p. 83) and vegetarianism (Adams and Fiddes cited in Parsons 2015, p. 142) are associated with the feminine. Moreover, James M. Cronin, Mary B. McCarthy and Alan M. Collins (2014, p. 20) found that hipsters espoused a vegetarian or vegan diet as a means of rejecting mainstream food choices and constructing an alternative identity. Consequently, by becoming vegetarian or only eating raw foods for example, the pro-ana user's food choices can simply be read as an aspect of normative femininity or an attempt to differentiate oneself from the mainstream, rather than cause for concern.

Such eating habits may successfully disguise an eating disorder, but they are also imbued with what Peter Naccarato and Kathleen LeBesco (2012) term 'culinary capital'. Drawing on a Bourdieusian framework, they argue that 'certain foods and food-related practices connote, and by extension, confer status and power on those who know about and enjoy them' (p. 3). Hence, as well as providing guidance on how to avoid eating, pro-ana online spaces recommend foods which can support weight loss, many of which rely on access to costly and even rare produce. Blogs such as *Heartthinspo* intersperse images of thin bodies with artistically displayed dishes of raw vegetables fruits, nuts, seeds and grilled meat. This may have the effect of disguising the blog's pro-anorexic intentions, but it is also demonstrative of culinary capital. The image gallery on *Heartthinspo*, for instance, implies that the acquisition of a slender and toned body necessitates a diet of natural foods and even a life of luxury as indicated by a photograph of a champagne bottle in an ice bucket amidst a sea view. The pro-ana user is depicted here as firmly middle-class, but hers is not merely a life of leisure, rather she works hard to achieve her slender figure, combining a healthy diet with exercise as images of women in workout clothing suggest. Nonetheless, the portrayal of a disciplined and even glamorous lifestyle is seemingly fragmented by a post in the middle of this image gallery bearing the statement, '#1 most awkward human being on this planet'. This claim to social unease, rather than simply undermining the author, makes her appear idiosyncratic, thus chiming with a contemporary form of femininity popularised by actress and singer Zooey Deschanel. According to Anthony P. McIntyre (2015), Deschanel's star text affects an awkwardness which renders her in need of the male competency she lacks, thereby ultimately reinforcing patriarchal gender norms. The author of *Heartthinspo* then, in her declaration of awkwardness, suggests that despite her sculpted body and desirable lifestyle, she is an exemplar of normative femininity who presents no threat to the status quo.

Such unthreatening femininity is exhibited by a member of *World of Pro-ana*, who, in a post to the forum, describes a diet of fruit smoothies and self-identifies as a geek:

> I had a blueberry and spinach smoothie for breakfast; for lunch I had a sugar-free juice and for dinner, a banana smoothie. Then I played board games at an independent bar – it was fun (sure, I'm a geek).

This user subscribes to a middle-class lifestyle and although she is restricting her food intake, her diet of smoothies, particularly those containing blue-berries, which are relatively expensive, bespeaks privilege. Furthermore, she self-identifies as a 'geek' as a result of spending her leisure time playing board games. The figure of the geek is referent of intersectional privilege in that the white, middle-class (and usually male) subject can more readily convert it into beneficial capital than can a racialised other – for the latter, this position is read as abject (Mendick and Francis 2012). The pro-ana user here confesses to her geekiness which serves to emphasise her individuality and distinguish her from the mainstream – an assertion which is reinforced by her noting that she plays games in an independent bar, as opposed to a more common-place high-street chain, for example. By differentiating themselves ·in this way, users discursively produce a privileged identity. *Fallen Ana*, for instance, features low-calorie recipes, such as 'salmon salad with fresh dill and lemon' and advises eating 'tofu, asparagus, lentils, low-fat cottage cheese, cranberries' in order to keep one's weight low and ward off suspicions that one is dieting. These foods require access to fresh ingredients as well as the time to prepare such dishes. Tofu, in particular, symbolises the appropriation of Asian foods undertaken by the Western middle-class: it 'becomes spice, seasoning that can liven up the dull dish that is mainstream white culture' (hooks 2015, p. 366). In short, food practices in pro-ana spaces interpellate users with culinary capital, as opposed to those whose tastes are less refined.

In pro-ana culture, food practices may connote social status, but they are also a means of disguise: in being seen eating foods such as salmon salad or passionately adopting veganism, the pro-anorectic can be perceived by those around her as quite simply a good, middle-class, healthy eater, rather than anorexic. The spaces examined thus emphasise the importance of *appearing* normatively feminine and healthy, even if the body is failing to function. Thus, when *Fallen Ana* details the complications an eating disorder could cause, it offers guidance on how to mask the outward manifestations of such issues. It lists, in alphabetical order, conditions from, 'Amenorrhea: The absence of the menstrual cycle' to 'Forgetfulness', 'Seizures' and 'Vision Impairment'. That the blogger acknowledges such symptoms but continues regardless, demonstrates the extent to which being thin is indica-tive of health and beauty whatever the cost (Parsons 2015, p. 111; see also Jones 2008, pp. 94–95). The blog advises using beauty products in order to disguise the superficial symptoms of illness and give the impression a healthy, feminine appearance:

> It's so important you look healthy: wear foundation and highlighter to give yourself a healthy-looking glow. Use lip balm to stop chapped lips, and wear nail varnish to stop your nails breaking and make them look healthy. Use leave-in conditioner on your hair for extra shine – if it's shiny it looks healthy.
>
> (*Fallen Ana*)

By advising that users should wear make-up to attain 'a healthy-looking glow', the blogger advocates 'cultivating an acceptable white feminine self' (Ahmed 1998, p. 40) In glowing, the subject is exhibiting a form of body management which rests on hegemonic whiteness. Guidance on how to present an *appearance* of health demonstrates the way in which the surface of the body is used to suggest one's affiliation with the middle-class and thus distance oneself from the working class (Skeggs 1997, p. 84). The use of make-up and hair products is recommended to mask the damage of anorexia and put forth an appropriate form of femininity. Pale skin, chapped lips, brittle nails and dull hair can all be rectified with a surface covering of cosmetics. As I argued in the previous chapter, discourses of denial and disguise blur the boundaries between what it means to be anorexic and what it means to practise normative body disciplining. Here, users endorse consuming refined foods and using cosmetics to create the appearance of a healthy, white, middle-class female; this is tacit acknowledgement that the thin ideal is situated at the intersection of privileged social categories.

'Lovely' girls and #grunge

As my critical enquiries have shown thus far, many pro-ana online spaces generate divisions with respect to gender, class, race and body size. Although this is communicated in numerous ways, broadly speaking users tend to champion either a polished look comprising the collation of images of slender women in brightly coloured gym clothing, of healthy food, and motivational platitudes, or, they espouse a grunge aesthetic, indicated by dark clothing, cigarettes, and statements of depression and suicide. These may appear to be juxtaposing attitudes: the former denotes enthusiastic self-worth, whereas the latter bespeaks apathy and self-loathing, yet both evoke white, middle-class individualism which disregards intersectional inequalities. The pro-ana user then represents herself as either an upbeat enthusiast of healthy eating and exercise or as a 'Sad Girl' (see Wollen cited in Mooney 2018) who is consumed by her own sorrow and disaffection. In both, heterosexual whiteness is common sense.

In a section of her website entitled, 'Why I'm pro-ana', the author of *Ethereal Anas* concedes, 'Let's face it skinny girls get all the guys. That's why I can't go near chocolate. If I do then food may as well be my boyfriend, and that's just embarrassing'. The author believes that there is a cultural chasm between thin women, whose slender bodies remunerate them with a heterosexual relationship, and fat women, who are destined for a life of loneliness, their only companion being food. This echoes mainstream narratives such as those of Frankie Essex discussed in chapter two, whose weight gain represented a threat to the maintenance of her heterosexual relationship, and the pro-ana marketing sites explored in chapter three where weight loss was framed as a means of alleviating loneliness. The author of *Ethereal Anas* may be angry that 'skinny girls get all the guys' (indeed much of her writing is in capital letters), but she uses this apparent knowledge as motivation to become 'skinny and pretty', because as she repeatedly exclaims, this is all she wants, and she would rather die this way than live as a fat girl. Nonetheless, the acquisition of a heterosexual relationship is presented as just one of many benefits to being thin, rather than the sole reason to diet. Put differently, users appropriate discourses of heterosexuality as one way of servicing their quest for thinness.

This occurs in *Guide to Ana*. In the about section of the site is a statement from the author stating that *Guide to Ana* 'is a gender-neutral space open to anyone with an eating disorder'. However, it repeatedly addresses a feminine subject (Do YOU want to be the fat girl?) and in its guidance on not giving in to hunger, it betrays the declaration of gender neutrality as follows: 'Men can carry you easily. They will be amazed how light you are' (*Guide to Ana*). This implicitly exposes the fragility of gender binaries, for 'no masculinity arises except in a system of gender relations' (Connell 1995, p. 71). In order for powerful, physically strong, masculinity to exist, there must be diminutive, physically fragile, femininity. Weighing so little that men can lift you with ease and even amazement shores up hegemonic masculinity. The author's claims to gender neutrality may imply that both men and women can be anorexic and therefore light enough to be lifted by a male counterpart, but it still resorts to heteronormative understandings of gender roles. Such frameworks, however, are utilised to inspire weight loss.

As well as asserting that thinness will please men, *Guide to Ana* lists numerous other reasons as to why the viewer should not let hunger defeat her, one of which is that she will 'have a delicate physique'. The desire to be 'delicate' recurs throughout the data examined in this study. In *Foreverproana*, a user writes that whilst she does not want to look like a child, she would like to have the body of 'a thin, delicate little teenage girl. Innocent-looking, lissom, pretty, beautiful'. Likewise, a #proanna search on Instagram produced a number of references to being 'tiny, fragile and delicate' and both #tiny and #girl appeared in posts across a range of searches on all platforms. In a 'thynspiration' search on Pinterest, for instance, #tiny accompanies images of very thin legs. The notion that the bodies depicted in these images are tiny, or that their posters desire to be so, takes the quest for ideal thinness into the realm of fantasy.

The fantastical nature of these spaces is underpinned by their invocations of fictional characters. Alice of Lewis Carroll's nineteenth century children's book, *Alice's Adventures in Wonderland* (2003) appears in various guises in pro-ana online spaces, with users creating posts using stills from the 1951 Disney film, *Alice in Wonderland*, and memes from the more recent (2010) film directed by Tim Burton. Alice is an important cultural figure in the study of girlhood (see Driscoll 2002) and in appetite (see Silver 2002; see also Falconer 2009). Equally pertinent to an interrogation of pro-ana culture, *Alice in Wonderland* is also, as Michael Hancher (cited in Hollingsworth 2009) puts it, 'a happily overdetermined and polymorphous text. It thrives in an indefinite number of forms, which amalgamate differently in the experience of each viewer, hearer, and reader, old or young' (p. xix). Pro-ana online spaces themselves thrive (and survive) because of their own polymorphism, which makes *Alice* ever more valuable to their culture. The pro-ana user interprets and utilises *Alice* to express their sentiments around extreme weight loss, but because the text holds numerous meanings, so does its appropriation. Arguably, pro-ana users adopt *Alice* imagery owing to the ability to shrink bestowed upon the protagonist (as opposed to the periods of growth she also experiences). #alicesdiet appears in the social media spaces analysed and is indicative of a number of different regimes, such as a 30-day programme which alternates minimal calorie intake with fasting as detailed in one Instagram post generated by #proanna. Other iterations of Alice's diet are more closely linked to *Alice* itself, where the user has 'Drink Me' and 'Eat Me' days as per Alice's experiences in the book. Unlike Alice, the pro-ana user must only shrink, and even on the 'Eat Me' days, may consume only minimal food. Anna Krugovoy Silver argues that despite initially representing Alice's voracity, the *Alice* books ultimately favour pre-pubescent femininity over womanhood, thereby castigating female hunger, whether it is sexual or for food (2002, p. 78). Alice's changing body size then denotes the conflict between girlhood and womanhood, and the latter's ultimate disavowal – therefore paying homage to Hilde Bruch's (1974) psychological explanation of anorexia as a rejection of adolescence and its subsequent popularising as a white, middle-class concern (Saukko 2009). In short, the appropriation of Alice in pro-ana online spaces reinforces normative understandings of anorexia.

By aspiring to unreal representations of femininity, users implicitly acknowledge that gender is 'a norm and a fiction' (Butler 1990, p. 173). Aside from Alice, many of the women deemed thinspirational in these spaces are on some level fictional, being as they are actors, models or celebrities. A recurring figure in pro-ana spaces is the character of Cassie Ainsworth, an anorexic teen from British television show, *Skins* (2007–2013). Although Cassie is fictional, the actress Hannah Murray who played her needed to be extremely thin for the role and as a result Murray and Cassie are conflated in pro-ana culture. My searches yielded content accompanied by both #cassie and #hannahmurray, thus affording both individuals thinspirational status. Murray herself could be described as one of the media's '"A1" girls [...] glamorous high-achievers destined for Oxford and Cambridge' (McRobbie 2009, p. 15). After achieving success as an actress from a young age, she went on to secure a range of major acting roles whilst also reading English at Cambridge University (Williams 2014). Hence, the elision of Murray and Cassie epitomises common sense understandings of the anorexic as a 'perfectionist "goody" girl, rendered neurotically compliant by the overly demanding middle-class family' (Saukko 2009, p. 66). Whether or not Murray has an eating disorder is irrelevant to pro-ana users because, either way, she projects the perfect thinspirational image.

Posts comprise stills of Murray in character, often together with quotations from *Skins*, the majority of which centre on not eating. In a #proanna search on Tumblr, Cassie is depicted in a screengrab from *Skins* emblazoned with the text, 'Crazy bitch. Never fucking eats'. Amongst other hashtags, the image is accompanied by '#hannahmurray', '#cassieainsworth' and '#cassie'. Thus, both actress and character come to represent 'proanna'. #hannahmurray alone generates numerous images of the actress, all of which depict her playing Cassie. One post is a gif of Cassie in the second episode of series one telling Sid whom she is trying to attract, 'I didn't eat for three days so I could be lovely' (Skins 2007–2013). 'Lovely' is Cassie's catchphrase throughout the series, and in this context, it is suggestive of middle-class, feminine beauty which is neither sexual nor vulgar. Femininity which is lovely conforms to the 'norms of niceness' (Griffin cited in Skeggs 1997; see also Wood 2016) which require respectable women to distance themselves from displays of sexuality. By not eating, Cassie hopes to be 'lovely' and in turn invite Sid's interest in a modest way. This is because, as Susan Berridge argues, 'despite [*Skins*'] emphasis on teenage nihilism, a closer examination reveals that it is underpinned by a more conservative sexual politics' (2013, p. 787). This chimes with the version of femininity espoused by many pro-ana users: ostensibly it is deviant, yet further interrogation reveals compliance with cultural norms. The term 'lovely' occurs throughout pro-ana spaces, with #lovelybones generating pro-ana content on Instagram and Tumblr, and the pin, 'lovelybonespo' appearing on Pinterest. Here, the pro-ana user is interpellated as a middle-class white woman with the potential to realise her loveliness through weight loss.

Searches for 'thinspiration' and 'pro-anorexia' on Pinterest evoke intersections of privilege. Contained in the motivational platitudes that dominate such search results, is a wealth of culturally specific markers indicating, for example, gender and nationality. One format users adopt is to list reasons to lose weight in bold fonts. A thinspiration search on Pinterest generated a number of such lists. One such post, which I quote verbatim because, as well as being adopted by pro-ana users, it appears across numerous mainstream weight-loss spaces, reads as follows:

> For the skinny jeans, for the mini skirts [sic], for the crop-tops, for the short shorts, for the bikinis, for the stares, for the fun, for the satisfaction, for the confidence, for your health, for your happiness, *for you.*
> (Fitness Images 2019; emphases in original)

The post catalogues the reasons for dieting, from the concrete to the abstract, and asserts that the most important reason to lose weight (and it is accentuated in a different colour), is 'for you'. Such rhetoric affirms that achieving thinness is ultimately for self-fulfilment: one may diet 'for the stares', in other words, for the approval or envy of others, but above all weight loss is an activity one undergoes for one's own good. This discourse recalls that of the magazines explored in chapter two where the reader is urged to 'skip the fad diets and focus on a happy, healthy you' (Glamour 2014, pp. 183–185) – ironically in this instance by incorporating Special K cereal into their diet.

The clothing to which this Pinterest thinspiration post urges individuals to aspire consists of items which highlight particular parts of a woman's body, such as the legs ('skinny jeans', 'mini skirts', 'short shorts') or the stomach ('crop-tops', 'bikinis'). These items all accentuate, and even expose, the female body and users are encouraged to enjoy 'the stares' slenderness will give them in minimal clothing; to revel in their postfeminist *to-be-looked-at-ness*. Not only do posts such as these reinforce heterofemininity, they also place the reader in a discourse which McRobbie suggests is regularly used in media reporting to highlight Western sexual freedom (2009, p. 27). She argues that this is 'a discourse which celebrates the freedoms of fashion-conscious "thong-wearing" Western girls in contrast to those young women who, for example, wear the veil' (ibid.). This Pinterest post then, seeks to motivate users through the promotion of a Western, heteronormative gaze.

Another post yielded by this thinspiration search on Pinterest enumerates '20 reasons to lose weight', such as: 'You will love you' and 'Be the skinny friend'. The fifteenth reason is, 'you'll get a prom date', thus it would appear that the user is addressing a teenage audience who may be planning to attend their end of year dance at school or college. Although it does not state that the 'prom date' should be of the opposite gender, the seventeenth reason to lose weight states that attracting men is of utmost importance: 'You know those cute guys you see around? They'll start to notice you too'. Slenderness here is framed as the key to successful heterosexuality, and as a separate post in this same thinspiration search claims, 'The more you work out, the weaker his knees get'. These spaces continually emphasise that a thinspirational body will put you in the thrall of men, even to the point of overpowering them. A person who is weak at the knees, here the male observer, is emasculated, having been stunned by the beauty of the slender woman before him. As such, whilst the traditional male gaze positions women as passive objects, here the postfeminist 'girlfriend gaze *cultivates* women's control over her own libido and turns it into "hotness"' (Winch 2013, p. 22, emphasis in original). In these posts – as in the Reddit posts examined in the previous chapter – women are urged to engage in compulsory heterosexuality as a means of empowerment rather than to reject it as oppressive. This is symptomatic of the way neoliberal individualism reframes structural inequalities as desirable. In their rigid focus on self-improvement, pro-ana users shore up, rather than criticise, intersectional marginalisation. Posts across the sample presuppose intersectional privilege and perpetuate the primacy of hegemonic identity categories. This is obfuscated by a neoliberal rhetoric which positions the individual as an autonomous being whose destiny is her own responsibility.

Such rhetoric though, is not always in the upbeat register of self-help and motivation, rather numerous posts emanate self-hatred and depression and are accompanied by #grunge, #grungestyle or #softgrunge, for example. Grunge was popularised during the 1990s and is typified by the nihilism of rock band Nirvana and a backlash against the consumerism of the previous decade (Arnold 2001, p. 26). It centres on a rejection of the status quo and is communicated through the diction of hopelessness. Whilst it has invited comparison to, and in many ways is borne out of, punk, scholars agree that grunge lacks punk's attention to race and class politics, instead exhibiting a sense of despair and alienation (Arnold 2001; Burke 2012; Shevory 1995). Given that their focus is more personal than it is political, it is fitting that pro-ana users identify with grunge. Specifically, Burke (2012) has drawn parallels between the pro-ana phenomenon and grunge culture, suggesting that grunge adumbrates pro-ana in its aligning of a thin body with distress. In the sample examined in this study, grunge is typically evoked either through images of thin young women coupled with hashtags and statements which directly reference grunge, or grunge is inadvertently summoned through allusions to self-hatred and suicide. Such pro-ana content chimes with sentiments promulgated by grunge icons such as Kurt Cobain, lead singer of Nirvana, who became renowned for the statement, 'I hate myself and I want to die', originally intended as the title of Nirvana's third album, *In Utero* (Cross 2002).

An image posted on Instagram produced by a #bonespo search is the epitome of grunge content: it features a young white girl with bleached blonde hair and dark eye make-up. She pulls at her face in an outward display of despair and attendant hashtags such as '#suicidal' and '#depressed' along with the caption 'I want to' followed by three gun emoticons, serve to emphasise her suicidal state. She also applies '#grunge' and '#grungestyle'. Her depression may be very real, but it nonetheless aligns her with a subculture which another image, this time yielded by #bonespo on Tumblr, suggests is 'cool'. The image depicts a skinny woman reclining in such a way that her jutting ribs are emphasised, and the user has affixed hashtags including, '#skinnier #bones #cool #grunge #hipster' – a combination which positions extreme thinness as characteristic of an alternative identity. If fashion can be understood as exhibiting the paradoxical desire to fit in and stand out at the same time (Simmel cited in Entwistle 2000, p. 116), then indicating an affiliation with grunge and hipster culture, as this pro-ana user does, grants membership of a particular group and rejection of the mainstream simultaneously. However, as Jake Kinzey (2012, p. 3) argues of the hipster, in their quest to be utterly individual, they simply end up being the same as everyone else. These pro-ana users may have angered the media and incensed Internet moderators, but their style is all too familiar.

According to Kinzey, 'if there is a musical movement associated with the hipster it is certainly indie' (2012, p. 25). Likewise, pro-ana grunge posts often combine statements of self-hatred with a penchant for indie music. An Instagram search for #ana yields a black and white blurred image emblazoned with the statement, 'I'm tired of feeling like I'm fucking crazy', a quotation from the song 'Ride' by American artist, Lana Del Rey (2012). Heather Mooney (2018) argues that Del Rey, who is often said to have popularised 'Sad Girl' style, 'refuses the normative expectations of the "empowered" can-do girl' (p. 178). Thus, her invocation in this post serves to further juxtapose the user's pro-ana identity with the upbeat enthusiasts discussed above. Moreover, Del Rey's apparent lack of authenticity as an artist is continually questioned (Vigier 2012) and she has subsequently been read as a 'quintessential current postmodernist expression of identity flux' (Barron 2018 p. 64). Her star text is thus ideally suited to pro-ana culture, because like *Alice*, she is polymorphous. As such, the hashtags alongside this post summon a range of meanings: distress is indicated through '#anxiety #suicidal #depressed', whilst other hashtags align the poster with an abundance of subcultures: '#pale #indie #hipster #punk #emo #grunge #softgrunge', as well as bands: '#arcticmonkeys #thestrokes #thewhitestripes #Nirvana'. This combination of hashtags places the user within a postmodern subjecthood where her identity is constructed through a range of cultural texts. The hashtag 'pale' here, which is commonly used in posts invoking suicide, grunge and depression, is not exclusively suggestive of skin colour. However, when accompanied by other hashtags evoking whiteness, '#pale' appears to indicate the hue of a distressed or unwell person's skin.

Although the Sad Girl's refusal to entertain upbeat femininity has been read as resistant (Mooney 2018), in pro-ana online spaces she falls short of meaningful protest. By aligning her sorrow with the pursuit of subcultural style, she positions pro-ana culture as a white, middle-class leisure pursuit rather than a critique of the status quo. At the same time, she turns her despair onto herself. As one user on *World of Pro-ana* writes: 'I hate myself and I hate my body. The way it looks and how it acts. It's so hideous it doesn't even let me have a physical relationship with my boyfriend. I just want to die'. Aside from understanding her body through the discourse of Cartesian dualism – a common reading of the anorexic body in Western culture (see Bordo [1993] 2003; Malson 1998), the user's anger is channelled inwards. It is directed not at structural inequalities, which in the case of this post could be at the impossible demands put upon women to realise an ideal body, instead it is turned on the self. This resonates with grunge culture in that '[it] occupies an emotional terrain in which the need for self-help devolves into the desire for self-annihilation' (Shevory 1995, p. 34). This not only presents dangers to the individual's well-being, it also reduces anorexia to individual psychopathology, which feminist scholars of the body have for so long contested (see Malson and Burns 2009, p. 1).

Conclusion

Pro-ana online spaces occur at the intersection of white, middle-class, heterofeminine, youthful, able-bodied privilege. Eating disorders can affect anyone, but pro-anorexia culture draws on hegemonic bodies to 'thinspire' its users. At the same time, in the data examined in this study, the non-white, lower class, disabled, or ageing body is othered or simply ignored. Users are ostensibly marginalised by dint of being pro-anorexic, yet they define themselves through both access to privilege and exclusion of groups who are not deemed to be in possession of embodied capital.

After addressing the key literature on intersectionality, this chapter showed that in order to be ideally thin, one must also be white. Although, as I have demonstrated, there are spaces dedicated to black thinspiration, for instance, they must be specifically sought. Furthermore, because pro-ana culture is archetypally postmodern, it appropriates elements of black femininity which have been historically denigrated (such as large breasts and buttocks) and renders them thinspirational on white bodies. This may seem strange and contradictory, but as I have argued, pro-ana online spaces are intrinsically intertextual, appropriating as they do images and discourses from the breadth of mainstream culture. As a result, these spaces reveal the extent to which common sense understandings of the thin ideal are centred on whiteness. As I argued, the ideal is not only constructed through the aesthetics of the body, but also through food choices. Users are urged to consume middle-class foods as a way of disguising their eating disorder. Displays of 'culinary capital' mask anorexia both offline and online, and in so doing, thinness is upheld as a marker of middle-class privilege.

In the final section of this chapter, I argued that pro-ana enthusiasts' modes of thinspiration are twofold: either they draw on motivational slogans and images, urging one another to never give up, or they espouse grunge culture and make declarations of despair and suicide. Users' endorsement of 'lovely' femininity reveals how heteronormative, middle-class ideals dominate contemporary thinness culture. What is more, they venerate fictional characters such as *Skins'* Cassie Ainsworth, thus aspiring to bodies which rely on illusion. Cassie embodies the cultural stereotype of the anorexic and, in users' adulation of her, they reinforce common sense understandings of what it means to be anorexic. This effectively disavows an intersectional approach to eating disorders and reinstates them within the realm of privilege. The Sad Girl or the proponent of grunge may resist the optimism of normative femininity, but she converts her sadness into style: by aligning herself with cultural icons ranging from Lana Del Rey to Kurt Cobain, the pro-ana user's sorrow and despair are funnelled into fashion and fandom. Whilst Burke (2012) warns that pro-ana culture is dangerous in its promotional of distress as a form of agency, its espousal of the optimistic anorectic is equally concerning: both approaches obfuscate and neutralise structural inequalities with their promotion of individualism.

Above all, the bodies adorning these spaces may be starved, but their owners do not look impoverished. As a result, rarely are 'real' images of emaciated lower class individuals in unfashionable clothing uploaded to these spaces. For the pro-ana subject, it is not enough simply to be thin, it is a young, white, physically able, middle-class body in stylish clothing which colonises these spaces. By appropriating texts from mainstream culture, pro-ana users reveal that intersectional privilege is essential to achieving the thin ideal, but rather than critique it they ultimately reinforce it.

References

Ahmed, S. (1998) 'Tanning the body: Skin, colour and gender', *New Formations*, 34, pp. 37–41.

Appleford, K. (2016) 'This big bum thing has taken over the world': Considering black women's changing views on body image and the role of celebrity', *Critical Studies in Fashion & Beauty*, 7(2), pp. 193–214.

Arnold, R. (2001) *Fashion, Desire and Anxiety: Image and Morality in the Twentieth Century.* London: I.B. Tauris.

Barron, L. (2018). 'Postmodern theories of celebrity', in Elliot, A. (ed.) *Routledge Handbook of Celebrity Studies.* Abingdon, OX: Routledge, pp. 70–84.

Berridge, S. (2013) 'Doing it for the kids'? The discursive construction of the teenager and teenage sexuality in *skins*', *Journal of British Cinema and Television*, 10(4), pp. 785–801.

Bilge, S. (2013) 'Intersectionality undone: Saving intersectionality from feminist inter-sectionality studies', *Du Bois Review*, 10(2), pp. 405–424.

Bordo, S. ([1993] 2003) *Unbearable Weight: Feminism, Western Culture and the Body*, 10th anniversary edition. Berkeley: University of California Press.

———. (2009). 'Not just "a white girl's thing": The changing face of food and body image problems', in Malson, H. and Burns, M. (eds.) *Critical Feminist Approaches to Eating Dis/orders.* London: Routledge, pp. 46–59.

Bourdieu, P. (1984) *Distinction: A Social Critique of the Judgement of Taste.* Nice, R. (trans.). New York: Routledge.

Brown, J.A. (2005) 'Class and feminine excess: The strange case of Anna Nicole Smith', *Feminist Review*, 81(1), pp. 74–94.

Bruch, H. (1974) *Eating Disorders. Obesity, Anorexia Nervosa, and the Person Within.* London: Routledge.

Burke, E. (2012) 'Reflections on the waif: Images of slenderness and distress in pro-anorexia websites', *Australian Feminist Studies*, 27(71), pp. 37–54.

Burton, T. (2010) *Alice in Wonderland* [Film]. Burbank: Walt Disney.

Butler, J. (1990) *Gender Trouble: Feminism and the Subversion of Identity.* New York: Routledge.

Carastathis, A. (2013) 'Identity categories as potential coalitions', *Signs*, 38(4), pp. 941–965.

Carbado, D.W. (2013) 'Colorblind intersectionality', *Signs*, 38(4), pp. 811–845.

Carroll, L. (2003) *Alice's Adventures in Wonderland.* Haughton, H. (ed.). London: Penguin.

Cobb, G. (2016) 'The Jenner genes definitely helped her': Kardashians, Jenners and the intersectional politics of thinness', *Critical Studies in Fashion & Beauty*, 7 (2), pp. 173–192.

Collins, P.H. (2004) *Black Sexual Politics: African Americans, Gender, and the New Racism.* New York: Routledge.

Connell, R.W. (1995) *Masculinities.* Berkeley: University of California Press.

Crenshaw, K. (1989) 'Demarginalizing the intersection of race and sex: A black feminist critique of anti-discrimination doctrine feminist theory, and antiracist politics', *University of Chicago Legal Forum*, 1(8), pp. 139–167.

Cronin, J.M., McCarthy, M.B., and Collins, A.M. (2014) 'Covert distinction: How hipsters practice food-based resistance strategies in the production of identity', *Consumption Markets & Culture*, 17(1), pp. 2–28.

Cross, C.R. (2002) *Heavier Than Heaven: The Biography of Kurt Cobain*. New York: Hyperion.

Davis, K. (2008) 'Intersectionality as buzzword: A sociology of science perspective on what makes a feminist theory successful', *Feminist Theory*, 9, pp. 67–85.

Del Rey, L. (2012) 'Ride', Available at: www.azlyrics.com/lyrics/lanadelrey/ride.html Accessed September 2018.

Disney, W. (1951) *Alice in Wonderland* [Motion Picture]. USA: Walt Disney Productions.

Driscoll, C. (2002) *Girls: Feminine Adolescence in Popular Culture and Cultural Theory*. New York: Columbia University Press.

Dyer, R. (1997) *White*. London: Routledge.

Entwistle, J. (2000) *The Fashioned Body: Fashion, Dress and Modern Social Theory*. Cambridge: Polity.

Falconer, F. (2009). 'Underworld portmanteaux: Dante's hell and Carroll's wonderland in women's memoirs of mental Illness', in Hollingsworth, C. (ed.) *Alice beyond Wonderland: Essays for the Twenty-First Century*. Iowa City: University of Iowa Press, pp. 3–22.

Fitness Images. (2019). *For the Skinny Jeans, for the Mini Skirts*. Available at: www.fitnessadvice24.com/fitness-images/for-the-skinny-jeans-for-the-mini-skirts-666 (Accessed July 2019).

Gilman, S.L. (1985) 'Black bodies, white bodies: Toward an iconography of female sexuality in late nineteenth-century art, medicine, and literature', *Critical Inquiry*, 12 (1), pp. 204–242.

Glamour (2014) Condé Nast, June.

Hollingsworth, C. (2009) 'Introduction', in Hollingsworth, C. (ed.) *Alice Beyond Wonderland: Essays for the Twenty-First Century*. Iowa City: University of Iowa Press, pp. xvii–xxviii.

Holmes, S. (2015) '"That perfect girl is gone": Pro-ana, Anorexia and *Frozen* (2013) as an "eating disorder" film', *Participations: Journal of Audience and Reception Studies*, 12 (2), pp. 98–120.

hooks, b. (2015) *Black Looks: Race and Representation*. Abingdon, OX: Routledge.

Jones, M. (2008) *Skintight: An Anatomy of Cosmetic Surgery*. Oxford: Berg.

Kinzey, J. (2012) *The Sacred and the Profane: An Investigation of Hipsters*. Winchester: Zero Books.

LeBesco, K. (2004) *Revolting Bodies? The Struggle to Redefine Fat Identity*. Amherst: University of Massachusetts Press.

Lelwica, M., Hoglund, E., and McNallie, J. (2009) 'Spreading the religion of thinness from California to Calcutta: A critical feminist postcolonial analysis', *Journal of Feminist Studies in Religion*, 25(1), pp. 19–41.

Lupton, D. (1996) *Food, the Body and the Self*. London: Sage.

Lykke, N. (2010) *Feminist Studies: A Guide to Intersectional Theory, Methodology and Writing*. New York: Routledge.

Malson, H. (1998) *The Thin Woman: Feminism, Post-Structuralism, and the Social Psychology of Anorexia Nervosa*. New York: Routledge.

Malson, H. and Burns, M. (2009). 'Re-theorising the slash of dis/order: An introduction to critical feminist approaches to eating dis/orders', in Malson, H. and Burns, M. (eds.) *Critical Feminist Approaches to Eating Dis/orders*. London: Routledge, pp. 1–6.

McGee, M. (2005) *Self-Help Inc.: Makeover Culture in American Life*. Oxford: Oxford University Press.

McIntyre, A.P. (2015) '*Isn't she adorkable!* Cuteness as political neutralization in the star text of Zooey Deschanel', *Television & New Media*, 16(5), pp. 422–438.

McRobbie, A. (2009) *The Aftermath of Feminism: Gender, Culture and Social Change*. London: Sage Publications Ltd.

Mendick, H. and Francis, B. (2012) 'Boffin and geek identities: Abject or privileged?', *Gender and Education*, 24(1), pp. 15–24.

Mohanty, C.T. (2013) 'Transnational feminist crossings: On neoliberalism and radical critique', *Signs*, 38(4), pp. 967–991.

Molina-Guzman, I. (2010) *Dangerous Curves: Latina Bodies in the Media*. New York: New York University Press.

Mooney, H. (2018) 'Sad girls and carefree Black girls: Affect, race, (dis) possession, and protest', *WSQ: Women's Studies Quarterly*, 46(3), pp. 175–194.

Naccarato, P., and LeBesco, K. (2012) *Culinary Capital*. London: Berg.

Nash, J.C. (2008) 'Re-thinking intersectionality', *Feminist Review*, 89, pp. 1–15.

Nasser, M. and Malson, H. (2009). 'Beyond Western dis/orders: Thinness and self-starvation of other-ed women', in Malson, H. and Burns, M. (eds.) *Critical Feminist Approaches to Eating Dis/orders*. London: Routledge, pp. 74–86.

Parsons, J.M. (2015) *Gender, Class and Food: Families, Bodies and Health*. Basingstoke, Hampshire: Palgrave Macmillan.

Pinterest. (2014) Available at: www.pinterest.com (Accessed July 2014).

PornHub. (2014) *Categories*. Available at: www.pornhub.com/categories (Accessed August 2014).

Puar, J. (2014). 'From intersections to assemblages', in Grzanka, P.R. (ed.) *Intersectionality: A Foundations and Frontiers Reader*. Boulder, CO: Westview Press, pp. 331–339.

Reddit. (2014) Available at: www.reddit.com/ (Accessed July 2014).

Sastre, A. (2014) 'Hottentot in the age of reality TV: Sexuality, race, and Kim Kardashian's visible body', *Celebrity Studies*, 5(1–2), pp. 123–137.

Saukko, P. (2009) 'A critical discussion of normativity in discourses of eating disorders', in Malson, H. and Burns, M. (eds.) *Critical Feminist Approaches to Eating Dis/orders*. London: Routledge, pp. 63–73.

Schott, N.D. (2017) 'Race, online space and the feminine: Unmapping "Black girl thinspiration"', *Critical Sociology*, 43(7–8), pp. 1029–1043.

Shaw, A. (2005) 'The other side of the looking glass: The marginalization of fatness and blackness in the construction of gender identity', *Social Semiotics*, 15(2), pp. 143–152.

Shevory, T.C. (1995) 'Bleached resistance: The politics of grunge', *Popular Music and Society*, 19(2), pp. 23–48.

Silver, A.K. (2002) *Victorian Literature and the Anorexic Body*. Cambridge: Cambridge University Press.

Skeggs, B. (1997) *Formations of Class and Gender: Becoming Respectable*. London: Sage Publications Ltd.

———. (2004a). 'Exchange, value and affect: Bourdieu and "the self"', in Adkins, L. and Skeggs, B. (eds.) *Feminism after Bourdieu*. Oxford: Blackwell Publishing, pp. 75–95.

————. (2004b) *Class, Self, Culture*. London: Routledge.

Skins. (2007–2013), E4.

Tomlinson, B. (2013) 'To tell the truth and not get trapped: Desire, distance, and inter-sectionality at the scene of argument', *Signs*, 38(4), pp. 993–1017.

Tumblr. (2014) Available at: www.tumblr.com/ (Accessed July 2014).

Vigier, C. (2012) 'The meaning of Lana Del Rey', *Zeteo: The Journal of Interdisciplinary Writing*, (November), pp. 1–16.

Villa, P.I. (2011). 'Embodiment is always more: Intersectionality, subjection and the body', in Lutz, H., Vivar, M.T.H. and Supik, L. (eds.) *Framing Intersectionality: Debates on a Multi-Faceted Concept in Gender Studies*. Farnham: Ashgate, pp. 171–186.

Webstagram. (2014) Available at: www.web.stagram.com (Accessed July 2014).

Wilkes, K. (2015) 'Colluding with neo-liberalism: Post-feminist subjectivities, white-ness and expressions of entitlement', *Feminist Review*, 110, pp. 18–33.

Williams, H. (2014) 'Hannah Murray interview: "I keep a sad face in my little box of tricks"', *The Independent*, 9 August. Available at: www.independent.co.uk/news/people/hannah-murray-interview-i-keep-a-sad-face-in-my-little-box-of-tricks-9656958.html (Accessed November 2016).

Winch, A. (2013) *Girlfriends and Postfeminist Sisterhood*. Basingstoke, Hampshire: Palgrave Macmillan.

Wood, R. (2016) '"You do act differently when you're in it": Lingerie and femininity', *Journal of Gender Studies*, 25(1), pp. 10–23.

5 Articulating pain

Investment or lament

Pro-ana online spaces appropriate discourses and images from mainstream culture, reframing them for their own purposes and in the process, they furnish texts with new meanings. As I have argued, there is a fine and shifting line between legitimate and illegitimate forms of weight loss: practices which are read as deviant in some contexts are read as normative feminine behaviour in others. Pro-ana texts thus draw on discourses of normative femininity in order to evade censorship. On the one hand this allows them to hide in plain sight, but on the other, it offers an opportunity to identify and critique normative conceptions of gender. In the latter half of chapter four, I determined two discursive representations of the pro-ana subject: the upbeat advocate of self-help and the self-hating proponent of grunge. In this chapter, I propose that the suffering subject of pro-ana online spaces approaches the pain of extreme weight loss either as an investment in to self-improvement or a lamentable state ultimately bent on destroying her. I suggest that both these approaches to pain are disciplinary: as Foucault (1979, p. 138) argues, 'discipline increases the forces of the body (in economic terms of utility) and diminishes these same forces (in political terms of obedience)'. By converting their pain into a worthwhile investment, users become economically useful and, by turning this pain inwards, they become politically compliant. In suffering to be skinny, pro-ana enthusiasts are rendered 'less socially oriented and more centripetally focussed on self-modification' (Bordo [1993] 2003, p. 166). This chapter then, explores how pain is presented as necessary for realising the thin body required of not only anorexia, but normative femininity. In so doing, it explores the extent to which pro-ana culture enacts an exposé of such demands.

The chapter is divided into three sections. The first attends to the cultural–historical context in which the coupling of pain and femininity is situated: it examines how the contemporary pro-ana user – albeit, not necessarily wittingly – draws on these cultural performances of suffering women to communicate her pain. This anticipates the second section of the chapter where I interrogate the discourse of 'no pain no gain' which pervades these spaces: in the modern West, the hard-working body in pain is an aspect of neoliberal self-improvement, and thus a prerequisite for the successful postfeminist female, but when pain is framed in this way its lived reality is obfuscated. In the last section, I explore the alternative to 'no pain no gain': the users who lament their suffering and provide candid accounts of the mental and physical pain of extreme thinness.

Normative femininity and the cultural performances of pain

In the introduction to this book, I outlined how feminist scholarship on anorexia has read it as operating on a continuum with normative femininity. Whilst for some this provides a welcome departure from the pathologising of anorexia as a disease, Su Holmes, Sarah Drake, Kelsey Odgers and Jon Wilson have found that for others, 'the feminist bid to place [*anorexia nervosa*] on a continuum with normative femininities may itself foster aspects of social and cultural stigma' (2017, p. 12). Indeed, throughout history, anorexia and femininity have been wedded to one another in ways that legitimise self-starvation and pathologise female body practices – and *vice versa*. Women, it would appear, are always already pathological subjects doomed to occupy 'a precarious balance between narcissistic gratification and an ever-present dissatisfaction fuelled by a deep-seated self-hate' (Davis 1995, p. 45). This legacy stems from Freudian psychoanalysis which has historically charged women with an innate masochism (see Bartky 1990; Malson 1998). Given that common sense understandings of anorexia locate it as a female phenomenon, it readily fits into such a paradigm. However, as Malson rightly argues,

> Constructions of anorexia as self-punishing and of "the anorexic" as "femininely masochistic" might be best viewed not as individuals' "feminine masochism" but rather as interpellations of (female) subjects within the already existing discourses and discursive practices which produce woman as masochistic.
>
> (1998, p. 166)

By the same token, although pro-ana online spaces are replete with narratives of compulsory suffering, it would be remiss to argue that they merely demonstrate individual users' masochistic tendencies. Rather, as I will show, these spaces are composed of a bricolage of cultural assumptions around femininity which users deploy as a means of expressing a pro-ana identity.

Before attending to the spaces themselves, it is important to state what I mean by *normative* femininity, particularly when femininity is neither substantive nor fixed (Butler 1990), but an 'ever-changing, homogenizing, elusive ideal' (Bordo [1993] 2003, p. 166). In line with Scharff (2012), I read it through Butler's (1990) notion of gender intelligibility whereby 'heterosexual conventions structure the coherence of sex, gender, and desire' (Scharff 2012, p. 14). Nonetheless, as chapter four explored, not only sexuality, but race, age, embodiment and class all offer themselves as matrices through which gender is constructed. As such, I understand normative femininity as a form of gender production which operates in tandem with – as opposed to critiquing – the status quo. This is not to deny that practices of femininity can provide enjoyment, or as Hannah McCann (2017) has argued, queer meaning. Rather, my concern is not only the way pain is central to normative femininity, but the extent to which it is *disguised* as pleasurable.

One way feminists – especially during the second wave – have understood feminine beauty practices, is through the lens of suffering. Whether it is the brief sting of plucking one's eyebrows, the day-long discomfort of walking in high-heeled shoes, or the longer-term pain of cosmetic surgery, 'no price is too great, no process too repulsive, no operation too painful for the woman who would be beautiful' (Dworkin 1974, p. 115). Femininity proper thus requires women to undergo painful procedures in order to achieve it and, such suffering is invariably presented as empowering and pleasurable, as critics of postfeminism Gill and McRobbie have shown. Gill notes that in postfeminist culture, even 'the application of boiling wax to the genital region and then its use to pull out hairs by their roots can be discursively (re)constructed as "pampering"' (2009, p. 105). The postfeminist subject is expected to suffer actively, for this is what it means to be a woman (McRobbie 2009, p. 98). McCann, however, makes an important intervention, arguing that 'it is not *femininity* that makes girls ill, but rather, it is the conditions under late capitalism that drive *all of us* to sickness' (2017, p. 14; emphases in original). Understanding this differentiation is crucial if we are to fully comprehend contemporary pro-ana culture: femininity is not the problem *perse*, rather it is the postfeminist neoliberal context in which it is situated.

The painful body modification activity with which women are targeted, such as dieting, exercise, cosmetic surgery and even hair-removal, are all presented as solutions to assuage the pain they are supposed to feel at failing at be properly feminine. Liz Frost argues that 'western consumer capitalism needs women to feel their bodies are inadequate, so that they spend large amounts of money on products to alleviate this sense' (2001, p. 29; see also Bartky 2004, p. 24). Pain in this context, whether physical or emotional, is a female economy, but the question remains, how does pro-anorexia, a user-generated phenomenon, fit into it? As Carole Spitzack says of *anorexia*, it 'offers images of females who at once support and undermine the performance criteria regulating gender in contemporary capitalism' (1993, p. 3) and Day and Keys have made similar arguments about pro-anorexia websites (2008a, 2008b, 2009). However, I argue that contemporary incarnations of pro-ana online ostensibly coincide with a capitalist agenda more than they critique it.

In order to communicate that they are pro-anorexic, users perform an identity which draws on cultural understandings of pain and suffering. This is not to deny the very real pain these individuals are likely enduring, but to argue that they communicate their suffering in line with previously established cultural tropes which signal to others their membership of a specific group. Erving Goffman uses the term 'front' to describe the figurative mask worn during the individual's performance of the self, arguing that 'when an actor takes on an established social role, usually he [sic] finds that a particular front has already been established for it' (1969, p. 37). Goffman may have been writing about human interaction in the physical world, but this applies equally to interaction online. In an Instagram search for the hashtag 'ana', a user posts what appears to be a selfie of a young girl slouching in a baggy black t-shirt, her head obscured from view. The image is captioned only with a heart emoji. When another user comments, 'Heya, wanna check out my page?' the original poster responds with a stream of hashtags, presumably intended to communicate her troubled state of mind. Through this list of words, we are able to garner that the user is struggling to recover from anorexia: '#ed #scared #fuckrecovery', that her mental health is suffering: '#suicide #depressed #selfharmmm #voices #anxiety #mentalillness' and she is unhappy with her physical appearance '#fat #ugly' The pain she wishes to communicate has been converted into hashtags, neatly categorising her with others who suffer similarly. As users learn that attendant to anorexia hashtags are those which invoke self-harm and depression, such posts become self-generating.

Using hashtags to express suffering might seem an unorthodox approach, but for pro-ana users it is an effective means of being heard. Elaine Scarry famously argued that language fails to adequately express physical pain (1996, p. 4). For Ann Jurecic (2012), this may be true of the extreme pain of torture, which Scarry examines in detail, but the same cannot be said of milder forms of pain. The problem here, argues Jurecic (2012, p. 44), 'is not how to find a language for pain, but rather how to make readers receptive to stories of pain'. The pro-ana user who deploys hashtags to communicate her suffering, is able to measure the receptiveness of her readers through the 'likes' she may receive to her post or, for example, when the hashtags she coins are adopted by others. Whereas, in the forums users engage in longer form discussions where they find like-minded others who are receptive to their suffering.

In chapter one, I attended to the female saints of the medieval period: women who were said to punish themselves through austere practices to show their devotion to God. Likewise, self-punishment, whether mental or physical is a key element of pro-ana identity. Pro-ana site, *Ethereal Anas* advises on engaging in painful activity as way of distracting oneself from the desire to eat, including a tip which recurs throughout pro-ana online spaces: 'Keep an elastic band on your wrist at all times. Whenever you think about eating, tie it even tighter and snap it'. Users are advised to abuse themselves in order to achieve their goals:

> Bite yourself [...] Tie yourself down if you have to [...] Put your favourite foods in the freezer [...] Spill tea, salt, pepper, or anything gross on your food "by accident" [...] Sit on your hands [...] Cut your hair short, then you won't be so upset when it starts falling out.
>
> (*Ethereal Anas*)

This advice chimes with Bell's description of the holy anorexic:

> The girl, that she may become more beautiful in God's eyes, may cut off her hair, scourge her face and wear coarse rags. To be more mindful of the Passion she may walk about with thirty-three sharp stones in her shoes or drive silver nails into her breasts. She stands through the night with her arms outstretched in penitential prayer and stops eating, taking her nourishment from the host.
>
> (1985, p. 19)

The contemporaneous pro-ana user may not act in such an extreme way, and unlike the pious women of the medieval period, she does not foul her food or self-mortify to become closer to Christ. Albeit, the outcome is the same: a starved and suffering body in pursuit of what she believes to be a higher purpose. In other words, anorectics – past and present – are embroiled in a quest for their own Holy Grail. Newer pro-ana online spaces may not draw on such religious rhetoric but their desire for self-punishment remains the same. Above all, users of these spaces – old and new – are engaging in performances of the self which have already been established by Western cultural beliefs around anorexia and femininity and they are now being perpetuated online.

Investing in pain

In contemporary culture, pain is all too often presented something we must endure if we are to be deserving of success: whether in the workplace or in our personal lives, pain must be acknowledged then overcome before we merit any kind of reward. Pain, as I argued above, pervades beauty culture: 'beauty is pain' as the old adage goes, and in some cases, tolerating pain for the purposes of an improved physical appearance is read as honourable. Jones argues that in makeover television for instance,

> [cosmetic surgery] is removed from vanity and narcissism and becomes something that requires motivation, something that tough and hardy people with a strong ethic of self-improvement consider: it becomes an act of courage, bravery and self-determination.
>
> (2008, pp. 53–54)

Similarly, in pro-ana online spaces pain is frequently understood as a compulsory investment one must make in order to realise, and be worthy of, the ideal body. Pain and hard work were often conflated in the sample analysed for this study, thereby reinforcing Hesse-Biber's argument that the fitness movement is a new form of *asceticism* (1996, p. 45). Whilst many pro-ana posts promote hard work and self-discipline, the gains such users seek are not pious. Rather, the pro-ana approach to self-discipline dovetails more with an *aesthetic* attitude to the body. The synthesis of hard-work and the pursuit of the body beautiful which pervades mainstream culture has led Simon J. Williams to suggest that 'the boundaries between the ascetic and aesthetic, in this context, become blurred' (2003, p. 33). The pro-ana user then does not engage in such drudgery out of religious service to God, rather she does so in the hope of realising the body she desires, and in the process, she draws on normative beauty practices.

Compulsory suffering is constructed in a number of ways in pro-ana online spaces, as can be seen in the diverse results generated by hashtag or keyword searches on social media platforms. For instance, one search for 'thinspiration' on Tumblr yields an amalgamation of different posts: from those depicting images of self-laceration and emaciated bodies, to those of motivational slogans and women in workout wear. These varying approaches to weight loss have all been posted by different users but are united by #thinspiration. Users whose quest for thinness involves self-harm tend to post images of their self-mutilated arms, legs or stomachs. In one post, a user is shown having carved the word 'fat' into her thigh with a sharp object. This evokes Franz Kafka's penal colony where 'the condemned man has the commandment he has transgressed inscribed on his body with the harrow' ([1919] 1992, p. 131). In this thinspiration post though, the transgression itself is inscribed on the woman's body. Still, the outcome is the same: both the condemned man and the self-punishing woman have their sentence etched into them, and for the pro-anorectic, being fat is the heaviest sentence of all. Conversely, other posts generated by the same 'thinspiration' search draw on the upbeat rhetoric of self-help, with motivational statements such as, 'Good things come to those who work'. This declaration appears to be an adaptation of the popular proverb, 'All things come to those who wait', which suggests that patience brings rewards (Simpson and Speake 2009a). Replacing 'wait' with 'work' illustrates the extent to which work has pervaded all areas of life under late capitalism: one cannot simply sit and wait, one must work to achieve one's desired future, whatever the cost. For Scarry, work itself is a form of pain, 'a diminution of pain: the *aversive intensity* of pain becomes in work *controlled discomfort*' (1985, p. 171, emphases in original). The pro-ana user who transforms the pain of anorexia into work on the self is able to render it worthwhile, hence, '*controlled discomfort*'. However, the 'good things' the user hopes to acquire through 'work' will almost certainly never materialise, for the toil to achieve the ideal self is ultimately 'a laborious fiction' (McGee 2005, p. 174). This is reinforced by another user's post which bears the statement 'don't stop until you are proud', yet such pride rarely manifests and users in these posts appear to be condemned never to stop. This is because femininity is a continual process of becoming (Driscoll 2002) and in the culture of the self-improvement, upon which pro-ana online spaces draw, '*becoming* is more desirable than *being*' (Jones 2008, p. 12; emphases in original).

As such, pain is often presented as something users actively and happily undergo, rather than that to which they passively and miserably submit.

During the research period, posts generated on Pinterest tended to be the most upbeat in tone, focusing as they do on motivating users. They frame pain as a necessary investment should one want to reap the rewards of the ideal body. A 'thinspiration' search on Pinterest, like the Tumblr search discussed above, yields numerous posts by a range of users, but all such posts evoke the extent to which hard work and suffering are necessary for achieving thinness. One post reproduces supermodel Kate Moss's infamous statement, 'Nothing tastes as good as skinny feels': her response when asked in an interview if she had any mottos, which led to public condemnation and outrage (Wardrop 2009). This quote appears regularly in pro-ana online spaces, its implications being that no food can bring as much pleasure as can being skinny. This is reinforced by an adjacent post which reads 'This month's diet is next month's body', emblazoned across the body of a slim and toned white woman. Such statements serve as a reminder that the work one does in the present will bring future prosperity. This is emphasised by another post featuring an image of a woman doing sit-ups, and the text, 'Stop saying tomorrow', beneath which reads the caption, 'No pain no gain!'. These posts are unforgiving and suggest that there is no excuse not to diet and exercise; if you want the ideal body, sacrifices must be made. The sentiment of 'no pain no gain' may find its roots in austere Puritan practices, but today, it is simply another tenet of self-improvement culture: it has permeated 'everyday parlance to describe that desirable results require undesirable associated by-products, such as in the finance sector (Pain 2009) and education (Rendón et al.1998)' (Kramer et al. 2012, p. 518). The problem with such a motto is that it can be used to justify even the most undignified suffering (Kilwein 1989) and the pro-ana user who welcomes the deterioration of her body in order to achieve ideal thinness is perpetuating this sentiment.

The term itself dates back to 1577 when it appeared in British poet Nicholas Breton's *Works of Young Wit* as: 'They must take pain that look for any gayn' (Simpson and Speake 2009b), suggesting one must endure pain, if one wishes to profit. It entered popular culture when it was adopted by Jane Fonda as her exercise slogan in 1982 to suggest that physical pain was necessary in order to achieve bodybuilding success (Kramer et al. 2012, p. 518). Fonda's use of the term made pain and gain about bodily improvement. On a superficial level, Fonda claimed to resist cultural norms of femininity, and she urged other women to do so too (Spitzack 1993, p. 17). However, her assertions of resistance ultimately fell short given that her espousal of a 'near-fatless ideal correspond[ed] to an archetypical male body' (Dinnerstein and Weitz 1994, p. 12). Therefore, 'no pain, no gain' in this context suggests that if women do not undergo the pain attendant with achieving the taut and toned body, they will never reap the gains which here come to stand in for the Freudian 'lack'[1] with which they have been blighted, simply by dint of being women. Fonda herself was able to gain legitimacy by reworking masculine discourses which value strength and muscle definition over softness and curves whilst still maintaining a feminine appearance. She therefore embraced the contradictory demands of femininity which require 'women to embody the "masculine" values of the public arena' whilst also being femininely attractive (Bordo [1993] 2003, p. 173). This is undergirded by cultural understandings of femininity as inadequate.

Fonda's legacy persists in the pro-ana online spaces examined. A 'thynspo' search on Pinterest yields numerous images and text, which clearly state that pain is equated with gain. For instance, an image depicting a slim white woman jogging is emblazoned with a statement light-heartedly cautioning the reader as follows: 'You'll get a lot more compliments for working out than you will for sleeping in'. Here, motivation is invoked with the promise of others' admiration (as per thinspiration content examined in previous chapters). At the same time, the post juxtaposes the disciplined, slim, early-riser who will be respected by others, with the lazy, implicitly overweight, late sleeper who will probably be disregarded. The hashtags accompanying this post are serious in tone: as well as alluding to health and fitness, they invoke the resolve with which the user is pursuing an ideal body: '#thynspo #eatcleantrainmean #sweat #muscles #strength #trainmean #eatclean #progress #diet #inspiration #determined #motivation #dedicated #pain #gain #exercise'. The user reiterates the need to train 'mean', thereby suggesting a no-nonsense approach to exercise. Further, by using the hashtags, 'sweat', 'muscles' and 'strength', her approach to weight loss more closely echoes the language of masculine bodybuilding (see Heywood 1998) than that of feminine loveliness discussed in the previous chapter. Consequently, pro-anorexia online spaces illustrate a conflict between active, masculine and passive, feminine forms of body disciplining, and active and passive forms of pain. A post on Instagram generated by #ana highlights this conflict. It features an image of a white, female athlete mid-run, emblazoned with the text 'There is no pain that I cannot endure and no pain that I will not fight through', a statement which echoes the 'militaristic and warrior analogies' used in bodybuilding (Fussell and Saltman cited in Bunsell 2013, pp. 118–119). On the contrary, the hashtags accompanying this post, such as '#bulimia #dead #cut #kill' do not imply that the user is *building* her body, rather they suggest that she is destroying it. However, she constructs her approach to pain as both noble and one in which she is complicit. Here, she is more the agentic edgeworker (Gailey 2009)[2] seeking 'embodied morality' through her extraordinary experiences (Gooldin 2008), than a passive sufferer whose pain has been externally imposed.

Whilst users may draw on bodybuilding discourses, they do so with the aim of decreasing, rather than increasing, in size. In particular, building muscle and strength is at odds with achieving very thin legs, which are coveted in pro-ana culture. As such, an image from a 'thynspo' search on Pinterest reads 'Push, push until those thighs don't touch' across a black and white photograph of a person wearing shorts to reveal skinny legs. The user here suggests that by working incredibly hard one will be thin enough to realise the sought-after thigh gap. Nevertheless, the implication is that this can be achieved not through exercise as the physicality of 'push, push' suggests, but through self-starvation as the user's comment below the image indicates: 'And if it means malnourishment, bring it on' – frivolous acknowledgement that there is a correlation between illness and realising the extreme thinness she desires. Users therefore appropriate discourses of hard work and exercise, not as a means of becoming healthier, but to achieve emaciation.

Pro-ana users communicate the importance of losing weight at any cost. The blogger whose tagline reads, 'I don't care if it hurts, I want to have control' (*Fallen Ana*) may be referencing the lyrics to 'Creep' by alternative indie-rock band Radiohead (Yorke 1992), but she also expresses the extent to which her life is consumed by a pain she believes is necessary in order to keep her appetite at bay. In her blog, she advises users to take cold showers and even suggests that they try to 'confuse' their metabolism into burning more calories (*Fallen Ana*). In the data gathered, users would often describe themselves in a battle to subdue the desires of the body. When one Instagram user in a #thinspoooo search posts in despair of her 'fat legs' and her yearning for a thigh-gap, a fellow user writes her a stirring poem urging her not to give up. The poem emphasises strength and independence, insisting, 'you're strongest when you stand alone [...] there's nothing you can't do'. This trope of the individual on a solitary quest corresponds with the ideal postfeminist neoliberal subject who is entirely self-reliant, as well as echoing the repudiation of dependence required of hegemonic masculinity. Ironically, in Western culture the [pro-]anorectic 'who starves herself to stave off cultural notions of dependency and weakness associated with fatness ends up having those same abhorred qualities projected upon her' (Saukko 1999, p. 44). Such projection emerges from research within psychiatry, which has conceived anorexia as 'a dependence disorder, specifically as 'an addiction to starvation' much like drug abuse (Brumberg 1988, p. 31).

A raft of discussions around anorexia examined in this study describe starvation in terms of a chemical high. In a thread on the sense of purity gained from fasting, one user on *Foreverproana* refers to the elation she feels as well as the strong sense of achievement:

> I just love fasting – that feeling of emptiness, no toxins, fats, chemicals. I feel clean and pure. And so proud! Even if zero calorie food existed, I still reckon I'd eat nothing and endure the pain. In fact, I like hunger pain – it means it's working.

She attests to loving the feeling of being able to subsist without food for so long and she also feels pride and validation from the discomfort of hunger; she may be suffering, but she reads this as a sign of success. Other users concur, responding with statements such as 'I love the high I get from fasting' and 'By the second day I'm euphoric' (ibid.). Whether or not users are addicted to self-starvation, Bordo argues that 'the ways in which the subject understands and thematises her experience cannot be reduced to a mechanical process' (Bordo [1993] 2003, p. 180). The anorectic may well feel euphoric from the high produced by starvation, but it is cultural understandings of the female body that frame this as indicative of success and moral purity. Another user in this thread describes fasting thus: 'For me, when I eat I feel dirty, fat and guilty. But when I fast I feel amazing. Clean and good, like fasting is the right thing to do' (*Foreverproana*). These users feel ecstatic when starving, but when the alternative is couched in uncleanliness and guilt they have little choice but to continue self-restricting.

Pro-ana marketing sites exploit these feelings of impurity, but unlike the user-generated pro-ana texts which construct pain as an investment into ideal thinness, the marketing sites portray a commitment to the pro-ana way of life as a *release* from suffering. *Prothinspiration Diet*, which promotes its own diet book, features a testimonial from the author who emphasises the 'pain' and 'suffering' caused by being overweight and suggests that the book can provide salvation:

> I promised myself that I would help others *suffering* from the same overweight problems like me. I committed to myself that what I would not let others *suffers* [sic] from what I *suffered*. I will show them the way out ... They can easily follow my footprints and *come out of that dark life*. I knew that I could talk to these women and inspire them to start taking steps towards *a new life* because I had been in their shoes. I knew the *pain and the depression* that those extra pounds bring with them ... So I wanted to help change others going through same *pain* and wanted to *bring them back to life*.
>
> (2014; emphases added)

Echoing my earlier discussion of the religious anorectic, weight loss here is described in terms of spiritual enlightenment, as having the potential to save the wretched from darkness. The verb to suffer occurs three times in this testimony and on many more occasions throughout the site. The author implies that, in being overweight, one is not truly alive. By implication, following this diet book will restore life, and a better one at that. Such a testimonial is evangelical in tone, but as Mary G. Winkler notes, 'when we speak of faith and virtue in the context of physical improvement, we have entered a thought world where the subject is thoroughly secular but the language is that of morality and theology' (1994, p. 217). In order to sell diet books, *Prothinspiration Diet* co-opts not only the rhetoric of pro-ana, but that of religious salvation.

The narrative of *Prothinspiration Diet* is not unique to pro-ana, it also echoes the paradigm used in makeover television to which I referred at the start of this section. Shows such as *Ten Years Younger* follow a 'submerged, quasi-religious discourse of ritual abjection and redemption' whereby women undergo an image overhaul comprising cosmetic surgery and new clothes in order to shuffle off the unsightliness of their former selves and emerge as an acceptable form of femininity (Tincknell 2011, p. 93; see also Jones 2008; Wearing 2007). The surgery administered by *Ten Years Younger*, and the diet advice meted out by *Prothinspiration Diet* may cause immense pain, but the postfeminist makeover paradigm teaches us that nothing is as painful as being physically unattractive. In short, many pro-ana online spaces articulate their suffering in such a way that it coincides with the compulsory pain required of the ideal postfeminist neoliberal subject.

Lamenting pain

Although many pro-ana texts convert the pain of anorexia into a worthwhile experience which comes with the reward of normative femininity, many do not. Instead, users write openly about depression or they express rage at the impossibility of achieving the thin ideal. In so doing, they highlight uncomfortable truths about thinness culture. It is not only self-imposed physical pain, such as cutting and hunger, which are represented in pro-ana online spaces, mental and emotional pain play a key part in the life of the [pro-] anorectic too. References to depression are ubiquitous, both via the deployment of #depression and more detailed discussions in the forums.

In *Foreverproana*'s subsection on mental health, one user asks if others are depressed and if they believe it is related to their eating disorder. The responders are generally in agreement that their depression is not related to their eating disorder:

> I don't honestly know why I'm depressed. I don't think it's related to my eating disorder, but they seem to go together/I've been depressed for most of my twenties now. It's not linked to my ED, but I don't exactly love my body/Same, anorexia makes it worse but I don't think it causes it.
>
> (*Foreverproana*)

Only one user claims that her depression is eating disorder related, and the thread is concluded by one subscriber who states: 'I think they are definitely linked: an ED can make you more depressed and depression can bring on an ED' (ibid.). Whether causal or not, depression and eating disorders are constantly aligned in pro-ana online spaces. It is, however, unclear what users mean when they declare that they are depressed or deploy '#depressed' in a post. On the one hand, they could be referring to a clinical diagnosis, on the other, they could be hyperbolically exclaiming their annoyance at not being as thin as they wish. There are certainly gradations of seriousness and flippancy with which this word is used and, whilst the thread referenced above certainly errs more on the serious side, 'depression' is often deployed offhandedly in these spaces.

It could be argued that pro-ana enthusiasts present the extent to which they suffer, both mentally and physically, as a form of capital. Discussions and posts on the level of pain and discomfort an individual endures often serve as a means of gaining the respect and admiration of others. This is illuminated in *Foreverproana* where users compile two lists on the pros and cons respectively of being skinny. The former consists of what they deem to be the advantages of having an emaciated body, the most referenced being the ability to wear children's clothes, to be physically smaller than men and to be able to fit into small spaces. The feminine ideal of taking up as little space as possible (see Bartky 1990) is pursued to its logical conclusion here. However, users also acknowledge that a drawback of such thinness is being verbally abused by men. One individual states: 'The other day, I was walking to the bus stop and I had loads of layers on – you couldn't even see my body properly but two lads shouted at me. It was so embarrassing – I'm not even that skinny' (*Foreverproana*). The individual appears confused as to why these men shouted at her – citing her covered body and not being 'that skinny' as reasons. This corroborates victim-blaming discourses wherein women are at fault for how men respond to them because of what they wear (or do not wear) and thus, 'the female body [...] is neither safe in the bikini where it is on full display or inside the burqa where it is fully veiled' (Duits and van Zoonen cited in Ringrose and Renold 2012, p. 334). Another user concurs, detailing a similar experience: 'Eww men are disgusting. I'm not that skinny either but I always get shouted at when I'm out – told I need more meat on my bones etc.' (ibid.). Whilst users bemoan such taunts, and fleetingly criticise men's sense of entitlement over the female body, these stories operate as opportunities for them to show off their extreme thinness using the words of others, rather than their own. Furthermore, by describing such incidences as 'embarrassing' or irritating, coupled with the assertion that they are not 'that skinny', users retain a sense of modesty which reinforces a normatively feminine identity.

As the discussion on the benefits of thinness dwindles, users begin to deliberate over its perceived problems and a participant instigates the second list on 'the cons of being skinny'. Here users discuss the pain and discomfort they undergo as a result of being so thin: examples range from the mildly inconvenient and comedic, to the more serious. One user complains of the annoyance of objects falling between her thighs, lacking as they do a buffer of fat which would prevent this:

> It's so annoying when I drop things and they fall through my thigh gap. Once I dropped a cigarette and it fell down the toilet. This evening a slice of cucumber from my salad fell through the gap and landed on the kitchen floor.
>
> (*Foreverproana*)

The user casually alludes to the sought-after thigh gap which many users complain is impossible to achieve. Therefore, predicaments such as dropping food and cigarettes through the gap may be 'annoying' but, they are also valued given that they only happen to those who have realised such an emaciated state. Another user initiates a list of problems which indicate that her body is struggling to maintain extreme thinness, and others add to it:

> Getting back pain in lectures because my bones dig into the chairs/Being unable to warm up from the cold and shivering for ages/Not sleeping properly cos of waking up so much from being cold/Standing up and feeling like I'm going to faint.
>
> *(Foreverproana)*

Users list reason upon reason as to why being thin is difficult, yet the subtext is that such problems are desirable and a sign that one is successfully starving. As one user writes after listing her ailments, '... I wouldn't change it for anything' *(Foreverproana)*. The suffering these individuals describe differentiates them from those who do not self-starve and simultaneously aligns them with their desired group.

These descriptions evoke an ethereal body: one with a gap through which objects may pass, one which bears so little fat that its bones rub directly against external surfaces, a body that is vulnerable to the cold and so weak it is barely able to stay upright. The ethereal thin woman has been explored in depth by Malson (1998) who found her anorexic informants drew on such cultural representations to make sense of their experiences. She argues that although the image of the ethereal woman dovetails with normative femininity, her liminality offers possibilities for transcending the certain death so often ascribed to anorectics. I suggest this applies to pro-ana contexts too: even when users are lamenting the pain of anorexia, by describing it in a way that makes them special or different may render such pain bearable. However, given that anorexia and the thin ideal operate on a continuum, such constructions of pain are at risk of being mined to reinforce thinness – and illness for that matter – as normative feminine attributes. In particular, the image of the ethereal woman resonates with the coveted consumptive look of the Victorian period that 'considered illness to be a source of female beauty, where in fact fashionable beauty was the source of illness' (Vandereycken and Van Deth 1994, p. 215). In such representations, normative feminine beauty and suffering are conflated. As Susan Sontag points out, during this time, 'agony became romantic in a stylized account of the disease's preliminary symptoms (for example, debility is transformed into languor) and the actual agony was simply suppressed' (1978, p. 29). Pro-ana subjects who espouse a romanticised or fashionable version of the effects of self-starvation then, may find that their extreme thinness is more readily accepted, but the painful lived experience of anorexia is obscured. In short, pro-ana online spaces depict women who are suffering deeply because of a culture which undermines their gender; however, when their depictions of pain dovetail with those prescribed by normative femininity, possibilities for resistance may be thwarted.

This is not to say that users uncritically accept idealised images of normative femininity: the sample yielded numerous images users had uploaded to denounce, either directly or indirectly. For instance, posts depicting women in stages of undress and in eroticised poses may elicit male appreciation, but they are also often accompanied by hashtags or an ensuing discussion which is anything but erotic. An image captioned, 'All that glitters' on the subreddit, *thinspirationpics* seemingly typifies the posts in this space: it depicts a woman semi-naked, her back arched and head thrown back in a pose simulating orgasm; in other words, it echoes the mainstreaming of pornographic traits described by Gill (2009, p. 94). However, in the Barthesian sense, it is also polysemous. The image evokes a troubling conflation of sexual pleasure and violence: this woman could have thrown her head back in desire, but equally, she could have been forced against the wall. Her ribs are exposed, her bones jut and her sinews are visible, yet her eyes are obscured, which intensifies the opacity of her pose. Her skin is damp, and the tiled surroundings suggest she is in a bathroom. On the one hand, the image evokes feminine power: it can be read as a woman who is in control of her body and her sexuality, but on the other, blue and grey lighting evokes coldness and is resonant of death: a body outstretched in a morgue. Either way, this image reproduces the cultural trope of female suffering, and as Rosalind Coward notes, 'not only do [such images] reinforce ideologies of sexuality as female submission to male force, but they also powerfully re-circulate the connection between sexuality and death which is so cruelly played out in our society' (1982, p. 18). The woman in this post echoes such a connection, evoking simultaneously the erotic and violent morbidity.

The title of the image, 'All that glitters', however, complicates such meanings. It appears to refer to the woman's skin, which shimmers in its dampness, and it is also an elliptical variation of the oft-quoted line from Shakespeare's *The Merchant of Venice*: 'All that glisters is not gold' ([1600] 1997, II.VII, 65). In the play, suitor to Portia, the Prince of Morocco unwisely chooses the golden casket and instead of winning Portia's hand, he is met with a written scroll which he reads aloud: 'All that glisters is not gold' (ibid.); in other words, not everything is as it seems. The *thinspirationpics* user, in applying this quote to the image of an emaciated woman, suggests that although she may outwardly gleam, her reality is more sombre. In the play, Morocco subsequently states, 'Gilded [tombs] do worms infold' (II.VII, 69): even if one rests in a golden vault, fate is the same for all: to be eaten by worms. Whether wittingly or not, pro-ana users acknowledge the immense pain, and even fatality, in maintaining extreme thinness. Nevertheless, the critique invariably falters at this point: users may expose the harsh reality of thinness culture, but in the moment where this might be used to mobilise resistance, they turn the critique on themselves.

This occurs in a post yielded by a 'bonespo' search on Instagram which depicts an image of a slim, tanned girl in a state of undress. This is accompanied by a caption describing how the user is feeling, along with a set of hashtags.

The description of the user's emotional state however is at odds with the image posted: a young woman posing suggestively; her lips are parted and her arms are behind her head as if to invite the viewer to look upon her; her face is in shadow, thus further drawing the focus to her body. Her tanned skin is accentuated by a white top, which could either be a bikini or her underwear, the ambiguity of which surely has the intention of titillation. However, the text accompanying this image is far from sensual. The author's username, 'hungertilithurts' references starvation and pain so as to display the magnitude of her weight-loss ambition. She indicates that her current weight is just over seven and a half stone. The ensuing text is an expression of her anger and frustration at not having lost enough weight, despite, as she suggests, not eating. She rages:

> How the f*** can I put on weight when I don't even eat?? I don't get it. Why?? I hate myself and I just want to take a knife and cut the fat off. Seriously I'd do a cleanse but I have nothing in me to get rid of!

The user is wracked with self-hatred and anger that she has gained weight despite apparently having not eaten. She assigns a number of hashtags to her post to reinforce how she is feeling:

> #thinspoooo #thynspoo #thin #skinny #starving #sad #depressed #size00 #anorexia #anamia #thygap #hipbones #bulimic #bonespo #blithe *#notme* #eatingdisorder #ednos #donteat.
>
> (emphasis mine)

These tags range from spelling variations of thinspo, the user's desire for a thigh gap, the sadness and depression she is experiencing, and a hashtag often used in pro-ana spaces: 'notme'. The regular deployment of #notme in these spaces is instructive: it is used on social media to signal that an image does not depict the user who has posted it. In this context, however, it also functions to expose the gulf between idealised standards of beauty and the way users perceive themselves. Here, the user directs her anger at herself, but it might be more usefully directed at the impossibility of achieving '"woman as image", forever unattainable, always invoking a sense of lack' (Thornham 2007, p. 43). Ultimately, for the pro-ana subject, the ideal will never be #me, because it is always held out of reach.

A search for #thinspoooo on Instagram produces a post by another equally incensed user who expresses her wrath in a monologue uncharacteristically long for this platform. The user's main source of anger is that her posts are being removed by moderators, and her diatribe is accompanied by an archetypal pro-ana image: a half-naked emaciated woman, reclining so as to emphasise her exposed ribcage – although she does not make it clear whether or not the image depicts her. The attendant hashtags predominantly evoke despair though, rather than anger: '#suicidal #selfhate #depressed #misery

#thygap #unwanted #fat #ugly #selfmutilation #mia #ana'. These terms recall a person who is suffering deeply: not only is she anorexic and bulimic, she cuts herself and is suicidal. That is, she has turned the anger and pain she feels on to herself. The caption, by contrast, is an outward projection of the user's anger which she appears to be directing at the moderators of Instagram. Replete with exclamation marks, swear words, capital letters and typographical errors, the user's fury is palpable. She argues that she only uses this account to 'help' her, as 'a way to vent' and that her followers stop her feeling 'so lonely'. She rages:

> So now my posts are being removed because they are apparently self-harm. How? I'm not telling people to hurt themselves! This account is the only thing that stops me feeling so alone. Stop telling me I need help. You try f***ing being in a treatment centre with actual crazy people! I've been there. Sure, I want to be thin and I'm depressed but that doesn't mean I'm crazy and should be locked up. Just leave me the hell alone.

The user is insistent on differentiating herself from those she deems 'crazy': her depression and desire to be thin, she tells us, is not 'crazy'. By accompanying her statement with a posed image, she suggests she simply wants to be slim and attractive like the woman pictured, and what is so 'crazy' about that? She claims that her behaviour is normal and, from a postfeminist perspective, it is, because she is merely expressing 'healthy signs of unhealthy femininity' (McRobbie 2009, p. 96). She is therefore understandably confused as to why this makes her 'crazy'. At the same time, this post highlights the discrepancy between image, text and hashtag, given that all three communicate different sentiments around what it means to be pro-ana.

I argue that posts such as these hold the potential to act as an exposé of the contradictions inherent in the aspirational culture of 'unhealthy femininity', and the older pro-ana sites are even more explicit about what this entails. In the tips and tricks section of *Ethereal Anas*, for example, the author unambiguously details what one should expect from extreme weight loss. She tells users: 'Relish constipation and enjoy being bloated [..] Take pride in your hair shedding all over the place [...] Halitosis means you are succeeding with anorexia because your gut is decomposing'. The author points to the trauma of hair loss, to digestive problems and bad breath, all of which are to be cherished, because they are evidence that the user is successfully losing weight. Femininity is presented here as bound, quite literally, to the disintegration of the body: hair falling out and guts rotting. Ironically, as the pro-anorectic becomes closer to disappearing, she nears her goal. These candid representations of the pain of anorexia thus operate as antidotes to the pro-ana texts which frame suffering to be skinny as a worthwhile investment: they show the viewer that pain may not ultimately yield gain.

Conclusion

This chapter has examined how pain is articulated in pro-ana online spaces. It has shown how many pro-ana online texts construct pain as a necessary by-product of achieving the thin ideal and filter it through discourses of hard work and self-improvement. Yet, it has also demonstrated how others denounce such suffering – even on the newer social media spaces – and rage against the culture of compulsory thinness. In short, I argue that together these contrasting articulations of pain expose the suffering inherent in not only anorexia but normative femininity too.

In the first section I interrogated the cultural history of pain and femininity, showing how cultural hallmarks as diverse as Freudian masochism, consumer capitalism and self-starving medieval saints have tethered pain and femininity in such a way that suffering to be a woman is seen as routine. The pro-anorexia phenomenon is thus situated within discourses of femininity which pre-date it by centuries: it holds striking parallels with the practices of the pious women of the Middle Ages, yet it also resonates with contemporary self-improvement culture. Thus, the fellowship of pro-anorexia may initially appear strange and perverse to many, however, upon closer examination the solidarity these women find echoes that of normative femininity, much of which Bartky points out, 'clings to the disciplines' (2004, p. 23). Western cultural understandings of femininity have taught us that women are supposed to suffer, therefore pro-anorexia is, regrettably, a logical step in a culture which demands women undergo physically painful procedures in order to be beautiful. If psychopathologies are invariably the crystallisation of what is wrong with a culture (Bordo [1993] 2003, p. 141) then pro-anorexia is a manifestation of cultural ills *par excellence*.

The second section of this chapter attended to the discourse of 'no pain, no gain' that pervades pro-ana culture. Here I showed how users frame the pain of extreme weight loss as a meaningful investment. Drawing on the language of hard work and dedication is one way pro-ana spaces are able to legitimise themselves, for, when bodily suffering is presented in terms of a noble quest, it is less likely to be read as pathology. Nonetheless, even when users adopt bodybuilding rhetoric for instance, they often disrupt its meanings by interspersing it with pro-ana lexis. This is both amplified and reversed in pro-ana marketing spaces which assume the grammar of pro-ana in attempts to reach new demographics with their weight-loss products. Such spaces present adherence to their guidance as a means of release from the pain of being fat. Despite this, whether user-generated or a front for weight-loss marketing, by articulating pro-ana practices in the language of postfeminist neoliberal self-improvement, these spaces are merging with mainstream diet culture. And in so doing, they expose the pain of normative femininity.

In the final section, I explored the way users lament the miserable reality of extreme weight loss. They rage against images of apparently perfect women, hashtagging them with terms such as 'not me' and 'depressed'. In spite of this, even when users discuss 'the cons of being skinny', there is still a sense that their suffering is desirable. As the posts analysed show, users recount their self-starving experiences to paradoxically distinguish themselves as pro-ana and in so doing they find common ground with a group of women who understand them. Although they lay bare the pain involved in achieving the thin ideal, users invariably turn their suffering inwards, blaming themselves for not being good enough. Put differently, they may acknowledge that 'All that glisters is not gold', but they remain steadfast in their desire to pursue it nonetheless. Such documenting of pain in pro-anorexia online spaces may reveal the suffering required of anorexia and of normative femininity, but users themselves 'do not undermine the oppressive power of beauty ideals' (Gimlin 2002, p. 146). What my enquiries show however, is the extraordinary will and commitment of a group of young women who will go to extreme lengths to achieve their goals. If such focus and determination could be harvested for political good, these women could organise a movement to destabilise the culture which insists they suffer. For this reason, censorship and vilification of these spaces is ever more problematic: pro-ana culture offers an important, albeit troubling, insight into twenty-first century femininity. Not only does it show how young people cope with disordered eating, it also shows how they negotiate the gendered constraints of the ideal body.

Notes

1 In his short essay, 'The Dissolution of the Oedipus Complex', Freud narrates the moment the girl child compares her genitalia to that of the boy, and in seeing his penis, 'perceives that she has "come off badly" and she feels this as a wrong done to her and as a ground for inferiority' ([1924] 1991, p. 320). Put differently, women, upon realising that they do not have a penis, according to Freud, come to understand their gender in terms of deficiency or lack.
2 Gailey defines edgework thus: 'According to Lyng (1990, p. 857), edgework includes activities that involve a "clearly observable threat to one's physical or mental well-being or one's sense of an ordered existence"' (2009, p. 95).

References

Bartky, S.L. (1990) *Femininity and Domination: Studies in the Phenomenology of Oppression*. New York: Routledge.

————. (2004) 'Suffering to be beautiful', in Bartky, S.L. (eds.) *"Sympathy and Solidarity" and Other Essays*. Lanham, MD: Rowman & Littlefield Publishers, Inc, pp. 13–29.

Bell, R. M. (1985) *Holy Anorexia*. Chicago: University of Chicago Press.

Bordo, S. ([1993] 2003) *Unbearable Weight: Feminism, Western Culture and the Body*, 10th anniversary edition. Berkeley: University of California Press.

Brumberg, J.J. (1988) *Fasting Girls: The History of Anorexia Nervosa*. Cambridge, MA: Harvard University Press.

Bunsell, T. (2013) *Strong and Hard Women: An Ethnography of Female Bodybuilding*. Abingdon, OX: Routledge.

Butler, J. (1990) *Gender Trouble: Feminism and the Subversion of Identity*. New York: Routledge.

Coward, R. (1982) 'Sexual violence and sexuality', *Feminist Review*, 11, pp. 9–22.

Davis, K. (1995) *Reshaping the Female Body*. New York and London: Routledge.

Day, K. and Keys, T. (2008a) 'Starving in cyberspace: A discourse analysis of pro-eating-disorder websites', *Journal of Gender Studies*, 17 (1), pp. 1–15.

———. (2008b) 'Starving in cyberspace: The construction of identity on "pro-eating-disorder websites"', in Riley, S., Burns, M., Frith, H., Wiggins, S., and Markula, P. (eds.) *Critical Bodies: Representations, Identities and Practices of Weight and Body Management*. Basingstoke, Hampshire: Palgrave Macmillan, pp. 81–100.

———. (2009) 'Anorexia/bulimia as resistance and conformity in pro-Ana and pro-Mia virtual conversations', in Malson, H. and Burns, M. (eds.) *Critical Feminist Approaches to Eating Dis/orders*. London: Routledge, pp. 87–96.

Dinnerstein, M. and Weitz, R. (1994) 'Jane Fonda, Barbara Bush and other aging nodies: femininity and the limits of resistance', *Feminist Issues*, 14 (2), pp. 3–24.

Driscoll, C. (2002) *Girls: Feminine Adolescence in Popular Culture and Cultural Theory*. New York: Columbia University Press.

Dworkin, A. (1974) *Woman Hating*. New York: E. P. Dutton.

Foucault, M. (1979) *Discipline and Punish: The Birth of the Prison*. Sheridan, A.M. (trans.) London: Penguin.

Freud, S. ([1924] 1991) 'The dissolution of the oedipus complex', in Richards, A. and Strachey, J. (trans.) *On Sexuality*. London: Penguin, pp. 313–322.

Frost, L. (2001) *Young Women and the Body: A Feminist Sociology*. Basingstoke, Hampshire: Palgrave Macmillan.

Gailey, J.A. (2009) '"Starving is the most fun a girl can have": The pro-ana subculture as edgework', *Critical Criminology*, 17, pp. 93–108.

Gill, R. (2009) 'Supersexualise me! Advertising and the "midriffs"', in Attwood, F. (eds.) *Mainstreaming Sex: The Sexualisation of Western Culture*. London: I.B. Tauris & Co. Ltd, pp. 93–109.

Gimlin, D. L. (2002) *Body Work: Beauty and Self-Image in American Culture*. Berkeley: University of California Press.

Goffman, E. (1969) *The Presentation of Self in Everyday Life*. London: Penguin.

Gooldin, S. (2008) 'Being anorexic hunger, subjectivity, and embodied morality', *Medical Anthropology Quarterly*, 22 (3), pp. 274–296.

Hesse-Biber, S. (1996) *Am I Thin Enough Yet? The Cult of Thinness and the Commercialization of Identity*. New York: Oxford University Press.

Heywood, L. (1998) *Bodymakers: A Cultural Anatomy of Women's Body Building*. New Brunswick, NJ: Rutgers University Press.

Holmes, S., Drake, S., Odgers, K., and Wilson, J. (2017) 'Feminist approaches to anorexia nervosa: A qualitative study of a treatment group', *Journal of Eating Disorders*, 5 (1), pp. 1–15.

Jones, M. (2008) *Skintight: An Anatomy of Cosmetic Surgery*. Oxford: Berg.

Jurecic, A. (2012) *Illness as Narrative*. Pittsburgh: University of Pittsburgh.

Kafka, F. ([1919] 1992) 'In the penal colony', in Pasley, M. (ed. and trans.) *Metamorphosis and Other Stories*. London: Penguin, pp. 127–153.

Kilwein, J.H. (1989) 'No pain, no gain: A puritan legacy', *Health Education Quarterly*, 16 (Spring), pp. 9–12.

Kramer, T., Irmak, C., Block, L.G., and Ilyuk, V. (2012) 'The effect of a no-pain, no-gain lay theory on product efficacy perceptions', *Marketing Letters*, 23(3), pp. 517–529.

Malson, H. (1998) *The Thin Woman: Feminism, Post-structuralism, and the Social Psychology of Anorexia Nervosa*. New York: Routledge.

McCann, H. (2017) *Queering Femininity: Sexuality, Feminism and the Politics of Presentation*. London: Routledge.

McGee, M. (2005) *Self-Help Inc.: Makeover Culture in American Life*. Oxford: Oxford University Press.

McRobbie, A. (2009) *The Aftermath of Feminism: Gender, Culture and Social Change*. London: Sage Publications Ltd.

Pinterest. (2014) Available at: www.pinterest.com (Accessed July 2014).

Prothinspiration Diet. (2014) *Homepage*. Available at: http://pro-thinspiration.com/index.html (Accessed June 2014).

Reddit. (2014) Available at: www.reddit.com/ (Accessed July 2014).

Ringrose, J. and Renold, E. (2012) 'Slut-shaming, girl power and "sexualisation": Thinking through the politics of the international SlutWalks with teen girls', *Gender and Education*, 24(3), pp. 333–343.

Saukko, P. (1999) 'Fat boys and goody girls: Hilde Bruch's work on eating disorders and the American anxiety about democracy, 1930–1960', in Sobal, J. and Maurer, D. (eds.) *Weighty Issues: Fatness and Thinness as Social Problems*. New York: Aldine de Gruyter, pp. 31–49.

Scarry, E. (1985) *The Body in Pain: The Making and Unmaking of the World*. New York: Oxford University Press.

Scharff, C. (2012) *Repudiating Feminism: Young Women in a Neoliberal World*. Farnham, Surrey and Burlington, VT: Ashgate Publishing Company.

Shakespeare, W. ([1600]1997) *The Merchant of Venice. The Riverside Shakespeare*. 2nd edn. Evans, G.B. and Tobin, J.J.M. (eds.). Boston, MA: Houghton Mifflin.

Simpson, J. and Speake, J. (2009a) 'All things come to those who wait', *The Oxford Dictionary of Proverbs*, 5th edn. Available at: www.oxfordreference.com/view/10.1093/acref/9780199539536.001.0001/acref-9780199539536-e-34?rskey=iqUuR4&result=1 (Accessed July 2016).

———. (2009b) 'No pain, no gain', *The Oxford Dictionary of Proverbs*, 5th edn. Available at: www.oxfordreference.com/search?source=%2F10.1093%2Facref%2F9780199539536.001.0001%2Facref-9780199539536&q=no+pain+no+gain (Accessed July 2016).

Sontag, S. (1978) *Illness as Metaphor*. New York: Farrar, Straus and Giroux.

Spitzack, C. (1993) 'The spectacle of anorexia nervosa', *Text and Performance Quarterly*, 13(1), pp. 1–20.

Thornham, S. (2007) *Women, Feminism and Media*. Edinburgh: Edinburgh University Press Ltd.

Tincknell, E. (2011) 'Scourging the abject body: The television make-over show and the reconstruction of femininity under neoliberalism', in Gill, R. and Scharff, C. (eds.) *New Femininities: Postfeminism, Neoliberalism and Identity*. London: Palgrave Macmillan, pp. 83–95.

Tumblr. (2014) Available at: www.tumblr.com/ (Accessed July 2014).

Vandereycken, W. and Van Deth, R. (1994) *From Fasting Saints to Anorexic Girls: The History of Self-starvation*. London: Athlone Press.

Wardrop, M. (2009) 'Kate Moss: "Nothing tastes as good as skinny feels"', *The Telegraph*, 19 November. Available at: www.telegraph.co.uk/news/celebritynews/6602430/Kate-Moss-Nothing-tastes-as-good-as-skinny-feels.html (Accessed July 2016).

130   *Articulating pain*

Wearing, S. (2007) 'Subjects of rejuvenation', in Tasker, Y. and Negra, D. (eds.) *Interrogating Postfeminism: Gender and the Politics of Popular Culture*. Durham: Duke University Press, pp. 277–330.

Webstagram. (2014) Available at: www.web.stagram.com (Accessed July 2014).

Williams, S.J. (2003) *Medicine and the Body*. London: Sage.

Winkler, M.G. (1994) 'Model women', in Winkler, M.G. and Cole, L.B. (eds.) *The Good Body: Asceticism in Contemporary Culture*. New Haven, CT: Yale University Press, pp. 215–231.

Yorke, T. (1992) *Creep*. London: EMI.

6 From counterhegemonic to counterpublic?

The political potential of pro-anorexia

Since its inception in the late 1990s, the pro-ana phenomenon has elicited a range of reactions, from anger and shock to sadness and fear. However, as this book has sought to demonstrate, pro-ana online spaces cannot be understood as a monolith: some resist societal understandings of anorexia as an illness whilst others deny that they are pro-ana, using discourses of normative femininity to justify their existence. Regardless of users' modes of expression, the phenomenon makes a radical statement about hegemonic thinness culture. Such statements can operate as a basis for political action, therefore, this chapter examines pro-ana online spaces' potential as counterpublics, asking if they constitute a *movement* capable of enriching the public sphere. In earlier chapters, I addressed the way pro-ana online operates as a subcultural space, distinguishing itself from the mainstream via its controversial stance on disordered eating, as well as aligning itself with the grunge and hipster subcultures. This chapter seeks to interrogate further the counter-discursive tendencies of the pro-ana phenomenon: I ask to what extent it is politically useful and if it can lead to a better understanding of, not only anorexia, but the gendered culture of compulsory thinness.

I approach this chapter in two main sections: in the first, I ask what it means for a movement to be considered a counterpublic. To do so, I draw on a range of historical and contemporary women-led publics, exploring what is involved in the formation of a counterpublic and what might be its limitations. In the second section, I turn to pro-ana online spaces themselves where I make a case for *postfeminist counterpublics*. A postfeminist counterpublic is inherently contradictory: if a counterpublic critiques the status quo, then postfeminism reinforces it. As such, here I argue that pro-ana online spaces are postfeminist enclaves, which also constitute groups of women who, on some level, critique the hegemonic order. Finally, in light of this, I ask if the political potential of pro-ana online spaces might be mined to bring about social change.

The private, the public and counterpublics

Jürgen Habermas defines the bourgeois public sphere as a 'sphere which mediates between society and state, in which the public organizes itself as the bearer of public opinion' ([1964] 1974, p. 50). Crucial to his definition is that 'access is guaranteed to all citizens' (ibid., p. 49); however, in practice, participation of persons who do not occupy positions of privilege is not assured. It was in the Enlightenment that the notion of the public sphere came to the fore (ibid., p. 50), and it was also during this period that women, who – since the time of Plato – had been associated with the private sphere, were mandated as such (Rose 1993, p. 363). As Gillian Rose points out, 'the realm of the public and the political was constructed as one of rationality, individuality, self-control and hence masculinity, since only men could be fully rational individuals, free from passionate attachments' (ibid.). Women, with their irrational temperaments and investment in emotions, were not seen as capable of political debate, and the private sphere in which they were located, not worthy of public discussion.

The bifurcation of public and private, of men and women, persists, and it goes some way towards explaining women's relative invisibility in politics (Siltanen and Stanworth 1984, p. 195). It also means that when political action is undertaken by women, there is the tendency to depoliticise it. As Fraser points out, 'the rhetoric of domestic privacy seeks to exclude some issues and interests from public debate by personalizing and/or familializing them; it casts these as private-domestic or personal-familial matters in contra-distinction to public, political matters' (1990, p. 71; see also Benhabib 1992, p. 100). Kathleen M. Blee suggests that the reasons for women's apparent 'invisibility' in political protest are threefold: it is borne out of longstanding assumptions of radicalism as essentially male, the limits of where we look for women radicals (formal settings such as unions and political parties), and how we go about looking (disregarding for example, the domestic arena) (1998, pp. 2–5). More recently, Jessica Winegar's (2012) research into the 2011 Egyptian revolution corroborates Blee's claims: she suggests that women's protest is often drawn from the private sphere or based on domestic tasks, skills, and expertise, and is, therefore, not recognised as political. In Egypt, it was the women who held the communities together: they cooked for male protesters and looked after the children; whilst the men were on the streets of Tahrir assuming the 'iconic image of the revolutionary [...] typically rais-ing a fist, throwing a rock, or standing in front of tanks' (Winegar 2012, p. 67). That is, cultural understandings of political protest favour this latter image over that of hidden domestic labour, which is no less important in the staging of a social movement.

Given that a number of groups are marginalised in the public sphere, the work of Habermas has been criticised by feminists such as Rita Felski (1989) and Fraser (1990, 2013), and by queer theorist, Michael Warner (2002, 2005). All three scholars make a case for counterpublics. Felski condemns the gender 'blindness' of the bourgeois public sphere and its patriarchal bias (1989, p. 165). She argues instead for counterpublics which 'seek to define themselves *against* the homogenizing and universalizing logic of the global megaculture of modern mass communication' (Felski 1989, p. 166, emphasis in original). Fraser concurs, calling for 'parallel discursive arenas where members of subordinated social groups invent and circulate counterdiscourses, which in turn permit them to formulate oppositional interpretations of their identities, interests, and needs' (1990, p. 67). Instead of a single overarching sphere then, scholars of counterpublics advocate for multiple publics (Asen 2000; Felski 1989; Fraser 1990; Warner 2002, 2005).

To explore how counterpublics operate, it is helpful to look at a set of historical and contemporary case studies, before attending to pro-ana online spaces. Here, I examine four diverse women-led publics to illustrate how different counterpublics operate: lesbian separatism, SlutWalk, the Me Too movement, and Toxic Links Coalition's (TLC) resistance of National Breast Cancer Awareness Month (NBCAM). Lesbian separatism, which was borne out of 1970s radical feminism, is an example of counterpublic withdrawal from the mainstream. SlutWalk, which first took place in 2011, follows the activist tradition of occupying public space and highlights a counterpublic's relationship with the media. The Me Too movement against sexual assault, which emerged from traditional activist circles in 2006, attracted mainstream attention as a Twitter hashtag in 2017 and demonstrates how online spaces can be utilised to mobilise a counterpublic. Finally, TLC's resistance of NBCAM illustrates the importance of the existence of multiple publics, rather than the binary of public and counterpublic. Each of these case studies, on some level, opposes hegemony; I follow Antonio Gramsci's definition of hegemony as outlined by Raymond Williams: hegemony is not fixed, rather it is a process which 'has continually to be renewed, recreated, defended, and modified. It is also continually resisted, limited, altered, challenged by pressures not at all its own' (1977, p. 112). This means that any group exhibiting counterhegemonic tendencies is in a pivotal position whereby it always risks incorporation by the hegemonic. If incorporation is resisted, a counterpublic is potentially formed. But, as Williams points out,

> all or nearly all initiatives and contributions, even when they take on manifestly alternative or oppositional forms are in practice tied to the hegemonic: that the dominant culture, so to say, at once produces and limits its own forms of counter-culture.
>
> (1977, p. 114)

How then might this play out in women's counterhegemonic spaces? Does the hegemony always prevail or do these spaces succeed in creating 'pockets of resistance' (Bartky 1990, p. 81)?

Lesbian separatism

To understand lesbian separatism, it is necessary to return to radical feminism – outlined briefly in the introduction to this book – because it was from radical feminism that lesbian separatism emerged. During the Civil Rights Movement in the mid-sixties, women were granted only supporting roles, 'useful at the typewriter, in the kitchen, and in bed, but expected to leave policy making to men' (Deckard 1983, p. 326). From here, radical feminism took root to address such side-lining and, although it was incredibly powerful, this new movement failed to represent certain groups of women – such as women of colour (Bryson 2003) and working class and lesbian women (Echols 1989, p. 203). This led to the formation of a group who named themselves 'Radicalesbians' (Deckard 1983, p. 341). Through the staging of protests, they ensured that, by September 1971, the National Organization for Women had recognised the legitimacy of lesbian women's oppression (Deckard 1983, p. 343). Despite these achievements, the lesbian separatist groups, which emerged concurrently, were only partly successful as counterpublics.

Having experienced discrimination in the women-only communities that had been established to provide a haven from patriarchal oppression, some lesbian groups had started their own collectives where they bought land, ran women-only bookstores and restaurants, and produced their own media (Shugar 1995, p. 57). Their withdrawal from patriarchal society was undoubtedly a powerful, symbolic statement, and as Marilyn Frye reminds us, all types of feminism are invariably constituted by separatism, a withdrawal from male-dominated spaces (1997). However, lesbian separatist spaces became enclaves 'where patriarchy was evaded rather than engaged' (Echols 1989, p. 5). Although the act of separating is a necessary phase in the formation of a counterpublic, its success relies upon its 'dual character' (Fraser 1990, p. 68): Janus-like, it must both separate from the wider public sphere and seek to re-join it, all the while resisting incorporation. The lesbian separatists though, were more focused on withdrawal than regrouping.

At the same time as withdrawing from patriarchal society, 'the focus [in these separatist groups] became one of personal rather than social transformation' (Echols 1989, p. 5). Ironically, this emphasis on the individual chimes more with liberal feminism, which has been criticised by radical feminists, than it does radical politics. Living a separatist lifestyle required a number of privileges; moving to a collective was not possible for all women, particularly those who had dependents and bills to pay. As a result, 'separatist ideology itself often appeared elitist or arrogantly middle-class' (Shugar 1995, p. 49) and contributed to the double oppression of certain groups of women, especially the poor and women of colour, who were subordinated not only by the patriarchy, but by other women. Writing on her experiences of living in a radical lesbian community during the 1980s, Kathy Rudy (2001) cites the danger in its singular approach to what it meant to be a woman and its debarring of complex identities, suggesting that this led to her disillusionment and subsequent departure from the collective. Valerie Bryson concurs: 'the idea that all women are united in a common sisterhood that transcends all man-made divisions can be dangerously misleading' (2003, p. 170). Hence, lesbian separatism inadvertently risked reproducing the bourgeois public sphere which, as Felski argues, is characterised by an indifference to inequality and the false belief that everyone's views are being represented (1989, p. 165).

Lesbian separatism is an example of a counterhegemonic group that ultimately fell short of succeeding as a counterpublic movement. In its formation of a separatist space, it may have created a haven for a number of women who were oppressed by the patriarchy, but for others, it was yet another group from which they were excluded. Furthermore, for a counterpublic to succeed, it must engage with wider publics if it is to bring about real social change. As Fraser argues, 'the concept of a counterpublic militates in the long run against separatism because it assumes an orientation that is *publicist*' (1990, p. 67, emphasis in original). It must seek to be 'transformative, not replicative merely' (Warner 2002, p. 88), lest it reproduces the hegemonic inequalities it seeks to counter. Such criticism can be levelled at SlutWalk; a phenomenon which has been condemned by feminists for its lack of inclusivity.

SlutWalk

In January 2011, during a routine address to law students on personal safety, Toronto police officer Michael Sanguinetti stated that 'women should avoid dressing like sluts in order not to be victimized' (SlutWalk Toronto Facebook 2011). His victim-blaming, slut-shaming comments prompted outrage, and in April of that year, two women, Heather Jarvis and Sonya Barnett, established SlutWalk Toronto in response (Nguyen 2013, p. 159). By the end of 2011, 'SlutWalks were organized in over 100 cities in 40 nations, mobilizing tens of thousands of women, men, and children' (Mendes 2015, p. 219). The movement quickly gained momentum and, in principle, had a global covering. In their mission to reclaim the term 'slut', participants marched with placards declaring that rape is the fault of the perpetrator and not the victim. Clothing choice was central to both the movement and the media reporting surrounding it: some protesters wore casual jeans and t-shirts, whereas others wore more revealing attire to emphasise their cause (Pilkington 2011).

SlutWalk has been widely criticised by the mainstream media and feminists alike for furthering the objectification of women and girls, for being heteronormative, and above all, for neglecting issues of race and nationality (Dow and Wood 2014). Keren Darmon cites the postfeminist mass media as the reason SlutWalks were so badly received, proposing that we might question

> the privilege that online spaces can really offer, if they lose (at least some of) their political and feminist edge and become both more personal and post-feminist on this journey into the mediated public sphere via the mass media.

> (2014, p. 702)

Nguyen levels criticism at the protesters themselves, arguing that

> many of the participants appeared to work within the postfeminist and Third Wave model insofar as they performed fierceness by revelling in female sexual power as end games [thereby] ultimately displac[ing] the somber and deadly issues of rape, domestic violence, sexual abuse, and street harassment.
>
> (2013, pp. 159–160)

Moreover, that this 'sexual power' was communicated primarily through women's right to freedom of fashion arguably misses the point; not least because it overlooks the fact that sexual assault takes place in countries where women are legally required to conceal their bodies.

Occurring at the backdrop of the public rape of a student in Delhi in 2012, 'SlutWalks were cast by some as nothing more than a Western import that had no relevance to the brutalized and victimized body sprawled across the Indian street' (Dhillon cited in Kapur 2014, p. 10) It is because of such limitations that the movement did not translate cross-culturally. David Greetham (2011) and Ratna Kapur (2012, 2014) have interrogated its reception in an Indian setting. Greetham notes that the term 'slut' was only really recognised by a small minority of upper-class Indian women and consequently when removed from its Western context, a SlutWalk could not hold the same meanings as it did in the west (2011, p. 719). Despite this, Kapur, who acknowledges the failings of SlutWalk and the 'Pink Chaddi Campaign' (a protest movement in response to attacks on young women in a pub in South India in 2009), suggests they hold value in that they constitute crucial moments in feminist history that allow for a reassessment of the most pressing issues (2012, p. 3). Rather than simply criticising SlutWalk for its failure to establish a successful feminist social movement then, we might utilise it as a springboard to ask what these protests can usefully tell us about contemporary feminism (Dow and Wood 2014; Kapur 2012; Mendes 2015). Bonnie J. Dow and Julia T. Wood urge us 'to recognize that feminism may never be able to speak for all women at all times' (2014, p. 37) and Kaitlynn Mendes argues that although feminism may have been ignored or derided in media reporting around SlutWalks, there was also evidence of feminist rhetoric being adopted without being directly referenced, thereby suggesting the extent to which it has penetrated public consciousness, even if it is not always practised (2015, p. 227). SlutWalks may not constitute a successful counterpublic movement in and of themselves, but they represent valuable lessons in feminist organising, and as Felski (1989, p. 166) points out, counterpublics are 'multiple and heterogeneous and do not converge to form a single revolutionary moment'. Ultimately, as we saw with the lesbian separatists, Slut-Walk excluded those without privilege and it personalised the political. At the same time though, it was a victim of the current postfeminist media that neutralised its politics, something to which all contemporaneous women-led publics are subjected.

#MeToo: an online public

The Me Too movement was started by Tarana Burke in 2006 as a way of bringing about empowerment though empathy for survivors of sexual assault from marginalised backgrounds (Rodino-Colocino 2018). In October 2017, following allegations of sexual misconduct against Hollywood producer, Harvey Weinstein, the online #MeToo movement emerged to draw attention to the ubiquity of sexual assault and sexual harassment. The hashtag was instigated by Hollywood actress, Alyssa Milano, who tweeted 'If you've been sexually harassed or assaulted write "me too" as a reply to this tweet' (2017). Milano was subsequently criticised for overlooking the original Me Too movement, but was quick to acknowledge Burke once this was highlighted (Rodino-Colocino 2018). According to Facebook, 'within 24 hours, 4.7 million people around the world engaged in the #metoo conversation, with over 12m posts, comments, and reactions' (Khomami 2017). #MeToo was, and remains, an important phenomenon, but it has its shortcomings – not least that it was founded by a woman of colour to support those from marginalised backgrounds and eleven years later surpassed by white, middle-class Hollywood.

For a counterpublic to be instigated, the private must become public and the silenced must speak out. During this process, it is not uncommon for groups to face criticism and for their assertions to be read as 'debased narcissism, a collapse of decorum, expressivity gone amok, the erosion of any distinction between public and private' (Warner 2005, p. 62). Of course, an insistence that certain matters should remain private merely operates as a gagging mechanism and a form of social control. Thus, the discussions #MeToo prompts should not be dismissed for this reason. The relative anonymity of the Internet has enabled marginalised persons to access information and support and the opportunity to engage in debate and potentially develop counterpublics (Dahlberg and Siapera 2007, p. 134; McDorman 2001). At the same time, 'as the media have become an almost oppressive force [New Communication Technologies] offer the possibility of reclaiming a degree of organizational autonomy' (McDorman 2001, p. 203). #MeToo then holds such potential. It sits under the wider banner of 'hashtag feminism', a term coined in a commentary and criticism section of *Feminist Media Studies* (Portwood-Stacer and Berridge 2014). In this collection of short essays, some scholars explore the radical potential of this new form of online feminism (e.g. Clark 2014; Horeck 2014), whereas others point out its limitations (e.g. Latina and Docherty 2014; Loken 2014). Some years on, feminist analysis of #MeToo has erred on the side of caution and questioned whether it will bring about real social change (Fileborn and Loney-Howes 2017; Mendes et al. 2018; Rosewarne 2017; Zarkov and Davis 2018). #MeToo may illustrate the omnipresence of sexual assault, but as Lauren Rosewarne (2017) puts it,

In an era where we have data up the wazoo on the prevalence of women's harassment and assault by men, why do you need to see me bleed so that you can believe that this is endemic?

From the outset, #MeToo relied on people (particularly women) coming forward with painful stories and broadcasting them to the world. Such an onus on the individual reinforces the notion that 'the widespread adoption of digital media may be shifting the burden of mobilization from organizations to individuals' (Walgrave et al. cited in Bennett and Segerberg 2011, p. 772), whilst also being indicative of neoliberal social structures that hamper collective action. At the same time, the hidden unpaid labour (both occupational and emotional) associated with these forms of digital activism is immense. Participants interviewed by Kaitlynn Mendes, Jessica Ringrose, and Jessalynn Keller described it as the 'emotional "tax" they experienced from listening to stories of abuse, harassment, misogyny and sexism' (2018, p. 239; see also Fileborn and Loney-Howes 2017). #MeToo may provide an alternative public sphere for women to break the silence around sexual assault and sexual harassment, but Burke's central concern is the extent to which, in its current form, it is not benefiting the marginalised, which was always her vision for the Me Too movement (Adetiba and Burke 2017, p. 5). Equally, Dubravka Zarkov warns that 'we should not assume that what is happening among the political and cultural elites will automatically "trickle down" to the streets' (2018, p. 6). Many people (myself included) felt pressured to speak out, yet lacked the resources or status to do so (see Zarkov and Davis 2018). As Bianca Fileborn and Rachel Loney-Howes (2017) remind us, 'there is a certain type of privilege that comes from being able to speak out. It is often white middle-class women who occupy online spaces, and victim-survivors from diverse demographic groups may be actively excluded'. In short, #MeToo may be another counterpublic in which only the very privileged can afford to participate.

Individualising discourses pervade #MeToo, meaning it risks personalising the political in similar ways to SlutWalk discussed above. As Burke points out, 'The conversation is largely about Harvey Weinstein or other individual bogeymen. No matter how much I keep talking about power and privilege, they keep bringing it back to individuals' (Adetiba and Burke 2017, p. 5). Individuals, therefore, become metonymies for wider structural problems: when people like Weinstein stand in for systemic inequality, the structures that perpetuate sexual assault and harassment are obfuscated and remain unchallenged. One of Zarkov's concerns then is that '*visibility* and exposure will be taken as a *solution* to the problem of sexual violence [...] that "making a person (especially the accused) visible" will be mistaken for "making the problem visible" ' (2018, p. 6; emphases in original). For #MeToo to succeed in bringing about real social change, the focus must be on transforming the structures that perpetuate inequality, *as well as* calling into account the individuals complicit in them; importantly, the impetus to do so should not sit with individual survivors alone. #MeToo has started an important conversation and has the potential to be a successful counterpublic if its original aim, as put forth by Tarana Burke, is kept in sight (both online and offline); otherwise it risks dissolving into the bourgeois public sphere.

Toxic links coalition's resistance of national breast cancer awareness month

Having examined case studies that feature counterhegemonic elements but may not fully succeed as counterpublics, it is necessary to look to an example which does. In her 2003 research into TLC's resistance of NBCAM, Phaedra C. Pezzullo demonstrates how counterhegemonic activity can launch a successful counterpublic movement. For over 30 years, NBCAM has been held every October to raise awareness of breast cancer and encourage early detection of the disease (Breast Cancer Awareness Month 2015). What is less well known is that it was started by pharmaceutical firm AstraZeneca, who instigated in-house breast-screening, which whilst effective for early detection, was chiefly a money-saving tactic to prevent loss of workers (Pezzullo 2003, p. 351). TLC, the activist group that works to draw attention to the environmental causes of cancer, claims that AstraZeneca, 'profits by first producing many of the toxins implicated in the breast cancer epidemic and then by selling the drugs used to treat the disease' (ibid., p. 353). In 1997, TLC sought to expose the inherent contradictions in AstraZeneca's sponsorship of NBCAM and to raise awareness of the environmental causes of cancer, using the month of October as a springboard. They did this by 'renam[ing] and, thus refram[ing], October as Cancer Industry Awareness Month (instead of NBCAM) in large part by sponsoring annual "Stop Cancer Where It Starts" tours' (ibid., p. 354). The 'tours' comprise TLC directly approaching institutions it believes produce and perpetuate toxic pollution (ibid, p. 347). Hence, TLC mobilised the counterhegemonic aspects of NBCAM in order to critique those which supported the status quo; here, the monopolisation of, and damage to, public health by the pharmaceutical industry.

Breast Cancer Action (which formed part of TLC's resistance to NBCAM) runs the 'think before you pink' campaign (Think before you pink 2015). It argues that the Pink Ribbon campaign, which promotes the wearing of a pink ribbon to raise awareness around breast cancer, 'obscures the harsh reality of breast cancer by creating a single story of triumphant survivorship based on positive thinking, beauty tips, and sanitized, carefully chosen images of women' (ibid.). The Pink Ribbon campaign, with its abundance of promotional material and corporate interest, operates as a brand itself, one which 'think before you pink' suggests has more benefit to its private sponsors than to women living with breast cancer (ibid.). Through grassroots activism, Breast Cancer Action seeks to expose the exploitative commodification of the counterpublic and its incorporation into the hegemony.

TLC's critique of NBCAM thus exemplifies the vulnerability of counterpublics to private and financial interests; once a counterpublic has the backing of a corporation, its mission is no longer fully supporting public interests (see also Habermas [1964] 1974, p. 55). In the case of NBCAM, AstraZeneca has a vested interest in women focussing on the *signs* of breast cancer rather than the *cause*; the former diverts them from the latter. This is exemplary late capitalist logic whereby markets are deployed to 'tame politics' (Fraser 2013, p. 218). When a counterpublic is co-opted by capitalism, it can be utilised as a means of shoring up the status quo, rather than questioning oppressive structures as originally intended. The public sphere then simply becomes 'a field for the competition of interests' (Habermas [1964] 1974, p. 54).

Pezzullo's case study is important to a study of counterpublics because it reveals their complexities. Ostensibly, NBCAM is a counterpublic itself given that it challenges the norms around what constitutes the public and the private by encouraging women to check their breasts so that early detection might increase the success of treatment. However, when the environmental factors highlighted by TLC are considered, NBCAM's mission is revealed to need revising. As such, Pezzullo (2003) argues that publics and counterpublics should not be read as a binary. Instead, by recognising both NBCAM and Cancer Industry Awareness Month as counterpublics, a healthy dialogue can ensue. This is because 'counterpublics are most likely to be successful when they mobilize diverse networks of social action with a view towards enriching the pluralism of the public sphere' (Coleman and Ross 2010, p. 92). At the same time, it is important to recognise that although TLC reveals the contradictions within NBCAM, the dialogue cannot end with Cancer Industry Awareness month. As Warner cautions:

> we cannot understand counterpublics very well if we fail to see that there are contradictions and perversities inherent in the organization of *all* publics, tensions that are not captured by critiques of the dominant public's exclusions or ideological limitations. Counterpublics are publics, too.
>
> (2002, p. 80; emphasis in original)

All counterpublics are susceptible to co-optation by the marketplace, which in its attempts to profit from such movements, voids them of political potency and results in their reinforcing existing hierarchies. Consequently, it is vital that new counterpublics emerge so that the status quo is continually challenged.

Pro-ana online spaces: *postfeminist counterpublics*

The counterpublic potential of pro-ana online is, in part, borne out of the range of marginalised positions its users occupy: firstly, their anorexic status means that they are pathologised by society at large; secondly, their embracing of this status ostracises them; thirdly, and perhaps most significantly, pro-anorectics are predominantly female-presenting, meaning that they are adversely placed within patriarchal society. The anonymity of the Internet then, combined with the reassuring presence of like-minded others provides them with a safe space, at least for a time until their censors block them. Ironically, it is the calls for censorship and media castigation which have made pro-ana online spaces so visible. That they use digital media in the first place suggests they are potentially open to being seen by broader audiences and, whether intentionally or not, they have formed their own public. They may have faced immense criticism, but through their use of websites, forums, and social media, users have been able to construct a counter argument, thus co-opting the power of their visibility to draw back, regroup, and provide a counter-narrative.

One way contemporary pro-ana users have crafted their own public is through their use of hashtags. Olszanowski (2015) proposes four categories that motivate individuals to use hashtags: to discover like-minded others, to find inspiration, to participate in challenges and/or communities, and to create an archive of images. The hashtag then can have a unifying effect but, upon entering wider publics, it is vulnerable to appropriation and subsequent derailing (both intended and unintended) as Anna Antonakis-Nashif (2015) found in her study of the feminist hashtag 'outcry'. #outcry was coined in response to sexism in Germany, and when it penetrated the mainstream, it prompted wider debate, but it was also mocked, hijacked, and neutralised. Antonakis-Nashif concludes that although hashtags can create empowering spaces, 'when entering mainstream media, the logics become different, the discourse gets abstracted and less subversive' (2015, p. 108). Her findings echo the response to SlutWalk discussed above, where its politics were all too easily distorted by the postfeminist media. Such distortion is a result of the dynamism of the hegemonic, which is ever-ready to incorporate that which may jeopardise its authority (Williams 1977, p. 113).

It did not take long for oppositional hashtags to emerge in response to #MeToo, one of which was #notme. In this instance, #notme was not cited to indicate pro-ana users unhappy with their appearance as I argued in the previous chapter, rather this was a campaign started by music producer Russell Simmons on Instagram in response to allegations against him of sexual misconduct (Abad-Santos 2017). Others followed suit and #notme was adopted across social media platforms by men seeking to show that they had not been perpetrators of assault, as well as by women asserting that they had not experienced it. Clearly, #notme does nothing to address the systemic abuse and inequality #MeToo highlights – it merely sidesteps it; however, what I want to point out here is the hashtag's endless polysemy and what #notme tells us about the current landscape. In a trawl of #notme, across a range of social media platforms, amongst the declarations from those who seek to absolve themselves of any blame for the culture of inequality and abuse, are images of thin women others aspire to be. These may appear to be two very different deployments of #notme, but, taken together, they provide insight into a culture that is underpinned by gender inequality. Moreover, both such uses of #notme stem from a worldview that focuses on the individual at the cost of the political.

Despite this, pro-ana users' individualism need not be antithetical to the formation of a counterpublic, for as Micki McGee (2005) has argued, a focus on the self can also be a catalyst for social change, provided it is founded upon acknowledgment of our shared vulnerabilities, rather than on difference and attempts to transcend human fragility. Dias's (2003) research into pro-ana sites is instructive here: she asks, 'whether women's behavior on these websites may be considered feminist without being overtly political, and conversely whether it can be considered political without being overtly feminist' (2003, p. 32). Dias reads pro-ana sites through the lens of third-wave feminism, concluding that 'the narratives in third wave collections, like the narratives on pro-anorexia websites, describe individual women's struggles with their identities as well as the contradictory nature of what each of them finds empowering' (ibid., p. 41). Dias' argument is important, and it holds much resonance for the time she was writing – in the early days of the pro-ana phenomenon. However, as this book has shown, the landscape of pro-ana online has changed considerably, not least because of censorship, but also because of the intensification of the postfeminist neoliberal climate in which it is situated. As a result, I propose a reading of pro-ana online spaces as *postfeminist counterpublics*. The users themselves may not be, to borrow from Dias, overtly political or for that matter, overtly feminist. But, they understand feminism as common sense (McRobbie 2004) adopting its rhetoric of freedom and choice to support them in their goals for extreme thinness, however problematic that may be. At the same time, their spaces are inherently contradictory and unstable, and their 'grammar of individualism' (Gill 2007, p. 162) means that they are susceptible to co-optation by postfeminist neoliberalism.

This is not to say that all pro-ana users wilfully embrace such assimilation into the mainstream. Pro-ana recovery site, *Let's change this*, expresses frustration at the media's distorted depiction of pro-anorexia, as well as what it terms 'the new generation of pro-ana', whereby users, such as those on social media platforms, present pro-ana as glamorous and 'cool'. In chapter three, I cited pro-ana forum *Beauty of Ana*'s annoyance at the pro-ana trend for 'underwear pics', hence, these spaces appear to be expressing their exasperation at the postfeminising of their culture, even if they do not describe it as such. At the same time, *Let's change this* refuses the pathologising of anorexia and states that its space is intended for individuals who seek to 'live with anorexia and not for it' (*Let's change this*). It even draws on academic research on pro-ana to support its claims that pro-ana online spaces can benefit users despite how the media have portrayed them. Users are acutely aware of the way they are being depicted and are using digital media to respond to this, whether through crafting their own language to evade censorship or making statements to defend their position. As the author of *Ethereal Anas* states on the landing page:

> Please understand that we made the choice to be like this. We are tired of being judged and misunderstood. Haters have no place here. An Ethereal Ana doesn't want to be helped, just accepted for who she is and

treated like a person. We have our own minds and we are capable of choosing for ourselves!

The author describes a chasm between the help she wants and that which is being forced upon her; a common theme in pro-ana texts. She asserts that her site provides support and understanding, contrasted with the ill-judged 'help' imposed from the outside, which she suggests is dehumanising. By stating that she and her fellow pro-anorectics are able to make their own choices, the blogger seeks to reclaim the agency that external 'help' has denied her. This statement both disrupts received understandings of anorexia as a passively-endured illness and responds to a public that has demonised those who resist 'help'. However, it also invokes 'choice feminism' in which 'women's choices [are read as] evidence of women's exercise of freedom [and] the troubled relationship between femininity and feminism is seemingly resolved' (Budgeon 2015, p. 306). Spaces such as *Ethereal Anas* may present a critique of anorexia treatment, but their protests are underpinned by the rhetoric of individualism that is hindering their counterpublic potential.

Pro-ana online spaces are vulnerable to incorporation by the hegemonic because, although they exhibit counterhegemonic viewpoints, many of their spaces also reproduce dominant ideologies, as earlier chapters of this book have demonstrated. Despite this, as Robert Asen and Daniel C. Brouwer warn '[…] to insist that oppositionality inheres in marginal identities is to overlook these people's mundane or hegemonically complicit activities' (2001, pp. 8–9; see also Dahlberg and Siapera 2007, p. 136). Politics aside, pro-ana online is an example of cultural history that offers valuable insight in to the lived realities of young women in the twenty-first century. In her ethnography of a queer activist group in Brighton, Aristea Fotopoulou (2017) found that the group's use of digital technologies, although contested by members, recorded their activity to public memory so that future queer activists might draw upon it. As Catherine Helen Palczewski notes, 'what happens within a movement in terms of identity creation, may be as important as, if not more important than, the outward directed rhetoric' (2001, p. 166). Censorship and deletion mean that archives of the pro-ana phenomenon are incomplete and fragmented, but its narrative still has the potential to be utilised in the formation of a counterpublic.

In spite of – and arguably because of – threats of censorship, pro-ana users remain steadfastly adaptive. From the outset, users instigated their own language with the terms 'pro-anorexia' and 'thinspiration' – coinages that have now entered the vernacular (see chapter three). Subsequently, as I have shown throughout this book, they developed an expansive vocabulary in an attempt to pre-empt erasure: hashtags ranging from 'thynspo' to 'blithe' signal that the discussion is pro-ana, and, for some time at least, can pass undetected by Internet moderators. The development of a new rhetoric is central to the success of a social movement as it has the effect of challenging and redefining hegemonic discourses (Fraser 1990; Malkowski 2014; Palczewski 2001). It would be remiss to argue that pro-ana users have crafted their own language with the intention of creating a social movement; rather, the constant attempts to censor their spaces mean they cannot converse in a language readily understood by those in authority. Coining and modifying hashtags is a practice of necessity, more than choice.

In order to remain online then, pro-ana authors are fiercely protective over their spaces. As such, they have faced criticism for their hostility to outsiders, leading Brotsky and Giles (2007) to describe the original spaces as more of a 'clique' than a community. If a group becomes a clique, it is much less conducive to the formation of a counterpublic whose success relies on an outward-facing approach. Indeed, it is not uncommon for established social movements themselves to flounder when the 'desire for community [...] produces a clique atmosphere which keeps groups small and turns potential members away' (Young 1990, p. 235). Now that pro-ana content exists primarily on social media platforms and less on forums, 'membership' *perse* is much less tangible, yet paradoxically content is more visible; differently put, pro-ana online is an open secret. References to 'secret' flood spaces, appearing in usernames, hashtags, and comments alluding to secretly starving and holding secret accounts. This accentuates the shameful connotations attached to eating disorders, whilst simultaneously suggesting that secrets are what unite these people. A search for #thynspiration on Instagram typifies the circulating of secrets in pro-ana online spaces: a user posts a thinspirational image of a model with a childlike appearance, the attendant hashtags signalling the meaning they attach to it. The hashtags combine allusions to extreme thinness, such as: '#skinnylegs #hipbones #chestbones #collarbones #thin #flatstomach', with references to eating disorders including: '#anorexia #ednos #bulimia' as well as: '#depression' and '#selfharmmm'. Again, the user indicates their distance from the image posted with, '#notme'. Amongst these hashtags are those to corroborate the post's secret meaning, including: '#secretsociety123, a coinage that is applied to both pro-ana and self-harm posts (see also Moreno et al. 2016), thus uniting those who self-starve with those who self-harm. Two of the users who 'like' this have secret usernames: 'secret_life_of_laura' and 'tinas_secret'. Through 'likes' and further hashtags, such a post is then made visible by other clandestine users and broadcast throughout pro-ana and self-harm networks.

Pace posts such as these, like those featuring #notme explored in the previous chapter, make bold statements about the unattainable standards of beauty that circulate in contemporary Western culture; they express the impossibility of achieving these standards and the accompanying misery it can bring. However, rather than enacting a critique against impossible ideals, users imbue them with life-threatening importance, turning their frustration upon themselves. This is symptomatic of the shift from second-wave feminism to present-day 'neoliberal feminism [which is] purging itself of all elements that would orient it outwards, towards the public good' (Rottenberg 2014, p. 431). Pro-ana users may adopt a counterhegemonic approach to compulsory thinness by implicitly stating that its requirements bear little difference to their own apparently deviant culture, nevertheless, they do not communicate beyond their networks, and instead their focus remains on the self.

Even the supportive slogans users share with one another invariably centre on the first-person singular, as results produced by a search for 'thynspo' on Pinterest demonstrate: posts here range from a user who asks, 'Why am I so obsessed with being skinny?' to another declaring 'My weight depresses me so much. No matter what I do I'm still fat'. Another user writes wistfully, 'Oh to be able to sit down without having rolls of fat' – the text is accompanied by an image of a woman with a concave stomach. Each post focusses on the individual's all-consuming focus on body weight, and each image depicts a woman alone, encapsulating the solipsism of self-improvement. The longest post generated by this search summarises pro-anorexia's individualism: 'Become skinny. Do your homework. Create the life you want to live cos *no-one* is going to do it for you'. This post is antithetical to any form of community and tells the viewer that they must be self-reliant and that their future depends entirely upon their own actions. As Gill and Orgad argue, such a rejection of dependence 'is the 'lifeblood of neoliberalism' (2015, p. 340). What is more, in line with many pro-ana texts, these posts are disdainful of fat, the continual castigation of which means pro-ana users are unlikely to connect with other groups who are marginalised because of their body type. Fat people and anorectics have more in common than it initially appears, but both groups are rendered inimical to one another by a culture that admires slenderness and is hostile towards fat (McKinley 1999, p. 110). This, combined with the fact that 'femininity in a neoliberal postfeminist society is promoted as a performance that one wins at' (Winch 2013, p. 157), makes potential alliances challenging.

A successful social movement must be premised on the uniting of disparate groups to create a cohesive front and as Wolf argues, the 'core of the [beauty] myth – and the reason it was so useful as a counter to feminism – is its divisiveness' (1991, p. 284). Further, John Downey and Natalie Fenton (2003) warn that,

> the "proliferation of subaltern counter publics" (Fraser, 1992: 69–70) does not necessarily lead to a multiplication of forces. Unless powerful efforts at alliances are made [...] the oppositional energy of individual groups and subcultures is more often neutralized in the marketplace of multicultural pluralism, or polarized in reductive competition of victimizations.
>
> (p. 194)

If these divisions were overcome, pro-ana advocates could engage with other counterhegemonic groups and launch an online counterpublic that could contribute towards actual social change. Mindful of the points raised by Wolf (1991) and by Downey and Fenton (2003), I propose two potential coalitions: 'Fat Acceptance'[1] and eating disorder recovery, both of which must be undergirded by a feminist anti-capitalist agenda. Forming alliances with these groups could present an affront to problematic cultural under-standings of women's bodies as too fat, too thin, and in need of constant surveillance.

Whilst there are always consequences to forming coalitions, the impact of the size acceptance movement as it stands has been on a small scale and has not yet led to significant social change (Sobal 1999). Perhaps this is in part because the Fat Acceptance movement is said to be largely US-based and its 'public face [...] remains predominantly white, middle class, and highly educated' (Donaghue and Clemitshaw 2012, p. 417). Moreover, The National Association to Advance Fat Acceptance (NAAFA) has been charged with 'reinforc[ing] rather than undermin[ing] the cultural fear and repudiation of fat' (Gimlin 2002, p. 140), and the online Body Positive Movement with 'foster[ing] corporeal performances that all too readily become mimetic of the very norms they seek to counter' (Sastre 2014, p. 931). Although these groups may offer crucial coping mechanisms and social support (see Smith et al. 2015), they currently fail to be critical of the wider ways in which the body is constructed (Gimlin 2002; Sastre 2014; Sobal 1999). As we saw in chapter two, women's magazines' embracing of the fat body – *Cosmopolitan*'s in particular – communicates that only certain types of fat bodies are acceptable. On entering the marketplace, Fat Accept-ance and Body Positivity have been neutralised, but alliances with other counterhegemonic groups, combined with a focus on intersectionality, could potentially re-politicise them.

The other proposed coalition is with online eating disorder recovery groups. This could enrich the debate around treatment of anorexia and pro-vide new avenues of support. At present, the exhortations to overcome anor-exia communicated via eating disorder recovery hashtags predominantly conceive it as a battle to be fought and won. This suggests that pro-ana, by contrast, connotes weakness and submission to illness. Recovery users adopt hashtags such as '#edsoldier or '#edwarrior' and '#fight' or '#beatana'. This conceptualising of the anorexic experience as a heroic battle often occurs in eating disorder narratives (see for example Gooldin 2008) and recovery dis-course (see Holmes 2017); it is yoked by a repudiation of anorexia and a privileging of masculine autonomy as conferred through the metaphor of the soldier or warrior. Thus, it contributes towards the discourses that construct anorexia in the first place: the '"male" virtues of control and self-mastery' (Bordo [1993] 2003, pp. 171–172; see also MacSween 1993), as well as 'our culture's fantasy of a disengaged, masterful, rational, and controlling self that creates the possibilities for endless and futile self-improvement' (McGee 2005, p. 173). The warrior approach to eating disorders then, risks playing into neo-liberal discourses of the self that value personal strength and individualism over communal support and reliance on one another. As such, acknowledgement that recovery may not always be possible – as many pro-ana online spaces assert – would temper this construction of the anorectic.

Hashtags such as '#antiana' '#antiproana', and '#prorecovery' may not always adopt warrior discourses, but the content they yield often takes the form of direct affronts to pro-ana spaces where users combine anti-ana hashtags with pro-ana hashtags in order to gain visibility in the latter space. For instance, in a #thynspo search on Tumblr, a user intervenes with a statement against pro-ana culture: 'Ana is not a person. Stop referring to anorexia as "Ana"'. Anorexia will not help you'. They then apply the following hashtags: '#antiproana #antipromia', as well as, '#proana #promia #thinspo #thynspo'. Undeterred, users continue to post pro-ana content, without even acknowledging the 'antiana' user. As Elad Yom-Tov et al. (2012) found, when pro-recovery groups impose their stance on pro-ana spaces, the latter merely become more entrenched in their pro-ana standpoint. As such, these individuals do not engage in the debate required to create a public in the Habermasian sense, rather they exist in enclaves where they reinforce one another's viewpoints. These issues must be overcome if successful counterpublic alliances are to be established.

Other spaces take a gentler approach to pro-ana and recovery, such as *Ana No more*, a site and forum, which describes itself as 'post-pro-ana'. By this, it means that it encourages users to move on from pro-ana as a lifestyle choice and instead actively seek recovery. Despite this insistence, it acknowledges that many aspects of pro-ana online spaces hold therapeutic value and provide much-needed support for those with anorexia (see also Smith et al. 2015; Tierney 2008; Yeshua-Katz and Martins 2012). This reinforces the heterogeneity of the pro-ana phenomenon and problematises calls for censorship. Thus, I argue that by continually critiquing what it means to be pro-ana, resisting (further) incorporation, and presenting a united front, effective alliances can be established.

The potential for pro-ana online spaces to form a successful counterpublic is borne out of their blurring the boundaries between what it means to be thin and attractive and what it means to be anorexic. However, this self-same discourse is what renders them susceptible to incorporation by the hegemony. It has been argued that in contemporary culture, anorexia operates as the frontier at which thinness is no longer desirable and has become pathological (Ferreday 2009, p. 202). I argue that the very notion of a phenomenon that is *pro*-anorexia and utilises media images of thin women to inspire self-starvation, disrupts the desirable/pathological binary and asks important questions about the meanings of thinness. As a result, it is capable of meaningfully critiquing the thin ideal but, in these postfeminist neoliberal times, political potential is being stymied. Ultimately, if pro-ana is to succeed as a social movement, it must be via intersectional feminism. To be clear, this is not to say that its spaces are anti-feminist, rather that they are a by-product of a culture that insists we are *post* feminism and readily converts critique into compliance.

Conclusion

This chapter has interrogated the political potential of pro-ana online spaces, asking to what extent they can be considered counterpublics. To begin with, I interrogated a diverse set of women-led publics. I showed how the lesbian separatists ultimately lacked engagement with wider publics which meant that, as a counterpublic, they were only partly successful. This, combined with their singular approach to identity, led to their demise. Although SlutWalk took a very different approach to feminist activism to that of the lesbian separatists – particularly as it relied on visibility – it fell short of an intersectional approach and, in turn, it did not translate cross-culturally. Simultaneously, whilst its politics were neutralised by postfeminism, it no less provides insight into contemporary feminist organising. At the time of writing, #MeToo is still in its early days. It has been criticised by feminists, but it has the potential to be a successful counterpublic, provided that is, it addresses wider, structural inequalities and benefits marginalised groups. Finally, TLC's resistance to NBCAM, as interrogated by Pezzullo, provides a useful framework for showing how a multiplicity of counterpublics is required to enrich the public sphere.

The latter half of this chapter focused on pro-ana online spaces themselves. I argued that in their current form, they may be counterhegemonic, but their potential as counterpublics is being hindered. Through networked technologies, pro-ana users are circulating counter-discourses and have created a vast and dynamic movement: they operate in contradistinction to dominant ideologies around health and medicine and counter traditional understandings of anorexia as an illness to be treated. Users have crafted their own rhetoric and they refuse censorship. By collating images of thin celebrities, low-fat recipes, and dieting advice from the mainstream and framing it as pro-anorexic, they expose the toxicity of compulsory thinness culture. For these reasons, pro-ana online has the potential to redress understandings of not only anorexia, but also body politics more widely. However, I propose that because of the postfeminist neoliberal context in which pro-ana online spaces are situated, they should be read as *postfeminist counterpublics*. Users' online raging and labelling of certain bodies as anorexic all constitute important cultural statements which speak volumes about femininity in contemporary society. They may espouse hegemonic femininity, but they also advocate women's right to control their bodies. It is this latter element of the phenomenon that must be mobilised in order to bring about social change, lest the all-powerful hegemonic consumes it. Pro-ana spaces may see women uniting over shared understandings of their weight-loss quests, but the tools of postfeminism they use to do so are ultimately reinforcing the status quo. As Bartky warns, 'unless new forms of female solidarity appear, women will be loathe to abandon the forms they know' (2004, p. 23) – and these new forms must allow women to come together in ways that do not damage their health or uphold painful gender norms.

Communication is integral to forming an effective counterpublic, but currently pro-ana online spaces operate more as enclaves where users may speak *against* dominant understandings of anorexia, but they do not speak *out*, meaning they lack substantial engagement with wider publics. The antagonistic way in which their spaces have been handled by the media, Internet moderators and society at large has not paved the way for productive debate or coalitions; instead, over time, pro-ana has begun to merge with the mainstream. The blurred boundaries between normative and pro-ana discourses that I have been speaking to throughout this book mean that where the ideals and ideas of the pro-ana public engage with the broader public, this engagement occurs as a form of depoliticised appropriation rather than negotiation. Nonetheless, like the case studies examined at the start of this chapter, the counterhegemonic activity of pro-ana online spaces constitutes an important story about the gender politics of the time; rather than censoring them or even asking what should be done about them, we should be questioning their entanglement with the mainstream.

Note

1 See, for example #fatacceptance: it has a similar approach to pro-ana in that it resignifies bodies which historically have been vilified and pathologised, as beautiful, posting images with motivational slogans and hashtags.

References

Abad-Santos, A. (2017) 'Russell Simmons starts a #NotMe hashtag to deny multiple accusations of rape and assault', *Vox*, 15 December. Available at: www.vox.com/culture/2017/12/15/16780872/russell-simmons-notme-rape-assault (Accessed March 2019).

Adetiba, E. and Burke, T. (2017) 'Q&A: Tarana Burke', *The Nation*, December, 4(11), p. 5.

Antonakis-Nashif, A. (2015) 'Hashtagging the invisible: Bringing private experiences into public debate: An #outcry against sexism in Germany', in Rambukkana, N. (eds.) *Hashtag Publics*. New York: Peter Lang, pp. 101–113.

Asen, R. (2000) 'Seeking the "counter" in counterpublics', *Communication Theory*, 10(4), pp. 424–446.

Asen, R. and Brouwer, D.C. (2001) 'Introduction: Reconfigurations in the public sphere', in Asen, R. and Brouwer, D.C. (eds.) *Counterpublics and the State*. New York: SUNY Press, pp. 1–32.

Bartky, S.L. (1990) *Femininity and Domination: Studies in the Phenomenology of Oppression*. New York: Routledge.

———. (2004) 'Suffering to be beautiful', in Bartky, S.L. (eds.) *'Sympathy and Solidarity' and Other Essays*. Lanham, MD: Rowman & Littlefield Publishers, Inc, pp. 13–29.

Benhabib, S. (1992) *Situating the Self: Gender, Community and Postmodernism in Contemporary Ethics*. Cambridge: Polity Press.

Bennett, W.L. and Segerberg, A. (2011) 'Digital media and the personalization of collective action', *Information, Communication & Society*, 14(6), pp. 770–799.

Blee, K.M. (1998) 'Introduction: Women on the left/women on the right', in Blee, K.M. (eds.) *No Middle Ground: Women and Radical Protest*. New York: New York University Press, pp. 1–15.

Bordo, S. ([1993] 2003) *Unbearable Weight: Feminism, Western Culture and the Body*, 10th anniversary edition. Berkeley: University of California Press.

Breast Cancer Awareness Month. (2015) *Homepage*. Available at: www.nationalbreast cancer.org/breast-cancer-awareness-month (Accessed October 2015).

Brotsky, S.R. and Giles, D. (2007) 'Inside the "pro-ana" community: A covert online participant observation', *Eating Disorders: The Journal of Treatment & Prevention*, 15(2), pp. 93–109.

Bryson, V. (2003) *Feminist Political Theory: An Introduction*. 2nd edn. Basingstoke, Hampshire: Palgrave Macmillan.

Budgeon, S. (2015) 'Individualized femininity and feminist politics of choice', *European Journal of Women's Studies*, 22(3), pp. 303–318.

Clark, R. (2014) '#NotBuyingIt: Hashtag feminists expand the commercial media conversation', *Feminist Media Studies*, 14(6), pp. 1108–1110.

Coleman, S. and Ross, K. (2010) *The Media and the Public: 'Them' and 'Us' in Media Discourse*. Chichester, West Sussex: Wiley-Blackwell.

Dahlberg, L. and Siapera, E. (2007) 'The Internet and discursive exclusion: From deliberative to agonistic public sphere theory', in Dahlberg, L. and Siapera, E. (eds.) *Radical Democracy and the Internet: Interrogating Theory and Practice*. Hampshire: Palgrave Macmillan, pp. 128–147.

Darmon, K. (2014) 'Framing SlutWalk London: How does the privilege of feminist activism in social media travel into the mass media?', *Feminist Media Studies*, 14(4), pp. 700–704.

Deckard, B.S. (1983) *The Women's Movement: Political, Socioeconomic, and Psychological Issues*. 3rd edn. New York: Harper & Row, Publishers, Inc.

Dias, K. (2003) 'The ana sanctuary: Women's pro-anorexia narratives in cyberspace', *Journal of International Women's Studies*, 4(2), pp. 31–45.

Donaghue, N. and Clemitshaw, A. (2012) '"I'm totally smart and a feminist … and yet I want to be a waif": Exploring ambivalence towards the thin ideal within the fat acceptance movement', *Women's Studies International Forum*, 35, pp. 415–425.

Dow, B.J. and Wood, J.T. (2014) 'Repeating history and learning from it: What can Slut-Walks teach us about feminism?', *Women's Studies in Communication*, 37(1), pp. 22–43.

Downey, J. and Fenton, N. (2003) 'New media, counter publicity and the public sphere', *New Media & Society*, 5(2), pp. 185–202.

Echols, A. (1989) *Daring to Be Bad: Radical Feminism in America 1967–1975*. Minneapolis: University of Minnesota Press.

Felski, R. (1989) *Beyond Feminist Aesthetics*. London: Hutchinson Radius.

Ferreday, D. (2009) *Online Belongings: Fantasy, Affect and Web Communities*. Oxford: Peter Lang.

Fileborn, B. and Loney-Howes, R. (2017) '#MeToo, rape culture and the paradoxes of social media campaigns', *Social Justice: A Journal of Crime, Conflict & World Order*, 4 December. Available at: www.socialjusticejournal.org/metoo-rape-culture-and-the-paradoxes-of-social-media-campaigns/ (Accessed October 2018).

Fotopoulou, A. (2017) *Feminist Activism and Digital Networks: Between Empowerment and Vulnerability*. Basingstoke, Hampshire: Palgrave Macmillan.

Fraser, N. (1990) 'Rethinking the public sphere: A contribution to the critique of actually existing democracy', *Social Text*, 25/26, pp. 56–80.

————. (2013) *Fortunes of Feminism: From State-Managed Capitalism to Neoliberal Crisis*. London: Verso.

Frye, M. (1997) 'Some reflections on separatism and power', in Meyers, D.T. (eds.) *Feminist Social Thought: A Reader*. New York: Routledge, pp. 406–414.

Gill, R. (2007) 'Postfeminist media culture: Elements of a sensibility', *European Journal of Cultural Studies*, 10(2), pp. 147–166.

Gill, R. and Orgad, S. (2015) 'The confidence cult(ure)', *Australian Feminist Studies*, 30(86), pp. 324–344.

Gimlin, D.L. (2002) *Body Work: Beauty and Self-Image in American Culture*. Berkeley: University of California Press.

Gooldin, S. (2008) 'Being anorexic hunger, subjectivity, and embodied morality', *Medical Anthropology Quarterly*, 22(3), pp. 274–296.

Greetham, D. (2011) 'Context and the "impossibility" trope', *New Literary History*, 42(4), pp. 719–738.

Habermas, J. ([1964] 1974) 'The public sphere: An encyclopaedia article', *New German Critique*, 3(1), pp. 49–55.

Holmes, S. (2017) '"My anorexia story": Girls constructing narratives of identity on YouTube', *Cultural Studies*, 31(1), pp. 1–23.

Horeck, T. (2014) '#AskThicke: "Blurred lines," rape culture, and the feminist hashtag takeover', *Feminist Media Studies*, 14(6), pp. 1105–1107.

Kapur, R. (2012) 'Pink Chaddis and SlutWalk couture: The postcolonial politics of feminism lite', *Feminist Legal Studies*, 20, pp. 1–20.

————. (2014) 'Brutalized bodies and sexy dressing on the Indian street', *Signs*, 40(1), pp. 9–14.

Khomami, N. (2017) '#MeToo: How a hashtag became a rallying cry against sexual harassment', *The Guardian*, 20 October. Available at: www.theguardian.com/world/2017/oct/20/women-worldwide-use-hashtag-metoo-against-sexual-harassment (Accessed October 2018).

Latina, D. and Docherty, S. (2014) 'Trending participation, trending exclusion?', *Feminist Media Studies*, 14(6), pp. 1103–1105.

Loken, M. (2014) '#BringBackOurGirls and the invisibility of imperialism', *Feminist Media Studies*, 14(6), pp. 1100–1101.

MacSween, M. (1993) *Anorexic Bodies: A Feminist and Sociological Perspective on Anorexia Nervosa*. London: Routledge.

Malkowski, J. (2014) 'Beyond prevention: Containment rhetoric in the case of bug chasing', *Journal of Medical Humanities*, 35, pp. 211–228.

McDorman, T.F. (2001) 'Crafting a virtual counterpublic: Right-to-die advocates on the Internet', in Asen, R. and Brouwer, D.C. (eds.) *Counterpublics and the State*. New York: SUNY Press, pp. 187–209.

McGee, M. (2005) *Self-Help Inc.: Makeover Culture in American Life*. Oxford: Oxford University Press.

McKinley, N.M. (1999) 'Ideal weight/ideal women: Society constructs the female', in Sobal, J. and Maurer, D. (eds.) *Weighty Issues: Fatness and Thinness as Social Problems*. New York: Aldine de Gruyter, pp. 97–115.

McRobbie, A. (2004) 'Post-feminism and popular culture', *Feminist Media Studies*, 4(3), pp. 255–264.

Mendes, K. (2015) 'SlutWalk, feminism, and news', in Silva, K. and Mendes, K. (eds.) *Feminist Erasures: Challenging Backlash Culture*. Palgrave Connect, pp. 219–234.

Available at: www.palgraveconnect.com/pc/doifinder/10.1057/9781137454928 (Accessed October 2015).

Mendes, K., Ringrose, J., and Keller, J. (2018) '# MeToo and the promise and pitfalls of challenging rape culture through digital feminist activism', *European Journal of Women's Studies*, 25(2), pp. 236–246.

Milano, A. (2017) 15 October, Available at: https://twitter.com/Alyssa_Milano/status/919659438700670976 (Accessed October 2018).

Moreno, M.A., Ton, A., Selkie, E., and Evans, Y. (2016) 'Secret society 123: Understanding the language of self-harm on Instagram', *Journal of Adolescent Health*, 58, pp. 78–84.

Nguyen, T. (2013) 'From SlutWalks to SuicideGirls: Feminist resistance in the third wave and postfeminist era', *Women's Studies Quarterly*, 41(3 & 4), pp. 157–172.

Olszanowski, M. (2015) 'The 1x1 common: The role of Instagram's hashtag in the development and maintenance of feminist exchange', in Rambukkana, N. (eds.) *Hashtag Publics*. New York: Peter Lang, pp. 229–242.

Palczewski, C.H. (2001) 'Cyber-movements, new social movements, and counterpublics', in Asen, R. and Brouwer, D.C. (eds.) *Counterpublics and the State*. New York: SUNY Press, pp. 161–186.

Pezzullo, P.C. (2003) 'Resisting "national breast cancer awareness month": The rhetoric of counterpublics and their cultural performances', *Quarterly Journal of Speech*, 89(4), pp. 345–365.

Pilkington, E. (2011) 'SlutWalking gets rolling after cop's loose talk about provocative clothing', *The Guardian*, 6 May. Available at: www.theguardian.com/world/2011/may/06/slutwalking-policeman-talk-clothing (Accessed October 2015).

Pinterest. (2014) Available at: www.pinterest.com (Accessed July 2014).

Portwood-Stacer, L. and Berridge, S. (2014) 'Introduction', *Feminist Media Studies*, 14(6), pp. 1090.

Rodino-Colocino, M. (2018) 'Me too, #MeToo: Countering cruelty with empathy', *Communication and Critical/Cultural Studies*, 15(1), pp. 96–100.

Rose, G. ([1993] 1999) 'Women and everyday spaces', in Price, J. and Shildrick, M. (eds.) *Feminist Theory and the Body: A Reader*. Edinburgh: Edinburgh University Press, pp. 359–370.

Rosewarne, L. (2017) '#MeToo and modern consciousness-raising', *The Conversation*, 19 October. Available at: https://theconversation.com/metoo-and-modern-consciousness-raising-85980 (Accessed October 2018).

Rottenberg, C. (2014) 'The rise of neoliberal feminism', *Cultural Studies*, 28(3), pp. 418–437.

Rudy, K. (2001) 'Radical feminism, lesbian separatism, and queer theory', *Feminist Studies*, 27(1), pp. 190–222.

Sastre, A. (2014) 'Towards a radical body positive: Reading the online "body positive movement"', *Feminist Media Studies*, 14(6), pp. 929–943.

Shugar, D.R. (1995) *Separatism and Women's Community*. Lincoln: University of Nebraska Press.

Siltanen, J. and Stanworth, M. (1984) 'The politics of private woman and public man', in Siltanen, J. and Stanworth, M. (eds.) *Women and the Public Sphere: A Critique of Sociology and Politics*. London: Hutchinson, pp. 185–208.

SlutWalk Toronto. (2016) *About*. Available at: www.facebook.com/SlutWalkToronto/about/?ref=page_internal (Accessed November 2016).

Smith, N., Wickes, R., and Underwood, M. (2015) 'Managing a marginalised identity in pro-anorexia and fat acceptance cybercommunities', *Journal of Sociology*, 51(4), pp. 950–967.

Sobal, J. (1999) 'The size acceptance movement and the social construction of body weight', in Sobal, J. and Maurer, D. (eds.) *Weighty Issues: Fatness and Thinness as Social Problems*. New York: Aldine de Gruyter, pp. 231–249.

Think before you pink. (2015) *Stop the Distraction*. Available at: http://thinkbeforeyou pink.org/past-campaigns/stop-the-distraction/ (Accessed October 2018).

Tierney, S. (2008) 'Creating communities in cyberspace: Pro-anorexia web sites and social capital', *Journal of Psychiatric and Mental Health Nursing*, 15, pp. 340–343.

Tumblr. (2014) Available at: www.tumblr.com/ (Accessed July 2014).

Warner, M. (2002) 'Publics and counterpublics', *Public Culture*, 14(1), pp. 49–90.

———. (2005) *Publics and Counterpublics*. New York: Zone Books.

Webstagram. (2014) Available at: www.web.stagram.com (Accessed July 2014).

Williams, R. (1977) *Marxism and Literature*. Oxford: Oxford University Press.

Winch, A. (2013) *Girlfriends and Postfeminist Sisterhood*. Basingstoke, Hampshire: Palgrave Macmillan.

Winegar, J. (2012) 'The privilege of revolution: Gender, class, space, and affect in Egypt', *American Ethnologist*, 39(1), pp. 67–70.

Wolf, N. (1991) *The Beauty Myth: How Images of Beauty Are Used Against Women*. New York: Harper Perennial.

Yeshua-Katz, D. and Martins, N. (2013) 'Communicating stigma: The pro-ana paradox', *Health Communication*, 2(5), pp. 499–508.

Yom-Tov, E., Fernandez-Luque, L., Weber, I., and Crain, S.P. (2012) 'Pro-anorexia and pro-recovery photo sharing: A tale of two warring tribes', *Journal of Medical Internet Research*, 14(6), unpaginated.

Young, I.M. (1990) *Justice and Politics of Difference*. Princeton, NJ: Princeton University Press.

Zarkov, D. and Davis, K. (2018) 'Ambiguities and dilemmas around #MeToo: #ForHow long and #WhereTo?', *European Journal of Women's Studies*, 25(1), pp. 3–9.

Epilogue

From the mainstream to the margins and back again

This book set out to capture the story of the pro-ana phenomenon at a time when its culture is becoming increasingly normalised. Pro-ana online continues to be framed as controversial and dangerous, yet the analysis reveals that it is circulating discourses that coincide with those perpetuated by the same mainstream that pathologises and demonises it. It occupies a pivotal space in contemporary culture, which works to its advantage and detriment simultaneously. On the one hand, pro-ana online spaces present an affront to the culture of compulsory thinness: through their diffusion of images and advice that they mark as pro-ana and their manipulation of hashtags, these spaces tacitly point out that the line between anorexia and ideal thinness is increasingly blurred. On the other hand, *because of* their discursive proximity to mainstream thinness culture, their political potential is being hampered by the postfeminist neoliberal climate in which they are located. As a phenomenon, and even as a concept, pro-ana is a critique of the thin ideal, however, the data explored in this study suggest that those who partake in it are not motivated by the desire to affect changes in eating disorder treatment or to bring down compulsory thinness culture, rather they are motivated by the desire to be thin. Furthermore, as pro-ana online spaces have altered over time, this desire has been paradoxically, amplified and obfuscated.

It was in chapter three that I explored in depth the changes that have taken place in the pro-ana landscape, showing how it has morphed from a website and forum-based phenomenon, to one which is predominantly played out on social media. Reflecting on this shift, I argued that pro-ana online spaces have changed for two principal reasons: censoring practices and the rise of image-centric social media. Censorship by Internet moderators has seen pro-ana users develop creative methods in order to remain online: this is enacted in various ways including disclaimers to disavow pro-anorexia, coining new hashtags to evade the blocking of key terms, and adopting the language of health and beauty. Tactics such as these may allow pro-ana online spaces to hide in plain sight, but they also mean that they are dovetailing with mainstream imperatives to body disciplining, the latter of which I explored in chapters one and two of this book.

Chapter one illustrated, through secondary research, how the medical gaze operates as a form of social control, paying particular attention to the impact this has had on women. It explored how the medical profession both eliminated women as practitioners and rendered them patients who were subsequently alienated from their own bodies. Because women – particularly those from the middle and upper classes – were seen as inherently sick, 'disorders' such as anorexia, hysteria, and agoraphobia came to be seen as characteristic of normative femininity. Despite this, these female maladies were also adopted by women as mechanisms of resistance. This chapter, therefore, began to address the possibilities for critique through not only anorexia but *pro*-anorexia. I suggested that, through pro-ana online spaces' defiance of medical authority and appropriation of its rhetoric, they have the potential to expose the gendered norms upon which it operates. Nonetheless, as well as appropriating medicine, pro-ana texts draw on discourses of thinness which emerge from popular culture. As such, in chapter two, I attended to the disciplining of the female body in the contemporary UK women's magazine. This chapter anticipated the blurred boundaries between mainstream culture and pro-ana online culture explored in chapter three. The magazines, I argued, perpetuate mutual self-surveillance through discourses that obfuscate such calls to discipline. For instance, the reader is repeatedly urged to *lose weight without dieting* and provided with endless advice on food swaps and 'guilt-free' treats, suggesting that she *can* have her cake and eat it. In the latter years, these contradictory discourses intensified: the magazines praise women who are said to embrace their curves, and they feature fat celebrities on their covers, yet, at the same time, they promote conformity to a body that is situated at the intersection of privileged social categories. Such contradictions are archetypally postfeminist and echoed in pro-ana online spaces, which deny that they are pro-ana whilst venerating extreme thinness and promoting white, middle-class heterofemininity.

This ideal was interrogated in depth in chapter four, which looked at the intersectional politics of pro-ana online spaces. I argued that, despite research continually showing that anorexia does not only affect young, white, middle-class women, pro-ana online spaces suggest that it does. Using intersectionality as a critical paradigm, I sought to show how postfeminist neoliberalism's 'apparent neutrality' (see Wilkes 2015) privileges white, middle-class heterofemininity. My analysis illustrated how the thin body in pro-ana culture is represented as antithetical to a non-white and lower-class 'other' – a discourse which has long been adumbrated by the mainstream. Moreover, pro-ana spaces advocate clean eating and the performance of an ethically aware persona, both of which may be deployed to disguise disordered eating, but they also require cultural and economic capital. Through analysis of the 'lovely' celebrities pro-ana users admire and of those they denigrate, I demonstrated how the thin ideal is tied to middle-class, white heterofemininity – and, for many users, a heterosexual relationship was seen as the 'reward' for achieving it. Despite this, I argued that, in the data examined, pro-ana subjects construct their desire for thinness in two contrasting ways: for some, it comprised upbeat motivational rhetoric and images of women in gym wear; for others, it involved a grunge aesthetic and statements of self-hatred and depression. These two very different manifestations of pro-ana culture are both underpinned by middle-class whiteness. In sum then, this chapter showed that the ideal pro-ana subject bears a striking resemblance to the ideal postfeminist subject.

The convergence of normative and pro-ana femininities may allow pro-ana online spaces to hide in plain sight but it also presents an opportunity to identify the contradictions within compulsory thinness culture, and in turn, critique it. Thus, in chapters five and six, I explored pro-ana culture's political potential in depth. In chapter five, I examined the articulation of pain in pro-ana texts. I first attended to the cultural–historical coupling of suffering and femininity before identifying two juxtaposing discourses of pain operating in pro-ana online spaces: as an investment or a source of lament. Articulations of pain as a worthwhile investment saw users adopting mantras such as 'no pain, no gain' and constructed suffering as essential to achieving ideal thinness. Such an address chimes with the refrain of the neoliberal subject who is engaged in a constant cycle of self-improvement, thus, by presenting suffering in this way, pro-ana texts merge with those of postfeminism and its painful lived experiences are obscured. By contrast, pain, when it was portrayed as lamentable, was accompanied by references to depression, anger, and self-harm. Like the invocation of grunge explored in chapter four, users wrote candidly of the suffering associated with anorexia. Although this more closely articulates the reality of anorexia, users ultimately turn this pain on themselves: they rage at their own bodies and despair that the thin ideal is '#notme'. As a result, I argued that although both these articulations of pain – the upbeat and the despairing – highlight the suffering required of normative femininity, they do not ultimately undermine it.

Nonetheless, pro-ana texts constitute an important cultural archive that speaks to, and about, twenty-first-century femininity. This archive exposes the extent to which denial and disguise pervade the culture of compulsory thinness and it reveals the blurred boundaries between disordered and normative body practices. Although this may not be intentional on the part of the users of these spaces, it is nonetheless a significant – as well as disturbing – statement. Therefore, in chapter six, I asked if the counterhegemonic elements of pro-ana online spaces could be harnessed to create a counterpublic. I looked at a selection of women-led publics before examining the counterhegemonic elements of pro-ana culture and their potential as counterpublics. I proposed that pro-ana online spaces should be read as *postfeminist counterpublics* whose political potential is hindered by the postfeminist context in which they sit. Although the pro-ana phenomenon contains the potential to destabilise contemporary thinness culture, I suggested that upon entering wider publics, the language of pro-ana is vulnerable to distortion and appropriation. This chapter, therefore, concluded that whilst all counterpublics are at risk of incorporation by the hegemonic, pro-ana online spaces are particularly susceptible. This is because, as I have argued throughout this book, in their current form, they perpetuate discourses of thinness that coincide with those of the mainstream – which censorship and media vilification have merely exacerbated.

As it stands, mainstream thinness culture and pro-ana online spaces remain thoroughly entangled: they appropriate one another's texts and utilise one another to establish weight-loss practices that are normal and weight-loss practices that are not. For instance, the notion that people are following pro-anorexia hashtags on social media to support weight loss renders *Cosmopolitan*'s diet tips innocuous and even sensible. However, what happens when both texts offer the same advice? Whether or not it is intended, this constitutes an important insight into the current bodily ideals demanded of women. If pro-ana users are appropriating mainstream texts to legitimise their spaces, then we must urgently address how this has become the norm; the mainstream co-optation of pro-ana only emphasises this need further. In a culture that continually seeks to incorporate dissident voices, one which has plundered punk culture, grunge style, and even the aesthetics of heroin users, why should 'pro-anorexia' or 'Concentration Camp Chic' (*A1 Thinspo*) come as a surprise? Pro-ana culture may have been cast as deviant, but it offers a telling interpretation of what it means to be 'normal' in the twenty-first century.

Directions for future research

As I emphasised early on, this book offers a snapshot of a dynamic and elusive online phenomenon. Whilst this means the study itself is a cultural artefact, it also means that it cannot be exhaustive. No sooner had I created an archive of pro-ana texts, the majority of the original content had been removed from the Internet: some posts and sites may have been forcibly erased and their authors banished; others may have left of their own accord. Either way, the pro-ana landscape is not what it was when I began this research. Social media architecture is constantly changing – for example, the introduction of the 'Stories' feature on Instagram in 2016, where users post content that automatically expires after 24 hours (Instagram 2016) may render pro-ana content further ephemeral, but the transience of Stories also presents a number of challenges for moderators for whom the policing of controversially deemed content is already an endless battle. Even as I write, pro-ana users are coining new hashtags, creating new spaces, and ensuring that images appear every day – all of which are vulnerable to deletion and vilification. Meanwhile, media reports criticising the phenomenon continue to circulate. As such, the limits of my own research constitute a recommendation for future research; that investigation into pro-ana online spaces continues.

As the denial and disguise I found in my own interrogation of these spaces persist, the phenomenon is merging with the mainstream and ever more losing its potential to critique the culture of compulsory thinness that pervades the Western world. One way though that thinness culture can be challenged is through sustained critical investigation into the culturally pivotal spaces that constitute pro-ana online: they may espouse postfeminist compliance with compulsory thinness, but they also adopt counterhegemonic discourses that offer a critique of such an ideal. Another recommendation for future research emerges from chapter four where I demonstrated the need for an intersectional approach to pro-ana online. Research that takes those who are underrepresented in pro-ana culture as its starting point would be worthwhile: for instance, LGBTQ+ persons' engagement with pro-ana online spaces has not yet been explored. Finally, as a result of my own position as an English-speaking Westerner living in the United Kingdom, the data explored were limited to the English language. However, during the collection period, pro-ana content in French, Spanish, and Russian, to name but a few, was generated. As I have argued, anorexia is not a solely Western phenomenon, yet the data I examined suggest that *pro*-anorexia is. By exploring pro-ana texts in non-Western contexts and in languages other than English, one could usefully investigate how the Western ideal of thinness (white, young, middle class, and heterofeminine) is negotiated. After all, anorexia, like the thin ideal, is culture-borne and culturally constituted; only with a continued focus on the contexts from which such 'disorders' arise, can we begin to understand how they become 'normal'.

The darker side of postfeminism

When I began this research, I anticipated being shocked by the images my data collection would yield. I was prepared to be astounded by the tips and tricks pro-ana users would share with one another in order to lose weight. I was expecting to be horrified by pro-ana, but I was not. What did disturb me was how familiar I found the images and the advice. To begin with, I questioned my search engine results – wondering if they were too *normal* to be pro-ana. Around the same time, investigative journalist, Jamie Bartlett was finishing *The Dark Net*, an exploration of the hidden or 'dark' Internet, which he describes as:

> an idea more than a particular place: an underworld set apart yet connected to the internet we inhabit, a world of complete freedom and anonymity, and where users say and do what they like, often uncensored, unregulated, and outside of society's norms.
>
> (2014, p. 3)

Bartlett locates pro-ana sites in this underworld, alongside pro-suicide sites, drug dealers, and political extremists, for example. But the pro-ana online spaces I was seeing did not arise from the underworld, nor did they operate 'outside of society's norms'; rather, they sat on the surface of the web, flanked by fashion blogs and fitness sites. What these spaces were showing me was not the dark side of the net, but the darker side of postfeminism.

Pro-ana culture speaks volumes, not only about femininity, but also about feminist politics in the twenty-first century. In the introduction to this book,

I advocated for the importance of continued attention to postfeminism (Gill 2016). This study underlines such a need. The data I examined showed no regard for feminism: it did not arise as a topic of conversation in the forums, nor was it addressed in any of the social media spaces. Yet the spectacle of feminism haunts the pro-ana phenomenon: this is because it is a product of feminism as well as a representation of its repudiation (cf. Scharff 2012). It epitomises the current contradictory cultural stance on women: a perspective that suggests they have the freedom to do as they wish, whilst, at the same time, promoting conformity to particular lifestyle choices. This contradictory combination exists in anorexia itself where the anorectic's bid for freedom is ultimately enslaving. This means that anorexia and postfeminist neoliberalism are perfect, and devastating, companions, adopting as they do a logic that centres on self-discipline and individualism, which I suggest offers some explanation for the phenomenon of pro-ana. Even in its early days, pro-ana sought to cloak disordered eating in the rhetoric of empowerment, and now, in efforts to stay online and avoid censure, it has embraced such a discourse wholesale.

Pro-anorexia is quintessentially postfeminist: it has selected and co-opted elements of feminism that are useful for its own ends, and it presents self-discipline as a form of empowerment. Both pro-ana and postfeminist cultures seek to transform painful and debilitating activities into pleasurable acts of self-improvement. Pro-anorexia is both constituted by, and a metaphor for, postfeminism. As I pointed out in chapter six, some users have declared themselves 'post-pro-ana' and are seeking to establish a new wave of eating-disorders support. There is certainly potential in their non-judgemental approach to both anorexia and pro-anorexia. However, at the time of writing, their online presence is being dwarfed by pro-ana content. The very concept of a phenomenon that is pro-actively embracing anorexia and uses mainstream images and advice to do so, demands continued attention. Ultimately, we cannot be truly post-pro-ana until, to use Gill's (2016) term, we are 'post-postfeminism'.

The twenty-first century has witnessed a renewed focus on feminism, as well as a backlash against not only feminists, but women in general. The abuse women are targeted with, online and offline, and the inequality that subsists is of dire concern and deeply damaging. However, we must also be mindful of the potential injuries to feminism when it enters the mainstream. In chapter two, I highlighted a shift in the magazine market's approach to the body: where earlier issues did not mention feminism and were critical of the fat body, latter issues covered feminist activism and urged women to have self-confidence, whatever their size. At the same time, this embracing of feminism and calls to body confidence are cloaked in individualism and contradiction: the onus is on individual women to say #metoo and show their pain to the world yet love the self-same body they are told must suffer. All the while, the work of trans-exclusionary radical feminists (TERFs), which reads trans people 'only as tools or victims of a patriarchal conspiracy to destroy feminism and harm girls and women' (Stryker and Bettcher 2016, p. 7), continues unabated. Ironically, arguments such as these play into the hands of the patriarchal system that seeks to exclude trans people and would readily destroy feminism at the same time. What I want to say is that, in these neoliberal times, we need to be cognisant that feminism can be all too easily co-opted into supporting the status quo; trans-exclusionary politics, when adopted by groups who also make claims to feminism, is, therefore, deeply concerning.

We must continue to ask what it means to be a feminist: does it mean paying attention to intersectional marginalisation, or in truth, does it only speak to the white, middle class? Because a worldview that disregards the marginalised has no place in feminist politics and can only serve the dominant order. This book has shown how a phenomenon with the potential to critique the status quo is being incorporated into the mainstream. In these troubling times of fake news, alt-facts, and post-truth politics, obfuscatory tactics are pervading contemporary culture more than ever. As a result, we must question that which critiques the hegemony as much we question the hegemony itself.

References

Bartlett, J. (2014) *The Dark Net*. London: Windmill Books.

Gill, R. (2016) 'Post-postfeminism?: New feminist visibilities in postfeminist times', *Feminist Media Studies*, 16(4), pp. 610–630.

Instagram. (2016) 'Introducing Instagram stories', *Instagram Blog*, 2 August. Available at: https://instagram.tumblr.com/post/148348940287/160802-stories (Accessed May 2019).

Scharff, C. (2012) *Repudiating Feminism: Young Women in a Neoliberal World*. Farnham, Surrey and Burlington, VT: Ashgate Publishing Company.

Stryker, S. and Bettcher, T.M. (2016) 'Introduction: Trans/feminisms', *Transgender Studies Quarterly*, 3(1–2), pp. 5–14.

Wilkes, K. (2015) 'Colluding with neo-liberalism: Post-feminist subjectivities, whiteness and expressions of entitlement', *Feminist Review*, 110, pp. 18–33.

Appendix
Information on pro-anorexia online spaces

All information describes pro-ana content as it appeared during the research period. As indicated in the main body of the book, almost none of this content exists any longer.

Table 1 Frozen spaces

Name	Type of space
Anamia Universe	Static website and private forum
Anything for Thin	Blog
Beauty of Ana	Static website, public forum and private forum
Beauty of Ana II	Static website, public forum and private forum
Ethereal Anas	Static website and private forum
Fallen Ana	Static website and public forum
Guide to Ana	Static website
Kneeling to Ana	Static website
Living pro-ana	Blog
Thinspo HQ	Static website and private forum
Thinspo NOW	Static website

Table 2 Active spaces

Name	Type of space
A1 Thinspo	Static website
All for Ana	Blog
Beach Thinspiration	Blog
Foreverproana	Public forum and private forum
Futurethinspo	Blog
Heartthinspo	Blog
Howtothinspo	Blog
Land of Skinny	Blog

(*Continued*)

Table 2 (Cont.)

Name	Type of space
Sunny Thinspo	Blog
Thinspirationpics	Public forum
Wasting for Thin	Blog
Workingforthin	Blog
World of Pro-ana	Static website and public forum
Your thinspo	Blog

Table 3 Marketing spaces

Name	Type of space
30 Days to Thin	Static website
Pro Ana Thinspiration	Static website
Pro Ana Tips	Blog
Prothinspiration Diet	Static website
Thinspiration	Blog
Thinspiration Pro Ana Tips	Static website

Table 4 Recovery spaces

Name	Type of site
Ana No More	Public forum and private forum
Let's Change This	Static website and private forum

Table 5 Search terms undertaken across social media platforms.

Search term (hashtag or keyword)	Platform
ana	Instagram[1]
bonespo	Instagram, Pinterest, Tumblr
pro-ana	Pinterest
proanna	Instagram, Tumblr
proanorexia	Tumblr
pro-anorexia	Pinterest
thin	Instagram
thinspiration	Pinterest, Tumblr
thinspo	Pinterest, Tumblr
thinspoooo	Instagram, Pinterest, Tumblr
thynspiration	Instagram

Note

1 As outlined in the introduction, all Instagram searches were undertaken via Webstagram, the searchable web browser for Instagram. However, for ease I refer to it as Instagram.

Index

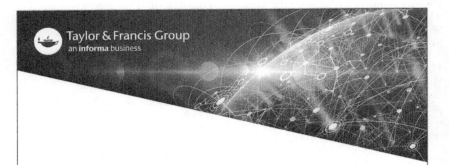